D1483810

Rationality in Economics

The Human Condition, I, 1934, by René Magritte, © ADAGP, Paris/DACS, London, in the National Gallery of Art, Washington, DC, Gift of the Collectors Committee, is reproduced by kind permission.

Rationality in Economics

Shaun Hargreaves Heap

Basil Blackwell

British Library Cataloguing in Publication Data
Hargreaves Heap, Shaun
    Rationality in economics
    1. Man. Rational economic explanations.
    Philosophical perspectives
    I. Title   *P*
    330
    ISBN 0–631–15666–6

Library of Congress Cataloging in Publication Data
Hargreaves Heap, Shaun 1951–
    Rationality in economics
    1. Economics. 2. Philosophy. 3. Rational
    expectations (Economic theory) 4. Uncertainty.
    I. Title.
    HB72.H43 1989 330 88–32777
    ISBN 0–631–15666–6

Typeset in 10 on 12 pt Times
by Vera Reyes, Inc.
Printed in Great Britain by Billing & Sons Ltd, Worcester

CONTENTS

to SBST

PREFACE

Did somebody once say that a little bit of economics was a bad thing? Or was it that a little bit of philosophy was a dangerous thing? Probably they have both been uttered more than once, and perhaps even by the same person. Anyway, it is my fortune to have fallen foul of both aphorisms.

I find it difficult to explain how it happened with economics. The closest that I can get to an explanation, and it is more of a description than an explanation, is that I have a love–hate relationship with the subject some of the time. During the rest of the time, my feelings are no less mixed, but they are perhaps best captured by the thought that economics is an irritation. The philosophical side of my fortune is much easier to understand.

I would not have written this book without the friendship and encouragement of a number of philosophers over the years. I studied some philosophy as an undergraduate, lived with some philosophers when I was in graduate school, and now I work with philosophers in the School of Economic and Social Studies at East Anglia. I owe a particular debt to Martin Hollis. He has provided an immensely useful set of comments on this text. He has also helped me towards a set of philosophical bearings through our joint work.

Angus Ross and Yanis Varoufakis, like Martin, read the whole of the first draft of the book. Their comments along with those from Steve Davies have much improved the text. I am most grateful to them. Finally, I would like to thank Christine Sharrock, Omega Scientific, for help with copy editing and members of staff at Blackwells for their aid and encouragement.

Well, to fall foul of two aphorisms which warn of 'badness' and 'danger' may be poor luck; it might even involve negligence. Or it might be good luck. I am undecided. But, I know a piece of serendipity when I see it: quite simply I doubt I would have completed this book without the time spent at a sublime part of the Norfolk coast.

Shaun Hargreaves Heap

1 AN OVERVIEW

1.1 Introduction

There is a familiar scene that has a parent pleading with a child over some matter. Finally, and in some despair, the parent exclaims: 'Oh be reasonable!' The child pays some attention to the remark, but replies with a suspicious look.

There is a long and a short story in this book. The short story is that the child was right to pay attention to the remark, and right to look suspiciously at the adult, albeit probably for the wrong reasons.

The point is that rationality matters deeply to economics, but it is a slippery concept.

The aim of the book is to support this proposition by providing a survey and an evaluation of how various rationality assumptions combine to produce explanations and prescriptions in economics. In particular, it is argued that mainstream economics is ill-served by its exclusive, formal reliance on the instrumental sense of rationality. One aspect of this 'poor service' is the damage done to discussions of policy: if economic theory is to exercise any claim to guide public policy then it must work with an expanded set of rationality postulates. Another aspect concerns the relationship between economics and the other social sciences. At the moment, we are encouraging the exclusive use of instrumental rationality by exporting it with great vigour to the other social sciences, when actually economists ought to be emphasising its limitations as a model of human action.

The long story goes something like this. I tackle a position in economics in part I of the book which denies that discussions of rationality *per se* really count for much. Most economists will readily recognise the view: it makes any assumption about behaviour provisional; it is only there as long as the predictions and explanations generated by it match the facts. So, no great care need be lavished on a particular rationality assumption, through reflecting on its a priori merits, because the test against the facts will sort out the good assumptions from the bad ones.

This position is buttressed by a crude empiricist methodology, which models economics on a version of the natural sciences. This version has 'facts' in the world that exist independently of our conjectures about them, and the task of the scientist is to go out and discover in an uncomplicated way the order connecting them. This methodological position also licenses the familiar distinction between positive and normative economics which strictly separates explanation from prescription and an image of the economist as some kind of technician, or perhaps, even better, as some kind of neutral commentator on social affairs: one who has a specialism in matters economic, and who lines up with other well-known media commentators on the news, sports and the like.

Doubtless, we will all see likenesses between particular economists and their equivalents in news and sports commentary. Nevertheless, however good the fit is here, the benign vision of neutrality cannot attach to these candidates. Even if this view of 'science' was ever relevant for the natural world, it certainly has no place in the social world. The 'facts' in the social world depend on our conjectures about them in a number of ways, and this undermines any simple methodology which subordinates theory and its assumptions about motivation to the 'facts'. For example, just consider the logic of the rational expectations argument. We form expectations using theory and these expectations affect our actions, the upshot of which becomes the 'facts' we observe. Of course, this is not to deny that there are elements of the world which exist independently of our conjectures about them, but they are not revealed transparently by the 'facts' as we encounter them.

The relationship between theory and empirical evidence is more complicated than is implied by the crude empiricist method. As a result of this complication, empirical evidence can never always be the decisive test of a theory. Instead, we often need other grounds for choosing between theories. The remainder of the book, then, is an examination of a kind of non-empiricist discourse about different theories which could fill some of the gap left by the collapse of the simple empiricist buttress.

'Rationalism' is the natural starting point for such a substitute methodology. Indeed, it has a long tradition in economics, stretching from the nineteenth century through the Austrians up to the present day. It begins with a self-evident proposition that human beings are 'rational' and deduces further theoretical propositions from this premise. Unfortunately, it is immediately apparent that this by itself is not going to get us very far in the evaluation of different theories because there is a range of contending assumptions about what is 'rational' behaviour. It would be no good to appeal to the empirical evidence, see which theory produces the best statistics and the like, because this makes it a short trip back to empiricism. Something else is called for, and parts II and III are an attempt at an answer.

Part II surveys three rationality postulates which have been used in economics and discusses the kind of explanations generated by them. Part III surveys, in turn, the prescriptions which emanate from those rationality postulates.

It would be disingenuous to claim that these parts of the book provide only a survey, with odd pointers to intentional and functional explanations and a few words on the practicality of the prescriptions. Although the analysis of how different rationality assumptions can be connected with various 'scientific' explanations is one of the purposes of the book, it is not the only one. There is an assessment of the quality of the explanations and prescriptions generated by these postulates. How well does this rationality postulate explain what went on, and does it gives us a handle on how and whether we might intervene to improve what went on? These are the questions I try to answer in parts II and III. That is, I go back to the gap left by empiricism and attempt to provide an answer to whether a theory is good one. Indeed, this is the main purpose of the book; to provide an evaluation of the major rationality postulates used in economics.

To explain how this evaluative argument is constructed in the book and what it amounts to, I need to backtrack a bit and fill in some more detail.

1.2 Different Senses of Rationality and their Explanations and Prescriptions

There are three pictures of an individual (or more generally the agent) in economics and each involves a different rationality postulate. It will be helpful for what follows, both here and later, if I give a brief outline of each and how they connect with explanation and prescription in economics. These thumbnail sketches are summarised in tabular form in figure 1.1. This will give a ready reference for the shape of the project, which can be consulted if confusion arises in some of the more detailed argument in subsequent chapters.

One postulate describes the individual (standing hereafter in this chapter for any agent) in terms of a set of usually well-behaved preferences and

Rationality	Explanation type	Form of prescription
Instrumental	Intentional (supra- and sub-intentional causality)	Consequentialist (i.e. Pareto optimality, utilitarianism)
Procedural	Functional (cumulative causation, hysteresis)	Rights based (i.e. capabilities, exploitation)
Expressive	True interest, experimental	

Figure 1.1   Taxonomy of rationality, explanation and prescription

motivates individuals with an instrumental rationality assumption. The person acts so as to satisfy these preferences best. I shall use the term instrumental rationality to describe this picture of an individual. This person is no stranger to most economists; he/she is the ubiquitous maximiser. Rationality is located in the means–end framework as the choice of the most efficient means for the achievement of given ends. This in turn generates intentional explanations of the sort which abound in economics, and prescriptive statements like those which come from the so-called three fundamental theorems in welfare economics.

The other two rationality postulates break with this categorisation of rationality in different ways. The second distances action from ends altogether, while the third takes rationality to be a concern with the ends pursued rather than with the actions taken in pursuit of them. To be more specific, the second vision portrays the individual as a rule follower, a person who follows norms, recipes or procedures for action. Such behaviour is procedurally rational. It is a vision which will be mostly familiar from the work of Simon (1982). However, Simon has the person following rules of thumb because the optimising calculations of the instrumentally rational person are simply not practicable. In this way, Simon's procedural rationality is a kind of ersatz version of instrumental rationality. By contrast, I want procedural rationality to stand for something more than this.

The idea of following procedures has deeper roots in the social science literature than Simon's person who has trouble with calculations. There is a tradition in the social sciences that locates the individual in a web of rules, roles and norms which define the expected behaviours associated with a person in that position (see Hollis 1987). The crucial feature of these procedures is that they are shared by others, whereas Simon's shortcuts are personal affairs. This larger tradition makes procedural rationality a source of historical and social location for individuals. It makes the individual irreducibly social in a way that is not found in the purely instrumental account because the person cannot ever be quite separated from these norms. This warrants a new sense of rationality because, unlike Simon, the following of procedures can no longer be regarded as part of the means by which one satisfies given ends. Instead, the following of shared procedures actually helps to define some of the ends which we pursue. It is also naturally associated with a characteristically different kind of explanation in economics (and the social sciences more generally): functional explanation.

By itself, there is little that the picture of the procedurally rational rule follower contributes to prescriptive statements in economics. However, when combined with the third version of rationality, there is more to be said. Expressive rationality reflects our concern with making sense of the world. We want to make the world intelligible to us so that we can act in it. In the modern world, the individual occupies a central position in the web of beliefs which produce this order, and consequently the concern with making sense has been focused on the individual and his or her preferences. The individual is self-consciously reflective about his/her preferences. It is not enough for a person to be guided by preferences; preferences must reflect an autonomous self. Of course, 'easier said than done' is the catch phrase here. Autonomy and self-respect come through taking one's preferences to be worthy of one's self and questions of worth are notoriously difficult to answer. Consequently, we have a picture of the individual who is groping for what is worthwhile: she/he experiments with and discusses this or that, much as a natural scientist would, when trying to make sense of something like subatomic physics which is as hidden from the naked eye as life is opaque.

Action which flows from this concern with autonomy is designated as expressively rational because it expresses our ideas about what is worthy in our selves, and by extension the sense which we make of the world. At first sight this may sound odd: how can action express ideas in this manner? It is here that we have one of the connections between expressive and procedural rationality which helps to make the all-pervasive role following of some social theory something more than the activity of cultural dopes. The rules, roles, norms or procedures which procedurally rational agents follow are information-generating devices; they encode expectations; and some of the information which is generated by following a rule or playing a role is information about what the person takes to be valuable and worthy in his/her life. Put slightly differently, the existence of publicly recognised norms enables action to become symbolic: the norms constitute a language which individuals can use to make statements about their ideas of what is worthy.

Again, action which is motivated by expressive concerns warrants the title of a new sense of rationality because it does not fit the instrumental model. Action is no longer a means to a given end. Action is implicated in the choice of ends; it is part of a groping towards who to be, what ends to have; and it would be better described as activity which is its own end.

Most people will probably recognise this third kind of individual more because it is sliced from a modern concern with existentialism than because it features regularly in the literature. Nevertheless, there are economic explanations which work on this conception of the individual: they are termed true interest and experimental explanations here, because of the particular slant which they give to explanations which work intentionally or functionally. In addition, the powerful critique of conventional welfare economics made by Sen, and of capitalism made by Marx, gains a purchase precisely because it employs this picture of the individual. Figure 1.1 refers to this kind of prescriptive statement as being 'rights' based while the prescriptive statements associated with instrumental rationality and individuals who are just a bunch of preferences are exclusively 'consequentialist'.

A brief sketch like this is bound to beg a lot of questions and the simple taxonomy given in figure 1.1 necessarily rides roughshod over the finer points. Treat it as a map, drawn to such a scale that there is very little detail of the terrain it covers, to be used, at best, as a guide to the whole area: useful for taking bearings every now and then along the route, so as to speak. The details are to be found in subsequent chapters. One final point should perhaps be made. Although each of these pictures of the individual is presented as a discrete description, it is not implied that any or all individuals should fit neatly into one category or another. Any individual may combine any or all of these perspectives on motivation. In short, real individuals can be multifaceted. Each of these types is but one dimension and real individuals can be anything from one to three dimensional, incorporating only one or all these visions.

1.3 Evaluating Rationality Postulates

It is the objective of evaluation which imparts the structure to parts II and III of the book. Chapter 3 sets out the stall of instrumental rationality in economics and chapters 4, 5 and 6 evaluate the explanations generated by this rationality postulate. The evaluation has two parts: one is straightforwardly evaluative in a normative sense (i.e. do I like this picture of rational agency?); the other concentrates on the scope of the intentional explanations. The normative evaluation is not central: it appears here and there and is only explicitly addressed briefly in chapter 6. It is the question of scope which gives the direction to the argument of these chapters.

The discussion of whether a particular rationality postulate constitutes a good recommendation of how to be in the world may seem odd in what is supposed to be an evaluation of explanations. But its strangeness is largely a product of the positive – normative distinction; and once this has been breached in part I, the appearance of normative considerations in part II will seem less grotesque. In a nutshell, one consequence of the arguments in part I is that theory helps build the world in which we live: through helping to create desires and/or beliefs, both of which contribute to action. Of course, we do not know the extent to which we are capable of creating the world in which we live. There may be severe natural constraints in the form of weather patterns, ecological laws, genetic endowments and so on. But as long as we believe that these factors are not all determining, then we are entitled to ask of a theory whether it presents us with a good view of the way people ought to be and to take the answer to this question as relevant in deciding whether to accept the theory or not.

Go back to the image of the economist as a neutral commentator. Once the crude empiricist method ceases to be tenable, so does this image: commentators are never neutral. Said in that way, it is obvious because we know only too well that our commentators are not neutral. Take, for example, the sports commentators who persistently refer to women athletes as 'girls', when men athletes are always 'men'. The exact significance of the feminist critique, that this kind of talk encourages a general perception of women as 'girls' may be controversial, but it cannot be denied that it has some effect through reinforcing this perception. The point, then, is simply that, unless I believe there is some natural constraint which is so determinist that it removes the choice about perception, I am entitled to say that I do not like the commentary because of the vision of women it contains. This is an important consideration, but it does not feature significantly in the book simply because there is no reasonable prospect of producing anything decisive from a discussion of how we ought to be in this sense. The reason for introducing it at this stage in the book rather than in part III, where these discussions normally reside, is pedagogic. It is to remind the profession that these questions are unavoidable: the claim to be just a 'positive' economist, who has left his/her normative predispositions at home, has no foundation. There is no disinterested activity of 'telling it like it is' in economics.

There are two aspects of the scope of the explanations generated by instrumental rationality which come under scrutiny. The first is the extent to which intentional explanations rely on institutional and informational props, which cannot themselves be explained in instrumental terms. This issue is explored in chapters 4 and 5. (It should be noted in passing that I am particularly sorry that I did not have Hodgson (1988) at the time of writing these chapters. Anyone interested in a fuller discussion of this issue should consult Hodgson (1988).) The second dimension of scope concerns whether the restrictions placed on preference orderings exclude recognisable sorts of human predicaments and behaviour. In particular, in chapter 6, I consider whether the phenomena of interdependent preferences and apparent preference changes fall within the scope of intentional explanations.

I conclude that instrumental rationality does suffer from significant deficiencies in the scope of its explanations. This is not to deny that it is also a very powerful explanatory assumption. The observation merely relates to the possibility that it can ever be the exclusive rationality assumption in economics. I can well imagine a shrug of the shoulders at this state: so, it cannot do everything, so what? Well, the answer is: exclusivity matters quite crucially because it affects the possibility of generating public policy prescriptions. Exactly how this possibility is affected will depend on the relationship which is envisaged between explanation and prescription: the need for other rationality assumptions in explanation means that prescriptions which are based exclusively on the picture of instrumental rationality are either inconsistent or indeterminate. In other words, the project of building a theoretical framework which is capable of producing public policy prescriptions is hopelessly compromised if it only uses the assumption of instrumental rationality.

Chapters 7 and 8 illustrate how procedural and expressive rationality can fill the gaps in explanation left by instrumental rationality. They give a survey of the use of these other rationality assumptions in economics in much the same way as chapter 3 surveyed the models embodying instrumental rationality.

There is some unfairness in this treatment of the various rationality assumptions. Instrumental rationality is subjected to the third degree, while the other two postulates get the kid gloves. Indeed, this way of staging the proceedings makes their appearance on the scene seem like the arrival of knights in shining armour. The justification for this 'unfairness' is to be found in the pre-eminent position of instrumental rationality in economics – life is tough at the top. Or to phrase it more ironically: mainstream economics responds in a Pavlovian fashion to almost every situation by turning it into one where agents have well-defined objectives which they are busy setting about satisfying; and my ordering of the discussion reflects that same habit.

Chapter 9, in part III, turns to the literature which has focused explicitly on prescriptions: welfare economics. It offers a brief survey of the welfare economics which has been built around the vision of instrumentally rational agents. This survey confirms the implication of the earlier argument: there is a mess in orthodox welfare economics and this is exactly what you would expect from a rationality assumption which has limited explanatory scope. Of course, the problems in orthodox welfare economics have long been acknowledged by practitioners in a way that the difficulties with orthodox explanations are not (see Sen 1979). The task of this chapter, then, is to draw out the anomaly of this difference in perception because the difficulties of welfare economics are the difficulties of orthodox explanatory economics. They can be traced to the same one-dimensional assumption about human agency: that we are only instrumentally rational. It is particularly helpful to make this connection because it forms the basis of the final argument in chapter 9 that Sen's approach to the impasse in welfare economics is to be preferred over that of the New Right.

Part III is rather short compared with part II because, unfortunately, orthodox welfare economics is known to be in trouble and with the exception of Sen, there is little work which is building procedural and expressive rationality into welfare analysis. Chapter 10 gives a summary of the arguments of the book and ends with a gesture towards a welfare economics which incorporates these neglected senses of rationality.

1.4 Final Comments

So, this book has three purposes: firstly, to substantiate the need for a non-empiricist discourse in economics, one which is concerned with the rationality of human action; secondly, to reveal how different rationality assumptions in economics generate explanations, how the explanations work, so as to speak; thirdly, to evaluate the rationality assumptions with respect to their capacity to explain economic behaviour and guide public policy.

The first is well-trodden methodological ground. It is largely an exercise of scene setting for the remainder of the book and it is undertaken in part I. The second draws heavily on the work of Elster and combines with the first to provide economists with what I take to be a minimal philosophical tool kit. These are not insignificant objectives because I think it is useful for economists to have an awareness of the architecture of their explanations, and it is important to loosen the hold which simple empiricist methodologies still seem to have over the profession. Nevertheless, it is really the third objective which drives the book.

I conclude that an economics based exclusively on the instrumental rationality postulate suffers from problems of scope in its explanations which necessarily compromise its capacity for generating public policy insights.

The reader will also notice that the tone of the argument often becomes shriller when neoclassical economics is discussed. This is because I associate neoclassical economics with the exclusive use of the instrumental rationality postulate. Those who accept this definition can read the book as a critique of neoclassical economics. Of course, people may object to this way of drawing a boundary around neoclassical economics – in which case, erase the words. What is important is the point about exclusive use.

But what is the real price of a bit of incompleteness in explanation? Does it really matter? Can neoclassical economics not live with it without too many sleepless nights? One way of answering this is to weigh up the explanations in chapters 6, 7 and 8 with those in chapter 3 and the instrumental components in chapters 4 and 5. I hope it surprises some neoclassicals to find how much goes on in economics which explicitly requires other rationality assumptions. But this is not the real reason why neoclassicals should be worried.

They ought to be concerned about the consequences which the problems of scope have for the capacity to generate public policy prescriptions. I believe all 'useful' theories in the social sciences must aspire to this capacity. The acquisition of knowledge in the social sciences about what 'is' the case is often interesting in its own right, but it is rarely valued exclusively because of its intrinsic worth. Most people value knowledge, in addition, because it enables them to intervene in the world, it is a source of guidance; and public intervention/collective action is one of the crucial arenas in which we need such guidance. Put baldly, knowledge is rarely for the birds; we value knowledge because it serves human interests, broadly understood. We wish to know amongst other things, of course, what kinds of public interventions/collective actions will enable us to act as freer and more autonomous individuals (see chapter 10 for a further discussion of the 'usefulness' of theories). Consequently, the capacity for a theory to generate public policy insights is not marginal – it is absolutely crucial.*

The major sources of the scope problems for the instrumental postulate are its failure to explain the institutional and informational structures that orchestrate instrumentally driven explanations. Institutions and information are really two sides of the same coin: they bear witness to a deep kind of interdependence between individuals which is the source of both a kind of freedom and uncertainty in the social world. Hence, another way of putting the difficulty encountered by the instrumental hypothesis is that it does not have much to say about freedom and uncertainty.

It is not new to complain about the absence of power, freedom and uncertainty in neoclassical economics. So, in this sense, this book is joining an established camp. What the argument of this book highlights, however, is that such discussions of power, freedom and uncertainty are not just optional features for a body of economic theory, to be debated as a matter of contingent relevance. They are necessary features if that theory is to make any serious claim to our attentions. Of course, there is a corollary to this argument for the camp of complainers, which is worth stating. That camp has to take seriously the project of constructing richer models of human agency because those complaints cut much more ice when set against the backdrop of such models.

If all this sounds a bit harsh on neoclassical economics, let me reiterate: the postulate of instrumental rationality is very useful; it just cannot be all there is. Parfitt (1984) puts it like this: 'Like my cat, I often simply do what I want to do. I am then not using an ability that only persons have.' There is another expression which trades on something that cats do not do: 'it's

---

* Indeed, Marx for one would see this even more clearly: this capacity lies at the heart of the difference between 'science' and 'apologetics'.

enough to make a cat laugh'. The point then is: can you imagine a neoclassical explanation of laughter?

A final word is in order about the audience that I am writing for. I hope to have left enough of the intuition in the descriptions of pieces of economic analysis to act as toeholds for the non-economist. This seemed important to me because I think economics has something to offer the other social sciences that is significantly different from the message which it usually sends. Nevertheless, the main audience is economists, and I have in mind a pretty general bunch of the species. This means that much of what I have to say on economics qua economics will be familiar ground, even if the ground shifts between specialists. 'So much the better', I say, and I make no apologies here since those parts will be that much quicker to read. The bits that I assume will be less familiar to economists are those which draw on philosophy and other areas in social theory. I trust that they will repay a second look even if they strike you as peculiar or if my explanation leaves something to be desired, because I think there is something wrong in economics which bears looking at through the eyes of philosophy and social theory.

Lest there be any misunderstanding at this early stage in the argument, I hasten to add that this is not a recipe for poetics or hand waving, or any of those other strange and 'dubious' habits which hard-nosed economists associate with philosophy and the other social sciencies. Economics after a good dose of philosophy and social theory can have all the rigour and empirical testing it likes. The point of the philosophy is to get this rigour and empirical testing back on the right track because it has become badly diverted by a vision of individuals as ludicrously simple 'pleasure' machines.

Part I

RATIONALITY

2 EMPIRICISM AND RATIONALITY

2.1 Introduction

This chapter is concerned with the epistemological argument for a rationality assumption in economics. What is meant here by a rationality assumption can best be appreciated through a comparison with the alternative empiricist methodologies.

There are a variety of empiricist methodologies in economics, but they share the common characteristic of making empirical evidence the ultimate arbiter of what is good or bad theory. So, for instance, any assumption with respect to what might or might not be rational behaviour has no special claim in this scheme. Such assumptions are only licensed directly by the empirical support they receive or indirectly by the empirical support that the predictions which are based upon them command. It is empirical evidence which is in the driving seat as far as theoretical development is concerned, and assumptions about behaviour are firmly planted in the back seat with the usual admonitions about back seat driving.

The contrasting claim of a methodology which begins with rationality is that all theory requires a prior assumption concerning what constitutes rational behaviour in order to generate explanations, and that the choice of assumption cannot be made exclusively by reference to the empirical evidence. The choice involves something more than a discussion of t statistics, R^2, Chow tests and the like.

Later chapters address directly the constituents of this non-empiricist discourse. This chapter is concerned with why one form of empiricism or another is not sufficient. It should be emphasised at the outset that the claim is only one about insufficiency. It is not being suggested that empirical work is redundant. The argument is simply that there is necessarily something more to judging theories in economics than 'consulting' the empirical evidence.

The next section sketches the empiricist methodological tradition in economics. There is no pretence that this is a genuine survey of this tradition. There already exist excellent references on this (see Caldwell, 1982 and Blaug, 1980). The purpose of this section is to remind the reader of the main features of what is still probably the typical economist's methodological position. Consequently, it concentrates on a famous and dominant version of the empiricist method in economics: the position that can be traced to Friedman's essay on positive economics.

This is followed by three sections which set out the principal difficulties of all empiricist methodologies. The major problems come under the heading of the Quine–Duhem hypothesis and concern the underdetermination of theory by facts and the theoretical impregnation of facts. These, along with the references to the philosophy of social science in the form of Popper (1963). Kuhn (1970) and Lakatos (1978), will be familiar to many economists. But there is also a brief discussion of the criticism which can be mounted by the hermeneutic tradition. This discussion is probably less familiar, drawing on for example Winch (1958). It is a useful introduction to some of the ideas that will surface again in the later chapters on procedural and expressive rationality.

These criticisms undercut the project of judging theories by the objective standard of the 'brute facts'. The question which then arises is whether there exists any other way of objectively judging theories. Is there another methodological approach which will enable us to anchor our theories? Or does this mean that social science must collapse into some form of relativism? Section 2.6 reflects briefly on the pre-existing methodological tradition of rationality in economics, which also claims to be the basis for judging different theories; and it touches even more briefly on other post-empiricist methodologies. It concludes that it will be difficult to resist the sirens of relativism unless a non-empiricist discourse can be established which will enable the evaluation of different rationality assumptions. This sets the challenge for the rest of the book.

2.2   Empiricist Methodologies in Economics

Empiricist methodologies in economics are usually explicitly modelled on a particular view of the natural sciences. Put baldly, the natural world is perceived as an ordered realm independent of our concepts, beliefs and hypotheses about it: the task of science is to discover that order, and the method is experimental. It is in experiment that scientific conjectures confront the facts of the world they hope to explain. This is the hallmark of the scientific method; its theories stand or fall according to how they fare in the test against the facts. It is the primacy of empirical evidence which marks the spirit of true science.

There is something vaguely heroic in this picture of science and the natural scientist which draws its sustenance from the Enlightenment and the secularisation of the modern world. It is a potent mixture of liberation and progress that seems to be responsible for its appeal. There is the insistence on the priority of the empirical evidence and the refusal to be guided by faith or vested interest which strikes a chord in the popular imagination; and there is the extraordinary material advance of the last 200 years which bears witness to the fruits of the approach. Of course, the image of the scientist may have changed but, I suspect, this spirit of science continues to inspire.

Lipsey (1963) trades on that feeling when he casts the social scientist in a similar role for an audience which is being introduced to economics. 'Einstein', he reminds us, 'started from facts' (p. v). The hallmark of the scientific approach is the answering of 'questions by an appeal to a carefully collected and co-ordinated body of facts' (p. 7). 'Over the last several hundred years the citizens of most Western countries have enjoyed the fruits of innumerable scientific discoveries.' This approach contrasts with others that 'might be to appeal to authority, e.g. Aristotle or the scriptures, to appeal by introspection to some inner experience . . .' (p. 6). Lest this mixture of progress and cocking-a-snook at one authority or another prove too heady, he concludes with a warning: 'having counselled disrespect for the authority of accepted theory, it is necessary to warn against adopting an approach which is too cavalier' (p. 16). It is too cheap to say that 'theory is for the birds'. To criticise a theory effectively on empirical grounds one must demonstrate, by a carefully made set of observations, that some aspect of the theory is contradicted by the facts.

While Lipsey (1963) acquaints the introductory student with the relevance of this picture of science to economics, it is Friedman (1953) who gives the classic statement of an empiricist position for the profession as a whole.* He associates economic theory with 'a language' and 'a body of substantive hypotheses designed to abstract essential features of complex reality'. The former is a 'set of tautologies' and 'its function is to serve as a filing system for organising empirical material and facilitating our understanding of it'. Whether the right features have been abstracted depends solely on the success of the resulting predictions: . . . 'Viewed as a body of substantive hypotheses, theory is to be judged by its predictive power for the class of phenomena which it is intended to explain . . . the only relevant test of the validity of a hypothesis is a comparison of its predictions with experience.' (pp. 8–9) Friedman goes on to note that these tests only ever provide the opportunity for falsification rather than verification, thus gesturing to the well-known problem of induction, i.e. the impossibility of grounding the principle of induction, the projection of past patterns into the future, without an appeal to the principle itself. He also doubts that the inability to conduct controlled experiments reflects any basic difference between the social and the natural sciences: 'Evidence cast up by

* There is something quite ironical in the canonical status which Friedman's article has achieved because, almost immediately after the positivist position has been set out, he undercuts it by admitting that other criteria like simplicity and fruitfulness must enter into theory choice (see for instance p. 10). Nevertheless, there is little doubt that the bald positivist statement captures well the profession's methodological position.

experience is abundant and frequently as conclusive as that from contrived experiments. . . .' (p. 10)

Taken together, the last two quotations constitute as clear a statement of an empiricist methodology in economics as one could hope for. It will be a familiar enough position to all economists and so requires no further elaboration here. However, two consequences of this methodology are worth signalling since the argument returns to them at a later stage.

Firstly and self-evidently, once empiricist nethodology is in place the foundations have been laid for the distinction between positive and normative economics. It is, in effect, precisely the same distinction and balance as was struck under the Enlightenment between science and religion. Positive economics is concerned with what is the case. It is a body of knowledge which is generated by following empiricist methodologies. The economist discovers the order in the social world just as the scientist discovers the patterns of the natural world. Naturally, as facts have been put in command of the evolution of this theory, it is value free. This is unlike normative economics, which is precisely concerned with how things ought to be. It starts with certain value-laden premises about what is good or bad and then sets out how these objectives might be achieved, often using the insights generated from the positive branch of the discipline about how the economy actually works. Thus, positive economics serves the normative branch just as Enlightenment science serves the spiritual goals given by religion.

Secondly, the economist who follows the empiricist creed is not really a hero in the Enlightenment mould. Rather, as Lipsey suggests, the practice of being a scientist these days is much more like that of a technician: remember 'the careful collection and co-ordination of observations'. What should not be lost, though, is that the image of technician is a popularising one which fits well with the twentieth-century suspicion of heroes. That any Joe Soap could be a scientist is important, and economists seem most adept at trading on this image. How often has the claim been heard from economists that they are only 'technicians'? At one and the same time, it has the virtue of an apparent modesty combined with a hint of the seriousness which lies behind such modesty. And, of course, these virtues are especially clear in the social sciences, where value judgements abound and seem to threaten to engulf whole disciplines. There is an undeniable comfort in being able to draw back from a morass of competing value judgements and, like the positive economist, 'modestly' aspire to no more than being a 'technician'.

The purpose of these remarks was to draw attention to the obvious attractions of an empiricist-based methodology of the sort commended by Friedman. Firstly, it seems to offer a very simple prescription for how to set about doing a social science which is drawn directly from the successes of the natural sciences. This is an obvious attraction and it should not be underrated. Secondly, it bestows on economists a self image which is psychologically flattering. This is probably less well recognised as an attraction; and it may seem, to some, equally less obviously relevant to a discussion of methodology. But the attractions of this sort of empiricist method do need emphasising. Otherwise, it becomes difficult to understand why it has exercised such a stranglehold on the profession because it is actually fatally flawed as method for guiding economics.

2.3 Duhem and Quine

One of the problems encountered by this vision of science is that there are no brute facts. There is, as Quine (1961) puts it, no 'unvarnished news' which can serve as an objective and independent test of hypotheses. Unfortunately, the 'facts' in economics are no different: they already have theoretical order built into them as well. So, they can hardly act in the simple manner suggested by Friedman, as the independent test of theories.

At one level, this dependence of facts on theory is plain from the historical record with respect to the development of any data series. Theory often seems to give the lead for the creation of particular data sets. National income accounting is a good example since it was heavily influenced by Keynesian economic theory. Equally, the partial nature of data on household, with its almost complete neglect of economic activity within the household, seems directly related to the treatment of the household in mainstream economic theory. This theory concentrates on the participation of the household in paid employment, treating it as if it were a single individual, while showing a marked lack of interest in what goes on inside the household, with the concepts of unpaid labour and a gender division of labour. The recognition of this type of influence of theory on the facts might be worrying for some versions of the hypothetico-deductive method where the experience of some initial set of facts is supposed to be responsible for the generation of the original hypotheses. However, it is not going to prove troublesome if hypotheses are not exclusively dependent on prior experiences but also rely on imaginative leaps of one kind or another. As long as the facts are always there and the historical record is read as one where the theory merely led us to collect the data on these facts, then the empirical evidence is still in the driving seat and capable of performing as judge and jury on theory.

However, the trouble is deeper than this. The 'facts' have a theoretical order built into them in at least two further and badly corrosive ways for empiricism. Firstly, a data series like the money supply or the general level of prices embodies theoretical order because there are a number of different definitions of the money supply and ways of aggregating prices, and the choice of one rather than another will reflect theoretical considerations. This can be of some consequence for empirical tests when the choice of one set of facts rather than another affects the falsification of different theories: witness the early studies of the demand for money where estimates of interest elasticity depended on which definition of the money supply was used (see Goodhart and Crockett, 1970).

Secondly, and this is where the social sciences differ significantly from the natural sciences, the facts do not stand independently of the theory because the beliefs that agents hold in the social world affect their behaviour and hence the outcomes which constitute the empirical evidence. Hahn (1980) offers a simple example of where this interdependence between fact and theory can undo quite dramatically any simple notion that the facts provide a decisive objective test for a theory.

Consider an economy which is in a 'Keynesian' non-Walrasian equilibrium position (as defined by Barro and Grossman, 1971, or Malinvaud, 1977), with a government which is expanding the money supply. Agents in the economy must form expectations with respect to the consequences of this expansionary policy: they either follow a simple 'monetarist' model which associates such expansions with increases in the price level and no change in output; or they use a simple 'Keynesian' model where output expands and prices remain constant. If agents hold monetarist beliefs then they will raise their prices individually in line with what they expect to be a general increase in prices consequent upon the expansion of the money supply; they have no desire to alter relative prices, otherwise they would have acted to achieve such a change before now. Hence, their behaviours will confirm their theoretical beliefs: the general level of prices will have risen, there is no increase in real demand and no reason to adjust output levels. Conversely, if they hold Keynesian beliefs they will expect an increase in real aggregate demand because prices are expected to remain constant and this warrants that individually they will boost their output, and so again their behaviours will confirm their theoretical beliefs.

What kind of sense would it make to talk about the facts as an independent check on the theory here? None! The facts are so deeply impregnated with the theory in this instance that it is the theory which is unambiguously in the driving seat. Nor need the example be construed as particularly special. Think of Akerlof's (1970) lemons model and the relation between the beliefs about encountering a 'lemon' in the market for second-hand cars and the actual likelihood of lemons dominating the market. It is the belief that second-hand car markets are dominated by 'lemons' which when acted upon leads to this dominance. Furthermore, the general point about the interdependence of fact and theory will arise whenever expectations are formed in the light of theory, i.e. whenever agents follow Muth's

(1961) general recipe for forming rational expectations and expectations affect agent behaviour. And the particular feature, where the facts become subordinate to the theory in the manner above, will occur whenever there are multiple rational expectations equilibria, as in Hahn (1980).

The second aspect of the Duhem–Quine criticism of empiricist methodologies relates to the inability to test single hypotheses. Quine (1961), echoing Duhem (1914), suggests that our beliefs form a 'seamless web', a 'field of force which touches experience only at the edges'. When these beliefs are tested, they 'face the tribunal of experience together' and, in assessing the verdict, we are always able to choose what to accept, revise or reject.

The point is usually well understood by economists because of the important role played by *ceteris paribus* conditions. Predictions are always issued subject to *ceteris paribus* clauses and, if the prediction fails, the economist is often able to claim that this is because *ceteris paribus* conditions were violated. This is an especially easy move to make when the *ceteris paribus* conditions refer to unobservables. The testing of homogeneity in consumer theory offers an obvious example. There is a convenient 'let-out' in the form of preference orderings which are unobservable but which must remain constant for a genuine test of the hypothesis – not to mention the host of other hypotheses that are jointly tested with homogeneity in consumer theory, which can be called upon in the creative interpretation of a poor result for homogeneity. It could be due to an incorrect functional form, dynamic specification and so on through the litany.

It is the same difficulty which is at the heart of the notoriously varied interpretations of the evidence which associates the money supply with the price level. The association does not constitute a test of the hypothesis that changes in the money supply cause inflation because there is at least one further hypothesis which is at stake in the interpretation of the empirical evidence: the endogeneity/exogeneity of the money supply. And it is precisely the ability to take different views on the matter of exogeneity/endogeneity which has fuelled much of this debate.

Indeed, the issue of exogeneity/endogeneity has a more general significance which is worth noting because it surfaces whenever classical statistical inference is used in economics. The standard test statistics all rely for their interpretation on a correct identification, among other things, of which variables are exogenous/endogenous in an equation system. Put bluntly, no statistical test can be conducted on a hypothesis concerning the significance of one or another variable which is independent of another hypothesis concerning exogeneity/endogeneity in the system as a whole (and a series of other hypotheses relating to 'correct' specifications. functional forms, error structures and so on). There seems to have been a vain hope once that these subsidiary hypotheses might be broken down and tested separately. For example, there is a battery of causality tests which refine the idea that causality can be judged by the temporal ordering between variables. As an outsider, it is difficult to judge how seriously these techniques were taken by econometricians as tests of exogeneity/ endogeneity. Fortunately, macroeconomists were wise at an early stage to the problem of making temporal ordering decisive, aided by the unsettling thought that it could hardly be the case that Christmas was caused by a prior increase in the money supply (see Kaldor, 1970)!

To conclude this section, the first difficulty with empiricist method-ologies arises because the facts, so to speak, do not constitute an independent jury. The second problem with empiricism relates to the necessary ambi-guity in the interpretation of a test which occurs because hypotheses are never tested singly. Theories are underdetermined by the facts. Hypoth-eses are jointly tested and this always leaves some discretion to the 'scientist' over what the implications of the test are for any particular hypothesis.

2.4 Popper, Kuhn and Lakatos

Some care is required here to avoid setting up a 'straw' empiricist method-ology which can easily be shot down. Most economists may subscribe to a Lipsey or Friedman type of empiricism, but that does not mean that it is the last word on the subject. For this reason, it is sensible to look at what philosophers of science have to say about method. Indeed, it is particularly important as there are some economists, like Blaug (1980), who believe that a correct reading of Popper can revive the flagging fortunes of empiricism.

The basis for such a claim lies in Popper's recognition that the Duhem–Quine hypothesis does create problems for empirical testing and the goal of falsifiability, which are to be the touchstones of scientific endeavor. Blaug puts it like this:

> It is because 'no conclusive disproof of a theory can ever be produced' that we need methodological limits on the strategems that may be adopted by scientists to safeguard their theories against refutation. These methodologi-cal limits are not superficial adjuncts to Popper's philosophy of science; they are essential to it. It is not always appreciated that it is not falsifiability as such that distinguishes science from non-science in Popper; what does demarcate science from non-science is falsifiability plus methodological rules that forbid what he first called 'ad-hoc auxiliary assumptions' later 'conven-tionalist strategies' and finally 'immunising strategies'. (p. 18)

Blaug acknowledges that there is 'no sure method of guaranteeing that the fallible knowledge we do have of the real world is positively the best we can possess under the circumstances'. Yet, he concludes: 'My own contention . . . is that the central weakness of modern economics is, indeed, the reluctance to produce the theories that yield unambiguously refutable implications, followed by a general unwillingness to confront those implications with the facts.' (p. 254) . . . 'The problem now is to persuade economists to take falsificationism seriously.' (p. 206)

Blaug perceives the problem as an indiscriminate use of those immunising strategies. We have failed to see that Popper explicitly proscribed such strategies because they undermined falsificationism. What is required is a redoubling of the guard against immunising strategies: there must be 'severe' tests; consistency with the evidence is not enough; competing hypotheses must stand in the same arena to see which fares best because this is a sophisticated form of falsificationism; there must be more attention to data collection, greater replication of results, reporting of all regression results to avoid data mining and so on. (See also for example, the Leamer (1983) and McAleer, Pagan and Volker (1985) contributions in the 'who will take the con out of econometrics' debate.)

This is all commendable stuff, and it may help to throw new light and perspectives on a particular data set. But it is not going to save empiricist methodologies. The trouble is that it fails to take to heart the earlier recognition that there is 'no sure way of guaranteeing . . .' and 'we cannot pretend that there is . . . a perfectly objective method'. The crucial point is precisely that: there is no 'sure way'; there is no 'objective method' which is impeded only because of the dastardly use of immunising strategies, like the unwarranted reliance on *ceteris paribus* clauses and data mining. If there was a 'sure way', then of course it would make sense to recommend vigilance with respect to immunising strategies. But there is not. The use of *ceteris paribus* clauses, or indeed data mining over functional form, is not necessarily a bad thing. It could be quite legitimate. The problem is that we do not know when these practices are legitimate and nor can we know by consulting the empirical evidence alone: this is the message of Duhem and Quine. To suggest that data mining or the use of *ceteris paribus* clauses should be avoided is no better than an injunction to use them liberally. Duhem and Quine are isolating a problem with empirical tests. The underdetermination of theory by empirical evidence means that so-called immunising strategies are built into science at the outset. This problem is not going to go away and the facts are not suddenly going to speak for themselves.

Kuhn (1970) does not really have much to say which is relevant on this. His concern is with the historical record in the practice of science. He finds very little evidence there of theories in regular battle with the facts. Rather, theories which would seem to be mortally wounded by the facts demonstrate extraordinary powers of resilience. The process of theory displacement is both more complicated and more gradual than an empiricist account would lead you to expect. It is best understood as a process of paradigm displacement, where paradigms are in important regards incommensurable and so they do not stand face-to-face in any straightforward test against the evidence. There is little here by way of a prescriptive nature, but Kuhn's reading of the historical record can hardly provide much comfort for the empiricist.

In contrast, Lakatos (1978) blends many of the Kuhn-type historical insights with a prescriptive model which goes under the title of the methodology of scientific research programmes. He suggests that all research programmes consist of two parts. There is a core of key metaphysical propositions and there is a protective belt of auxiliary hypotheses. The belt absorbs the impact of contrary evidence and to that extent the theory responds to the evidence. But, in so doing, it shields the core of the programme. So, for example, one might characterise the neoclassical research programme in economics as having a core of individualism, with agents maximising well-behaved objective functions, and a protective belt which contains hypotheses about things like information and perhaps institutional context. Hence, when the research programme is confronted by an anomaly, say the apparent failure of agents to exhaust all mutually beneficial trades in the labour market, the belt adjusts to accommodate the observation by allowing for less than perfect information or an institutional context like unions where insider/outsider problems are important. (See Latsis (1976) for more detail on the application of Lakatos to economics.)

Research programmes are then to be judged by whether they are 'progressive' or 'degenerate'. They are progressive when adjustments to the belt in response to unwelcome facts throw up novel predictions, and degenerate if they absorb new facts by *ad hoc* adjustments which serve only to protect the core from the latest embarrassment. At first glance, this looks like a tempting alternative guide for judging theories. It seems to be substituting a comparative dynamic standard for the comparative static standard which normally characterises empiricist methodologies. But suspicions begin to be aroused the moment the guide is set to work. Consider the relaxation of the perfect information assumption in the example above: how is this to be judged? A first idea is that it is progressive: look at the countless applications of imperfect information assumptions from lemons models through to reputation models in oligopoly games. However, on second thoughts, to acknowledge imperfect information in this way begins to look like an own goal because it sits uneasily with the core assumption of individual utility maximising behaviour. After all, there is the old conundrum of how to know what the optimal acquisition of information is, which suggests that imperfect information demands an alternative model of individual behaviour to the maximising one. Perhaps, then, it was wrong to characterise the neoclassical core as containing individual objective maximising behaviour. But, once you allow a redefinition of the core to prevent this unwelcome thought, it looks as if the methodology of scientific research programmes has found an Achilles heel to rival the flexible use of the *ceteris paribus* conditions in the basic version of empiricism. The point is that since the core of a research programme is not self-evident it seems likely that any particular unwelcome inference on the progressive/ degenerate scale can be avoided with a simple redefinition of what constitutes the core.

Consider another possible line of defence. Suppose it is agreed that the research programme is degenerate. Why should adherents to the programme treat this as an indication that the programme will remain in this state of torpor hereafter? What prevents the argument that this is a temporary slough? Might not the adherents gesture with good reason to the revived fortunes of the 'classical' paradigm in macroeconomics to substantiate their own unwillingness to scrap their programme?

The worry here is that the assessment of whether a research programme is progressive or degenerate, and indeed what to do about such an assessment, will vary with the eyes of the beholder. It can be expressed more generally by asking what kind of criterion is being suggested by the methodology of scientific research programmes. It certainly looks empirical in the sense that it appears that we are asked to count up the number of novel predictions emanating from adjustments in the belt. And if this is the case, then the earlier problems with empirical tests are bound to surface in one form or another. Alternatively, if it is not empirical, then we need to know much more about the currency of the non-empirical discourse which is being suggested.

2.5 Rules and Meaning in the Hermeneutic Tradition

Before I discuss what an alternative rationalist methodological approach might look like, it will be helpful to mention a critique of the empiricist method which comes from a different quarter. This attack emanates from the hermeneutic tradition and it serves both to introduce the idea of the primacy of conceptual categories which is also central to the rationalist approach and to illustrate the dangers in the form of a collapse into relativism which can occur if this idea is allowed a free rein.

Winch (1958) disputes that the social sciences should emulate the empirical method of the natural sciences by building on some of the arguments which are to be found in Wittgenstein (1953) and Weber (1922). Roughly speaking, it is the combination of Weber's insistence on the internal point of view with Wittgenstein's idea of rule-governed behaviour which generates the conclusion that the project of the social sciences is understanding rather than predicting or explaining what has happened.

The important part of the argument as far as this chapter is concerned is the Wittgenstein element. It turns on a recognition that, while the external world exists, truth and indeed other descriptions of the world do not exist in the external world: these descriptions are a human creation and if we are to understand how they are created we must look at the language in which they are constructed. Winch puts it like this:

> 'What is real?' involves the problem of man's relation to reality which takes us beyond pure science. . . . For it is not an empirical question at all, but a conceptual one. It has to do with the force of the concept of reality. An appeal to the results of an experiment would necessarily beg the important question, since the philosopher would be bound to ask by what token those results themselves are accepted as 'reality'. (p. 9)

> Our idea of what belongs to the realm of reality is given for us in the language that we use. The concepts we have settle for us the form of the experience we have of the world. It may be worth reminding ourselves of the truism that when we speak of the world we are speaking of what we in fact mean by the expression 'the world': there is no way of getting outside the concepts in terms of which we think of the world. . . . The world is for us presented through those concepts. That is not to say that our concepts may not change; but when they do, that means our concept of the world has changed too. (p. 15)

Winch continues the Wittgenstein refrain by arguing that concepts and meaning in language are not created by language acting as a mirror for nature. This is obvious in the literal sense that 'river' does not correspond more closely in its sounds or shape to water passing between two clearly visible land masses, while 'ocean' corresponds better to water which ebbs and flows in a particular way which is associated with absence of any land mass in close proximity. The existence of foreign languages further illustrates that it cannot be the sound or shape of the word which reflects nature. Nor is it that words are like signs and symbols on a map, where there is a one-to-one mapping between the signs and symbols and their physical counterparts in the natural world. It is not a question of consulting the legend of the map to unlock the meaning of a word through its association with some feature of the natural world. This is clear if one reflects on the difference between 'winking' and 'blinking'. There is, of course, an important difference between the two but we do not recognise it by virtue of the physical differences which are manifest in the natural world when one activity is undertaken rather than the other. Physically, 'winking' looks identical to 'blinking'. We could never learn the rich difference in meaning between the two through a microscopic study of the physical activity itself because the difference is not to be found in the physical activity itself. Instead, it is to be found in the rules which contextualise the action. These rules might be loosely referred to as the cultural context of action.

A celebrated example from one of the founder figures in modern linguistics, Saussure, makes the same point in a slightly different way. When we say 'it is the same train which leaves Geneva for Paris at 8.25 each morning', it is, of course, not literally the same train. There are not the identical engine and wagons each day, with personnel to match. Yet there would be no misunderstanding if we talk of the train as the same. And this is because we understand very well in the context of rules governing what constitutes 'sameness' and 'difference' in railway travel in our society (i.e. principally time of departure) that they are the same train.

In Winch's hands, the Wittgenstein assault on the correspondence theory of truth is turned into a radical proposal for the social sciences which echoes the earlier nineteenth-century hermeneutic tradition. It is a controversial argument that turns on combining the idea of a language game, which is what is being hinted at in the examples above, with the idea that there are no meaningful private languages. The force of the point about language games is that it does not make sense to think of language as reflecting some prior set of concepts or mirroring the real world because you cannot get outside the game to make this kind of observation of correspondence. It is just like a game of chess: the rules have not been formulated to satisfy some antecedent urge to move pieces of wood around a board. Instead, the rules help to define pieces of wood like a knight or a castle and create reasons and purpose for their movement which are wholly internal to the game. This is not to deny that we talk about the 'real world' and we make claims using concepts like 'truth', but in doing so we are operating within a game. The rules of the game help to define the concepts of 'truth', 'sameness' etc. rather than to express something which is prior to the game itself.

If concepts on this account are internal to the language game, then concepts could still be tied to the individual if it is also possible for individuals to have private languages. But Wittgenstein forestalls this move by arguing that the rules of language games are never exhaustive. They are not fully extensive: there are always gaps left open by the rules and consequently you can always interpret a set of rules in different ways. This is one of the paradoxes of following a rule, and it means that the following of a purely private rule as in a private language is going to be beset by a problem: you can never be sure when you are following a rule or breaking it. The way we get out of this problem of needing to follow rules for meaning to be established is to follow social rules and allow society to define what counts as following a rule.

This lays the basis for a thoroughgoing kind of relativism because concepts and meaning have neither external reference in the world nor internal references in ourselves. The purpose of social science, then, cannot be to discover the way the social world really is through the judicious collection of evidence, experimentation and the like, since we have created the world with our language (the thought is variously referred to by sympathisers and critics as the social construction/destruction of reality). Instead, the object of a social science is to understand how we have created the world through bringing to the surface the rules which have sometimes explicitly, but more often implicitly, gone into the construction of that world. And this can be done as easily from the philosopher's armchair as the scientist's laboratory!

This is not the place for a serious evaluation of Winch's argument (see, for instance, MacIntyre, 1973). It is interesting because it throws a slightly different perspective on the Duhem–Quine arguments about empirical evidence; and in doing so it implicates social rules in the observation of this changed relationship between theory and evidence. This and the idea of rule-governed behaviour will be developed in chapters 6, 7 and 8. The main purpose of this brief review of Winch at the moment has been to bring out two points in the development of the argument of this chapter. The first is the primacy of conceptual categories in relation to empirical evidence because this helps to make sense of minimalist rationalist claims for the foundation of knowledge. Secondly, it sounds a relativist warning. This can be quickly appreciated by reflecting on the new objective for social science of 'understanding' rather than 'explanation'. Consider the question of how such an approach would face the problem of different 'understandings' of some particular social setting. There is no sense in trying to decide which 'understanding' is correct: all that can be attempted is an 'understanding' of those 'understandings'; and in a similar fashion, it is not possible to judge the accuracy of this 'understanding' of 'understandings' because the only licence we have is to 'understand'. In short, one 'understanding' will always be as good as another because there is no other meter which would enable an evaluative comparison.

As Winch puts it, there are as many realities as there are forms of life because 'reality' is a concept which is internal to the matrix of rules which constitute the practices of that society. This is a serious challenge to the traditional project of the social sciences, and in a general sense it is easy to see how it has arisen. In the empiricist account 'facts' provided an external and objective test for theories, and once the objectivity of facts came under suspicion so did the anchoring of theories in anything objective. This opened the gate to a purely 'subjective' or relativistic account of theory, which is epitomised by the work of Winch; and it looks as if it is going to be difficult to resist going through the gate unless there is some other way of bringing objectivity back into the discussion of theories. At this stage, it becomes natural to consider rationalist methodologies because it is exactly their claim that there is another source of 'objectivity' which can be used to anchor theories. The next section provides a brief sketch of this methodological approach and other post-empiricist responses that can be found in the economics literature.

2.6 Rationality

So far little has been said about what an alternative methodology might look like. The argument has been directed at denying the foundation of empiricist-based methodologies. Virtually nothing has been said on the possibilities and prospects of a non-empiricist discourse, except for the worrying thoughts on a collapse into relativism at the end of the last section. Yet, there need be no great mystery here because there has always been an alternative methodological tradition in economics, one which is based on the claim of a priori knowledge. The contemporary Austrian school are, perhaps, the most vocal exponents of this tradition, but it has its roots in the nineteenth century (see, for example, Blaug, 1980).

In this tradition, economics is concerned with a prioristic reasoning. It begins with self-evident propositions about human action (i.e. that they are 'rational') and builds deductively upon them. von Mises, (1949, 1962) is the most unambiguous exponent of this view, calling it praxeological reasoning, and he has some of the most trenchant things to say about the relation between theory and empirical evidence:

> Without theory, the general a prioristic science of human action, there is no comprehension of the reality of human action . . . experience concerning human action is conditioned through praxeological categories. . . . If we had not in our minds the schemes provided by praxeological reasoning, we should never be in a position to discern and grasp any action (1949, pp. 39–40)

> What assigns economics its peculiar and unique position . . . is the fact that its particular theorems are not open to verification or falsification on the ground of experience. . . . The ultimate yardstick of an economic theorem's correctness or incorrectness is solely reason unaided by experience. (1949, p. 858)

> As a method of economic analysis econometrics is a childish play with figures that does not contribute anything to the elucidation of the problems of economic reality. (1962, p. 63)

The argument here for the primacy of a priori categories bears a strong similarity to that of Winch (1958). It is the same idea that the conceptual categories must come first: 'the a priori categories are the mental equipment by dint of which man is able to think and to experience and thus to acquire knowledge' (1962, p. 18). And it is cashed-in in exactly the same way through a complete relegation of empirical evidence to the status of 'childish play.' The prescription is likewise sedentary: 'The economist deals with matters that are present and operative in every man. . . . The economist need not displace himself; he can in spite of all the sneers . . . accomplish his job in an armchair.' (1962, p. 78)

What marks von Mises out as different from Winch is the further particular commitment to individualistic a priori categories – or to put this in the terms of the previous section, von Mises is parting company with Winch and Wittgenstein over private languages. Ultimately, as he says, there are only individuals in history, and the crucial feature of individual action is that it is purposive: 'Whether or not he aims at accumulating wealth, he always aims at employing what he owns for those ends which, as he thinks, will satisfy him best.

There is only one motive that determines all actions of all men, viz., to remove directly or indirectly, as much as possible any uneasiness felt.' (1962, p. 76)

In effect, this would seem to be a claim to be able to ground economic theory a priori in an individualistic kind of instrumental rationality. This is plainly going to be a controversial move because Winch uses the same kind of argument to support a different type of project in the social sciences.

Before addressing that controversy, it is probably sensible to make a brief parenthetic remark about Hayek, if only to avoid any confusion which might otherwise arise. Hayek is a commanding figure in the Austrian tradition but he has never been quite so dogmatically a priorist as von Mises. His commitment to the foundation of individualistic purposiveness is every bit as strong as that of von Mises. However, he also accepts that empirical evidence and testing has a methodological role, albèit a subordinate one. His reasons for casting it in this subordinate role are more closely related to the individualistic foundations than von Mises's ruthless application of the logical primacy of a priori reasoning. It is the fact that, in the final analysis, it is individuals that provide the key to explanation which means that knowledge about the economy is necessarily imperfect. You could never have a full knowledge of everyone's tastes to enable predictions of a particular kind. You might be able to issue general predictions of the sort that a fall in price will prime demand because this does not require any specific knowledge. But the moment that you wanted to know something more detailed about the change in demand, the lack of knowledge of individual tastes eats away at the quality of the predictions. The problem is even more complicated because individual behaviour also depends on the imperfect knowledge he/she has of other agent's behaviour. As this knowledge changes, so does behaviour, thus complicating the task of prediction because the world is always on the move, moving towards equilibrium, but rarely is it ever there.

Actually, this emphasis on the role of information exposes further interesting similarities between the Austrians and Winch, because Winch has an analogous argument about the difficulties of forming predictions in the social world. The terms of the argument are rather different at first sight because they relate to the open-ended nature of rules in Winch: the fact that such rules can never be exhaustive. But this difference should not be exaggerated because Hayek (1969) also recognises that the problems of information in a society are bound up with what he calls the 'rules of conduct'. Indeed, Winch uses two nice examples to illustrate his line of argument, and it would cause no surprise to find either of them in an Austrian tract on the same theme. In one, he argues, it would not be possible through a minute study of the rules governing music composition in the time of Haydn and Mozart to predict a Beethoven. In the other, he quotes Humphrey Lyttleton's reply to a question about the direction of jazz: 'If I knew where jazz was going I'd be there.' It is difficult to imagine a better example of the force behind the rational expectations argument in economics that exposes at the same time the difficulties in the formation of such expectations which Austrians would be quick to draw attention to.

As with all parenthetic remarks, this one is showing alarming signs of developing a momentum of its own. So, I will return to the main strand of the argument: von Mises and a priori knowledge as an alternative source for the 'objective' foundations for economic theory.

There is an obvious difficulty with the von Mises position. He has singled out instrumental rationality as a necessary starting point for all economic theory, but, using the terms of the previous section, what is there to prevent the accusation that this conception of rationality is internal to the particular language game of twentieth-century industrialised countries? Stated more simply, supposing I argue that I know a priori that rational behaviour sums to something other than this, how could this claim be disputed? Appeals to empirical evidence alone would take us back to an empiricist method; and a gesture to widespread agreement amongst individuals in our society over what is rational behaviour is not going to head-off the suspicion that a priori knowledge is conventional knowledge masquerading under another name. In other words, once you leave empiricist methodologies, there is nothing obvious to halt a slide into relativism. The claim of rationalism seems merely to have channelled the relativist impasse into a discussion of what constitutes rational behaviour.

Alas, this also appears to be the conclusion reached by other economists in the post-empiricist methodological literature. For example, McCloskey

(1983), in an engaging article, argues that something other than empirical evidence is responsible for persuading us to hold one theory rather than another; and that something else is best understood as coming under the venerable title of 'rhetoric'. 'Rhetoric' probably conjures up a picture of a sorcerer's book of tricks on the art of persuasion, and this is not far off the mark. It is certainly not a scientific activity that persuades an audience by grounding some theories 'objectively' while others fail the test.

Although McCloskey stops short of making the connection with relativism, it is difficult to escape this conclusion. After all, 'rhetoric' comes into play precisely because there are no objective foundations: it is licensed by the recognition of a relativist position. In a nutshell, style assumes an importance exactly when there are no matters of substance which can be used to distinguish one theory from another.

It is difficult to resist much of McCloskey's argument. One can understand many of the developments in economics through the rhetorical tools which have been deployed on their behalf. However, it also says too little. There is more to how an explanation 'works', how it persuades. Some of what is mising can be filled in by the arguments of Katouzian (1980) on ideology and the professionalisation of the discipline, or more generally through the development of a perspective on the sociology of knowledge. But the important omission is philosophical.

In effect, McCloskey says too little because too much has been conceded to relativism. There is a philosophical contribution that can be made which opens up the space between empiricist objectivity and relativism; and this book is an attempt to set out some of that contribution. It is operating on the terrain created by the rationalist approach and it hopes to go some way towards answering the question, which the rationalist position must address, on the merits of one rationality assumption rather than another.

2.7 Conclusion

Empiricist methodologies are extremely attractive. They imply that there is a straightforward way of choosing between theories which is based on their 'objective' properties – their relation to the 'facts'. They also yield a distinction between positive and normative economics which permits the economist to take on the attractive role, at least in the social sciences, of being a technician. However, these methodologies flatter to deceive.

'Facts' do not give the theories they support an objective status because the 'facts' are always impregnated with theory and theory is typically underdetermined by the 'facts'. The question which every social science then has to face is whether there is any other way of judging theories objectively. If there is not, then, as the argument has been developed so far in this chapter, a collapse into relativism looks likely and the project of the social sciences becomes one of 'understanding'.

The alternative methodological position in economics grounds theories on the a priori knowledge that agents are rational. At first sight, this looks a promising strategy for halting the drift into relativism and preserving the project of explanation and prescription in economics. However, as it stands this methodological tradition leaves plenty of room for relativist play over how to cash in exactly what constitutes rational behaviour. One of the main objectives of the rest of this book is to forestall that free-for-all by developing a non-empiricist discourse which evaluates different rationality assumptions.

It should be made clear that a non-empiricist methodology does not necessarily mean that there is to be no recourse to empirical evidence. The conclusion to be drawn from the first four sections is only that empirical evidence must be dislodged from a pre-eminent epistemological position. It cannot occupy such a role, and if economists wish to preserve the project of explanation and prescription then they must look afresh at the rationality assumptions with which they go to work. But this does not mean that the evaluation of different rationality assumptions will not have an empirical dimension. Empirical evidence still matters: it just no longer rules the roost. Rorty (1987) brings out this changed relationship between theory and empirical evidence: 'The world can cause us to hold certain beliefs, but it cannot propose a language for us to speak . . . the fact that Newton's vocabulary let us predict the world more easily than Aristotle's does not mean that the world speaks Newtonian. The world does not speak: only we do. (p. 3)' It is worth pausing to elaborate on this altered relationship because it is easy to flip-flop between epistemological poles when what is actually required is some analysis of the uncomfortable terrain in between the clear positions of empirical objectivity and relativism. It is one thing to notice that there is no 'unvarnished news', to agree that our experience of 'reality' is always mediated through our own conceptual categories about what 'reality' is; but this is not to deny that there is an objective world which is independent of conjectures about it. The problem is that this objective world is not known to us directly. Nevertheless, it can still exercise an important influence on our capacities for action, and so we have every reason to grope towards an imperfect understanding of it.

It will be plain to most people that there are natural constraints, including those of human nature, in the world. For instance, however much I believe in the desirability or moral virtue of unpowered flight, I am not going to be able to throw open the windows of my fourth floor office and take off! The property of unaided human flight is not just an attribute of some forms of life and not others. There is a natural constraint here which is discovered empirically and I would be crazy, and probably short-lived, if I ignored it in any plans for a glorious social life on the wing.

Hence, the inability to judge theories objectively with reference to the facts does not mean that relativism has won the day. Instead, it licenses relativistic considerations in the more limited form: it introduces a welcome kind of scepticism about all claims to objective knowledge, without undermining the thought that there are objective constraints on action. In effect, we are forced into a strange world where the claims of both objectivity and relativism must be acknowledged; and in this world, empirical evidence is not decisive but it remains relevant. This is put in terms of the terrain between objectivity and relativism and not just the objectivity of facts because it will become apparent in subsequent chapters that a similar perspective attaches to the rationalist claims of objectivity. The discussion of rationality can usefully narrow the options much as empirical evidence on unaided human flight does, but in important cases it does not prove a decisive consideration. (For a fuller philosophical survey of attempts to transcend the either–or oppositions of objectivity and relativism, see Bernstein (1983).)

As far as the remainder of the book is concerned, this means that although it is a non-empiricist methodological approach, empirical evidence will not be out of place. Nevertheless, the cutting edge of the argument is conceptual. We can say things about the requirements of the rationality assumptions which will have to be built into theories if they are to serve as albeit imperfect guides for intervening in the world. Part of what we can say actually comes directly from the argument of this chapter. What has been concluded about the prospects for knowledge in the social sciences ought to be included in a model of rational action. It is our rationality which tells us that there are limits to our ability to anchor our knowledge securely and this must be built into the beliefs entertained by rational agents as they grope towards a consequently always imperfect understanding of the real constraints they operate under. It is this thought that what we can say about the foundations of knowledge, as rational agents, ought to feed self-reflexively into our models of a social world containing rational agents which partially motivates material on expressive rationality in chapter 8.

Finally, there is one loose end to be tidied up. The distinction between positive and normative economics, and with it the image of economist and technician, cannot be sustained once 'facts' have lost their objective status. Instead, if the leading edge of theory is always in a terrain between objectivity and relativism, where empirical evidence and considerations of rationality help to narrow the options but do not prove decisive, then there is always going to be room for values, rhetoric and other considerations to guide the acceptance of one theory rather than another.

But there seems nothing in this to cause alarm. Indeed, quite the reverse seems to be the case. Rorty's observation that it is us who do the speaking ought to be quite inspiring. The implication to be drawn from this methodological discussion is that we do create in important respects the world within which we live. This creation may be constrained by objective features, but it remains in part an act of creation and so it should not be surprising that our choice of what theories to hold should be guided in part by the way we would like to see the world. And the creative image of the economist that flows from this should be as good as source of comfort to us as the rhetorical jest of being technicians.

Part II

RATIONALITY AND EXPLANATION

3 INSTRUMENTAL RATIONALITY

3.1 Introduction

Instrumental rationality equates the 'rational' action with the choice of the means most likely to satisfy a given set of ends. For example, using a pedestrian crossing is the rational action because it is the best way of satisfying the objective of crossing the road with minimum risk of a road traffic accident. It is the dominant rationality assumption in the social sciences and it yields a type of explanation which is normally referred to as intentional. The action of using the pedestrian crossing is explained by reference to the intention of getting to the other side with minimum risk.

Within this category of intentional explanation, it is helpful to distinguish a pure intentional explanation where the action/outcome can easily be traced to a motivating intention, as in the use of the pedestrian crossing, from more complex forms where the intentionality combines with other causal elements to produce either a supra-intentional causal or a sub-intentional causal explanation. In both these cases, the element of intentionality is transformed and is only opaquely related to the outcome because the causal mechanisms intervene and operate 'behind the backs' of individuals and their intentions.

Supra-intentional causality refers to situations where individual actions are causally connected in such a way as to produce unintended consequences. This is what Smith (1976) foreshadows in that celebrated passage at the beginning of *The Wealth of Nations* when he asserts that: 'It is not from the benevolence of the butcher, the brewer or the baker, that we expect our dinner, but from their regard to their own interest.' (p. 18) It is a point which is more fully developed in his argument against restraints on trade.

> He generally indeed neither intends to promote the public interest . . . he intends only his own gain, and he is in this, as in many other cases, led by an invisible hand to promote an end which has no part of his intention. . . . By pursuing his own interest he frequently promotes that of society more effectually than when he really intends to promote it. (p. 477)

The causal element works like an 'invisible hand', in Smith's words, to produce consequences which are not intended by individual actors. As such, it modifies the consequences which flow from intentional actions rather than undermining the sovereignty of the intentions themselves. The same cannot be said about sub-intentional causality.

Sub-intentional causality refers to cases where the causal component affects the intentions themselves. Unknown to the agents, their beliefs and desires are being shaped by causal processes. Freud in his analysis of the unconscious roots of some actions offers one model of such sub-intentional causality. Cognitive psychology provides many others. Since the causal element here undermines the intentional component, the discussion of this type of explanation is held over to the critical review of instrumental rationality in the next three chapters (in particular chapter 6).

Some examples of how the instrumental rationality assumption has been used to generate intentional and supra-intentional causal explanations in economics are given in the next two sections. Necessarily, this is not an exhaustive survey: at best, it picks out some highlights. The discussion is designed to give an idea of the scope of this rationality assumption in economics by mentioning some central parts of economics which use it, and by sketching how the explanations offered in those parts of economic theory can be related back to the rationality assumption. This will be familiar ground for most economists because the reliance on instrumental rationality is one of the hallmarks of neoclassical economics. Consequently, the discussion can be easily skimmed. What should not be missed, though, in any quick skim is the fact that it is not only neoclassical economics which uses this rationality postulate. The postulate is to be found throughout economics.

The discussion of these two sections is divided between parametric and strategic decision settings. The parametric decision environments of the next section yield simple plans of action for agents, while the strategic settings of the third section produce a rather richer set of behaviours, like pre-commitments and reputation building. The fourth section offers a preliminary evaluation of this rationality postulate. It is preliminary in the sense that it only establishes the areas where instrumental rationality needs to be pressed, in the course of a proper evaluation; and in this way, it sets the stage for the next three chapters.

3.2 Instrumental Rationality in a Parametric Environment

An instrumentally rational action is defined with respect to a given set of objectives: it is the action which best satisfies those objectives. If the objectives can be expressed mathematically then the rational action can be simply understood as the action which maximises the objective function; and provided the objectives are also mathematically 'well behaved', a quite extraordinary range of insights concerning rational action and its consequences can be derived.

The most familiar example comes from consumer theory. Suppose that the preferences of an agent over any arbitrarily defined commodity bundles x, y, z etc. satisfy the following conditions, where R means 'is preferred to or is indifferent between', P means 'strictly preferred to' and I means 'indifferent'.

1 Reflexivity: for any bundle x, xRx. That is, x is always as good as itself.
2 Completeness: for any two bundles x and y, either xRy or yRx. That is, any two bundles can always be compared.
3 Transitivity: if xRy and yRz, then xRz. That is, the preference ordering must not exhibit internal inconsistencies.
4 Continuity: for any bundle x, define $A(x)$ as the at least as good as x set and $B(x)$ as the no better than x set; then $A(x)$ and $B(x)$ are closed. That is, given any two goods in a bundle it will always be possible by reducing the amount of one fractionally and increasing the amount of the other fractionally to define another bundle which is indifferent to the first.
5 Non-satiation: xPy when x contains more of at least one good and no less of any other than y.
6 Convexity: if xRy, then for $0 < \pi < 1$, $\pi x + (1 - \pi)y$Ry. That is, mixtures of indifferent bundles are preferred to either one of the bundles.

When (1)–(4) hold the preference ordering can be represented by a utility function which is unique up to a positive monotonic transformation. That means that a function $U(x)$ exists such that when xPy then $U(x) > U(y)$, and when xIy then $U(x) = U(y)$. But there are any number of such functions: it is only an ordering and any positive monotonic transformation of the function will preserve the ordering. With the addition of (5) the action which best satisfies these preferences is restricted to the surface of the budget constraint. Condition (6), whilst not always necessary, makes the utility function quasi-concave.

So, when (1)–(6) hold, the action of the instrumentally rational agent can be defined as the maximisation of a well-behaved utility function (in the sense of being differentiable and quasi-concave) subject to a budget constraint which, for a given price vector, constrains the bundles of commodities that can be purchased. In short, the instrumentally rational action is the one that best satisfies these well-ordered preferences.

Without any further specification of the detail of these preferences, it is well known that a number inferences can be drawn concerning the demand for commodities. For example, it is easy to demonstrate the Slutsky negative own price substitution result which underpins the so-called 'law' of demand. Let x be the vector of goods purchased when p is the price vector, and x' the vector of goods when the price vector changes to p'. The Slutsky own price substitution effect of the change in prices from p to p' is defined by considering the bundle x'' which would be purchased using the price vector p' when this is combined with a compensating variation in income to enable the purchase of the original bundle x (i.e. income changes so that $y=p'$ $x=p'x''$ or $p'(x-x'')=0$). In other words, it nets out the income effect associated with the price change and focuses on the pure price effects. Consistency/transitivity demands that, if x'' is chosen when x is available, then x'' cannot have been available when prices were p since x was chosen. Hence $px''>px$ or $p(x-x'')<0$. Combining the compensating income definition p' $(x-x'')=0$ with this consistency requirement yields $(p'-p)$ $(x''-x)<0$, which is the Slutsky condition. (For a full range of inferences see Deaton and Muellbauer, 1980.)

Perhaps the apex of achievement, as far as applications of instrumental rationality are concerned, is neoclassical general equilibrium theory. Let us assume that there are many agents in the economy each with preferences satisfying these conditions and that there is an initial distribution of factor endowments which can be traded. Suppose further that production occurs under conditions that are in many respects analogous to those of consumer theory: they can be captured in a like manner by a function which is differentiable and strictly quasi-concave. Finally, assume firms maximise profits subject to this production constraint under competitive conditions. Then it can be demonstrated that a price vector exists which equates the supply with demand for each commodity, including factors of production (see Arrow and Hahn, 1971), and furthermore that an equilibrium price vector produces an allocation of commodities which is Pareto optimal. That is, there is no reallocation of factors that can be made to produce a different bundle of final commodities so as to make one person better-off without at the same time making another person worse-off (see chapter 9 for a sketch proof).

Arrow and Hahn (1971) are right to claim this as a quite extraordinary result. The latter part is the formalisation of the Mandeville slogan of 'private vices, public virtues', which inspired Smith's analysis of the 'invisible hand'. As Arrow and Hahn (1971) suggest:

> It is important to understand how surprising this claim must be to anyone not exposed to this tradition. The immediate 'common sense' answer to the question 'What will an economy motivated by individual greed and controlled by a very large number of different agents look like?' is probably: There will be chaos. (p. vii)

Of course, as Arrow and Hahn (1971) make clear, it is one thing to demonstrate that the 'invisible hand' could go to work to bring Pareto-optimal order to this prospective chaos; it is quite another to suggest that this will always happen. Nevertheless, the example reveals neatly another aspect of theories which are built around instrumental rationality and intentional explanations: they yield a category of events which are unintended consequences of the action. Elster (1983a) refers to this type of explanation as supra-intentional causal: it is the 'intentional explanation of individual actions together with the causal explanation of the interaction between individuals' (p. 84) which explains the unintended consequences. So, it is not from the benevolence that the butcher, the brewer etc. but it is the structuring of the interaction between the private self-interests around the competitive markets which produces the unlikely public virtue of a Pareto-optimal result.

Recognition of unintended consequences plainly opens up the domain of events which might be explained with the aid of an instrumental account of rationality. Anything that cannot be directly traced back to intentions is no longer immediately ruled out of court: it could still be potentially explained with reference to unintended consequences. Hence, it would seem to add to the explanatory power of this rationality postulate. However, it is worth noting in passing that this greater explanatory power does not come without cost.

First, the explanation ceases to work through intentions alone; it relies on the additional causal elements. This is not necessarily damaging to the cause of instrumental rationality. The explanatory 'honours' need not be shared with some other sense of rationality as long as those causal elements, like the competitive market context, can be explained with reference to instrumental rationality in another piece of analysis. Secondly, it is no longer possible to make a straightforward normative claim about states of the world which are grounded in instrumental accounts of rationality. The point here is that it is tempting, if you accept the instrumental description of agents, to assume that when such action has been freely chosen the outcome must be alright. Everything is for 'the best in the best of all possible worlds' if we choose it, seems to be the natural Panglossian inference. But, once unintended consequences are recognised, such an unqualified inference becomes illegitimate.

Of course, if the influence of the invisible hand element was always benign, then there would be no reason for striking out the Panglossian conclusion. But this is not always so. Another standard example of supra-intentional causal explanation is pollution, and here there is a frustrating gap between intention and outcome because the unintended consequence is negative. Pollution is the unintended consequence of instrumentally rational actions by agents when the causal element of interaction is subject to negative externalities because property rights are poorly defined. The invisible hand does mischief here, and that is why it complicates the welfare properties of events which can be explained intentionally.

Intentional and supra-intentional causal explanations are not restricted to neoclassical economics. They also form an important part of the explanations offered by Marxist economics. For example, much of Marx's concrete analysis of capitalist dynamics posits instrumentally rational capitalists who seek to maximise profits. The same could be said of neoRicardian economics. Indeed, whenever it is assumed that profits are equalised, it is likely that what supports this is the assumption of profit maximisation because it is the drive to winkle out any extra profits which ensures equalisation of the profit rate. Profit maximisation, in turn, can be related in Marx to another objective which capitalists seek to maximise: profits provide the funds for accumulation. 'Accumulate, accumulate! That is Moses and the prophets . . . Therefore save, save, i.e. reconvert the greatest possible portion of surplus value, or surplus product into capital!' (Marx, 1967a, p. 595)

The difference with Marx does not lie in the use of instrumental rationality in generating explanations; rather it is found in the further argument over the origin of the objectives of profitability and accumulation and in the reasons behind capitalists' assuming these roles under capitalism. For example, it is sometimes argued, albeit controversially, that Marx locates the drive towards maximising profits and accumulation in the competitive pressures of capitalism (see Nell, 1980). Similarly, a few pages after this quote, Marx is most concerned to point out that there is nothing natural or pre-ordained about capitalists' occupying the role of accumulators. Accumulation can go on without capitalists, he remarks in a characteristically barbed tone, instancing some parts of Indian agriculture: 'Here production and reproduction on a progressively increasing scale, go on their way without any intervention of that queer saint, that knight of the woeful countenance, the capitalist abstainer.' (p. 598)

Marx also makes plenty use of supra-intentional causal explanation. The communist manifesto lists a host of unintended consequences which follow from the bourgeois drive towards accumulation: the 'cosmopolitan' character of production; 'torn away the sentimental veil from the family'; 'subjected the country to the rule of the town'; in a curiously modern note, the bourgeois drive 'batters down all Chinese walls'. Finally there is the ultimate unintended consequence: the 'bourgeoisie . . . produces, above all, its own grave diggers'.

It may not always be easy to trace the causal elements that come into play to produce these unintended consequences. The same observation is often made with another famous example in Marx of unintended consequences: his analysis of the law of tendency of the falling rate of profit, where the drive towards accumulation undermines the incentive towards accumulation because the rise in the organic composition of capital tends to produce a falling rate of profit. However, these difficulties are not what is at issue: the point is that Marx makes copious use of supra-intentional causal explanation. And anyway, these problems do not always attach to

Marxist analysis. For instance, the underconsumptionist strand of Marx's crisis theory can be easily rerun through a simple Keynesian model to flesh out the causal mechanisms. This strand of Marx's argument works through noting that 'the labourers as buyers of commodities are important for the market. But as sellers of their own commodity – labour power – capitalist society tends to keep them down to a minimum price' (Marx, 1967b, p. 316). So, cutting wages may appear to each individual capitalist to improve profitability, but when all capitalists do it there is the unintended consequence of a reduction in the demand for goods and services from workers which can reduce profitability by leaving goods unsold on shop shelves.

Uncertainty can be introduced into this account of rational action. Provided that uncertainty can be captured by a probability distribution over the events (or states of the world) which determine the relation between actions and outcomes, then it only requires the addition of a few more axioms for a simple extension of the basic model: utility maximisation becomes expected utility maximisation in the world of uncertainty.

Firstly, define a prospect vector associated with each action as the pairings of the range of possible outcomes with the probabilities of their occurrence. To keep it simple, think of the outcome as income: so a prospect vector P associated with some action consists of a vector of £x, where each element (x_i) is coupled with a probability of p_i of the particular state of the world arising when that action yields x_i. So, the action is like the purchase of a lottery ticket: if 'so and so' happens then you get 'this'; if 'the other' happens you get 'that'. The prospect combines the 'this' and 'that' with the respective probabilities of the events occurring.

Now, assume that the earlier axioms of consumer theory apply to the ordering of these prospects. Further, there are some axioms relating to ordering and definition of probabilities which need not detain us, and there is the more controversial axiom of 'strong independence'. This implies that, when two actions (A and B) yield different consequences (£x and £y) under one state of nature and the same £z under the other state of nature, and A is preferred to B, the same preference will be shown in another situation where there are the same different consequences (£x and £y) but a different common consequence (£w). It is the latter axiom that is crucially responsible for giving the utility function its additive structure. To be specific, $U=U(P)$ defined by the earlier axioms is transformed into $U=pU(x)$, thus yielding the interpretation that agents maximise expected utility, where utility is defined with respect to commodities/outcomes as ordinarily understood in the standard discussion of consumer theory.

There is another sense of strategic uncertainty which can also be introduced into models that embody instrumental rationality. This is discussed in the next section. For the moment, I conclude this section by reflecting that, since many decisions appear beset by uncertainty, these developments with respect to the inclusion of uncertainty would again seem to expand significantly the explanatory potential of this canon of rationality.

3.3   The Strategic Dimension of Instrumental Rationality

Interdependence was effectively ignored in neoclassical consumer theory through the assumption that agents treated the medium of interaction, the price vector, as exogenous. In contrast, game theory is built around agents' appreciating their interdependence. The equilibrium concept most frequently used in non-co-operative game theory relies on the instrumental version of rationality: it is the Nash equilibrium.

The Nash equilibrium is defined by a vector of strategies where each player's strategy is a best response to each other player's strategy. For example, consider a game that might be played amongst two oligopolists. Each oligopolist has a choice of pricing its commodities high or low. The outcome where both price high is preferred by each firm to the one where both price low because it enables them to reap some of the industry's monopoly profits. The best outcome occurs when an oligopolist lowers price while the competitor keeps the price high because this enables the low price oligopolist to expand market share enormously. Conversely, the worst situation arises for a high price oligopolist when playing against a low price oligopolist because there is an extreme loss of market share. Figure 3.1 depicts these preference orderings with some normalised pay-offs.

The Nash equilibrium here is the [low, low] strategy pair. Low is the best reply to itself, and there is no other strategy pair where each is the best reply to the other. The example might be regarded as illustrating the advantages of collusion in such an industry, since a collusive agreement which guaranteed the [high, high] strategy pair would produce a superior outcome for both. In this way, the analysis might contribute to the explanation of why such collusive arrangements are negotiated, and in-

		Firm A	
		High	Low
Firm B	High	1,1	−1,2
	Low	2,−1	0,0

Figure 3.1   Oligopoly game

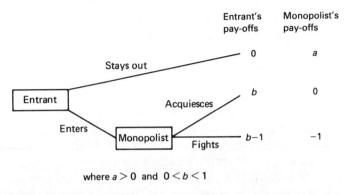

where $a > 0$ and $0 < b < 1$

Figure 3.2   Chain-store game

deed, further, why such agreements require careful policing because there are incentives towards cheating.

A selective list of examples where game theory has been applied to help explain economic behaviour could be developed to match the survey of the previous section. Rather than develop such a list, I focus on two new types of behaviour which can be understood with the help of game theory: the acts of pre-commitment and reputation building. They share a common feature of being more complicated behaviours than the simple maximising plans of the previous section. They both involve taking one step backwards in order to advance two steps later. Yet, they can both be traced back to the instrumental account of rationality with the aid of game theory.

Suppose there is a monopolist and a potential entrant to the market. The monopolist prefers it if the entrant does not enter, but finds it more costly to fight than acquiesce when there is entry. The entrant meanwhile prefers entry to no entry when there is acquiescence, but prefers to stay out if there is a fight. These preferences are captured by the normalised pay-offs in figure 3.2

One obvious ploy here for the monopolist would seem to be to threaten to fight an entry, thereby deterring the entrant since the entrant prefers not to enter if there is going to be a fight. However, such a threat would not be credible. As the game stands with common knowledge, the entrant realises that the monopolist prefers to acquiesce when there is entry, and so the entrant ignores the threat and enters, and the monopolist acquiesces. In the language of game theory, the ploy is not part of a perfect equilibrium because the response of fighting is not a Nash equilibrium strategy in the sub-game after there is entry.

A second thought is that things might be rather different if the game was repeated a number of times. In the original version of this game, Selten (1978) casts the monopolist as a chain-store operator facing entry in each of the geographic markets where he/she enjoys a monopoly. The idea then becomes that it might be rational from an instrumental point of view for the monopolist to fight entry in one market (one play of the game) if that helped build a reputation for 'toughness' which forestalled entry in other markets (later plays of the game). It is certainly an appealing thought. It works by closing an apparent gap between short- and long-term interests through the rational creation of reputations. It also offers support for instrumental rationality because it promises to preserve an intentional explanation in a variety of situations which otherwise do not look too encouraging since agents appear to be acting against their own (short-term) self-interest. For instance, the continuation of a strike by a union, when the costs of continuation outweigh any possible gain in the form of employer concessions, might be construed as instrumentally rational if the union was guarding a reputation for toughness which would pay dividends in future plays of the industrial relations game.

Unfortunately, this promising line of argument does not stand up to a close examination. To appreciate the problem, consider the last play in the sequence of repeated plays of the game. In this play, the monopolist has no need to guard a reputation for toughness because there are no future plays of the game . The last play is just like the one-shot version of the game, and consequently the monopolist will acquiesce if there is entry and the entrant realising this will enter. As there will be entry and acquiescence in the last play, that means that the monopolist has no need to carry over a reputation from the penultimate play of the game to the last play. Hence, the monopolist need pay no attention to reputation creation in the penultimate play of the game, and the returns from playing the game in that period are exactly the same as the one-shot version. So, the monopolist will acquiesce in the penultimate play if there is entry, and recognising this the entrant would enter in that play. But this means that the monopolist does not need to carry over a reputation from the play before the penultimate one, and so on. The game unravels back to the present with entry and acquiescence in all time periods.

The logic of this backward induction process is quite ruthless. Furthermore, it will take hold even when there is uncertainty about the time period of the last play (i.e. over how many plays of the game remain). Provided the probability distribution over the last play is bounded from above, i.e. as long as the game will end some time even if the time is not known for certain, then there is definitely a last play of the game and the backward induction process can take hold. It is only when there is a possibility of the game going on for ever that the backward induction process is prevented from taking hold (see Hargreaves Heap and Varoufa-kis, 1987). Or, to put the point more precisely, to forestall the backward induction process it is necessary in every play of the game that there is a non-zero probability of the game continuing; and when the probability distribution is bounded from above, there is always one period for which it is not true to say that there is a non-zero probability that the game will continue for another play.

Interestingly, this result can be modified, by the introduction of some imperfect information, to restore the thought about reputation creation. Kreps and Wilson (1982) demonstrate that a sequential equilibrium is possible in this game which has no entry in early stages followed by reputation building in the later stages when there is sufficient initial doubt in the mind of the entrant about the motives of the monopolist. (A sequential equilibrium is the analogue to the perfect equilibrium concept when there is this kind of imperfect information.)

To be specific, suppose the entrant's doubt is captured by a probability p that the monopolist is 'tough' and prefers fighting to acquiescing when there is entry. In terms of the normalised pay-offs in figure 3.2, the 0 and -1 are inverted to reflect the changed preference ordering for a 'tough' monopolist, as contrasted with the 'weak' one currently depicted there. When $P > b^n$, where n is the number of plays of the game remaining, there is no entry by the entrant. With no entry, the monopolist is not called upon to do anything, and so there is no new information on his/her motives. Consequently, there is no reason to revise p. Eventually, with p constant, as n falls $p \leqslant b^n$ here. The reputation creation phase begins. There is some likelihood of entry now which is matched by some other probability that the monopolist will fight. If the monopolist fights, there is new evidence on toughness and the probability assessment of toughness is revised up to $p = b^n$ for the next play of the game. In the next play of the game, the same process of entry and possible reputation building repeats itself. Should a monopolist acquiesce on one of these occasions of entry, the monopolist is revealed to be weak, and p goes to 0. Thereafter, there is entry and acquiescence in all future plays of the game.

The underlying rationale for this result is something like this. The first thing to notice is that, if $p > b$ by the last play of the game, then entry in that last play is not certain. Once entry in the last play is not certain, the backward induction process cannot take hold and other results become possible. Secondly, it is perfectly possible with reputation-creating behaviour for the current probability to be considerably less than p, and for the entrant to maintain an expectation that it might rise to $p = b$ by the last time period. Thus, a lower p now can be consistent with doubt over entry in the last period. The final part of the proof revolves around recognising that reputation-creating behaviour is risky for the monopolist. The weak monopolist can only build a reputation if it can tempt the entrant to enter. Otherwise there is never any new evidence to warrant a revision in p. But the weak monopolist will never tempt the entrant in if it always fights entry. There must be some positive probability of a weak monopolist acquiescing to get a possible entry from the entrant. As reputation building is risky, the monopolist does not engage in it until it is absolutely necessary to keep the reputation on course for the critical terminal value. The rest is mathematics. When the current p is above the value necessary to keep it on course for reaching $p=b$ by the last time period, the monopolist does not need to tempt the entrant in. The entrant realises that the 'weak' monopolist will only acquiesce with some positive probability when he/she has to start building a reputation. Consequently, he/she stays out until the stage of the game has been reached when reputation building has become imperative.

Another way the monopolist could forestall entry is through the use of a strategy of pre-commitment when there is not this pattern of imperfect information. For example, the monopolist might invest in excess capacity. This could plausibly alter the preference ordering between fighting and acquiescing when there is entry. If costs rise steeply when there is excess capacity, then sharing a market with the entrant could be very costly (see Dixit, 1980). Of course, investing in excess capacity does not come without cost. But if the cost of this strategy in the commitment part of the game, when the entrant offers his/her best response, is less than the gain from the chain-store part of the game (i.e. a in each play), then it is instrumentally rational to make this pre-commitment.

Again, it would be a mistake to think that game theoretic applications of instrumental rationality are confined to orthodox economic theory. Recent 'explanations' of exploitation in Marxist economics have used co-operative game theory. Roemer (1982a) gives an account of capitalist exploitation of a coalition S of agents by the complementary coalition S' in the following terms. S is capitalistically exploited if

> 1) If S were to withdraw from society, endowed with its per capita share of society's alienable property (that is, produced and non-produced goods) and with its own skills, then S would be better off (in terms of income and leisure) than its present allocation;
> 2) If S' were to withdraw under the same conditions, then S' would be worse off (in terms of income and leisure) than it is at present.
> 3) If S were to withdraw from society with its own endowments (not its per capita share), then S' would be worse off than at present. (p. 285)

A number of different kinds of exploitation can be distinguished according to the withdrawal rules. Agents are feudally exploited when the equivalent withdrawal rule in (1) is 'with its own endowments', while agents are socialistically exploited when withdrawal is 'with all endowments, alienable and inalienable'. Further, this analysis of exploitation can be connected with a discussion of class (see Roemer, 1982b). More generally still, Elster (1985) has given a game theoretic interpretation to a range of Marx's insights with respect to collective action.

3.4 A Preliminary Evaluation

This review of some of the areas in economics which have relied on instrumental rationality is enough to convey its central importance to the subject. Yet, there is still room to doubt the scope of the explanations that come from instrumental rationality alone. The worry about scope has two dimensions.

Firstly, the constraints on preferences in section 3.2 may seem harmless enough. Indeed rather more than that, it may seem that the analysis has been attractively economical: little has been said about an individual's preferences and so it is likely that the conclusions will enjoy a wide applicability. But an axiomatic approach of this sort can be deceptive. It is not always obvious what actual types of preferences will fit an axiomatic bill. Do these axioms allow for interdependence between individual preferences? Or can they only apply to selfish preferences? Are there plausible sorts of preferences that pose problems of indeterminacy for instrumental rationality and hence also for intentional explanations?

These are the sorts of questions that it would be useful to have answered before deciding on the explanatory scope of this rationality postulate. At the very least, we can already suspect that this analysis, by taking an individual's preferences as given, sidesteps cases of sub-intentional causality. How important such cases might be and what concrete preference structures might have to be excluded to avoid problems of indeterminacy and the like are the subjects of the discussion in chapter 6.

Secondly, a moment's reflection on this quick survey will reveal that the explanations generated by instrumental rationality rely quite heavily on an exogenous informational and institutional structure. There always seems to be some background institution or information set which helps bring the explanations to life, particularly for the supra-intentional causal variety.

How do agents, for example, in neoclassical general equilibrium theory know the price vector which determines their opportunities for trade? Invoking the fictional auctioneer merely deflects the query on to one about institutions. Nor will the alternative Edgworthian bargaining approach help very much, because the point rebounds as one about information when it is asked how agents come to know the full range of possible coalitions.

These are not idle questions, products of some exaggerated sense of the curiosity. The answers matter because the results of the analysis are sensitive to the choice of institutional or informational setting, and so these 'props' are not passive 'fillers': they contribute significantly to the explanation. Contrast a competitive equilibrium with a conjectural equilibrium, or a competitive market with a market for lemons, if you doubt the significance of information sets in explaining what happens in markets. Likewise behind any competitive equilibrium price vector, there lurks a distribution of property rights. Change the property rights and the price vector changes. Or why competitive markets? Competitive markets are crucial in the supra-intentional causal explanation of the invisible hand: they are the institutions which structure agents' interaction to produce the causal element in the explanation. Equally, it is the particular form of property rights that structures interaction to contribute the causal element in the supra-intentional causal explanation of pollution. Or, consider Samuelson's (1958) overlapping generations loan model of interest: in the simplest case, the interest rate is negative, but it becomes zero when the institution of money is introduced. Finally, notice how exploitation changes with the differing withdrawal rules in a society in Roemer's model. Institutions can make a quite decisive intervention!

The second worry about the scope of intentional explanation, then, concerns the degree to which it relies on exogenously given information sets and institutional structures. We need to be clear what this worry might or might not amount to. It is only ever going to be a substantial criticism of instrumental rationality, and with it an economics which is based exclusively on this rationality assumption, if these institutional and informational props cannot themselves be explained intentionally by reference to the actions of instrumentally rational agents. If instrumental rationality can be marshalled to explain information sets and institutional structures, then it will not count against instrumental rationality that, in some concrete explanations, it treats these as given. Instead, it will be seen as an analytical device which simply divides the material to be explained into more conveniently sized packages.

The next two chapters take up this question. They consider explanations of information sets and institutions which attempt to work through instrumental rationality. Without wishing to pre-judge that discussion, it is worth anticipating here a position that would make light of any problems which might arise in the intentional explanation of institutions and information sets, at least as far as an economics based exclusively on instrumental rationality is concerned. This position, in an abbreviated form, runs something like this: 'So what, if information sets and institutions cannot be explained using instrumental rationality alone?' 'Why should this bother economists?' 'We can't be expected to do everything: there's a division of labour in the social sciences and if you want to know about institutions talk to sociologists or political scientists!' 'If they have to use some other sense of rationality, that's all well and good but it is not going to disturb my reliance on instrumental rationality.'

In effect, the argument amounts to a doubt about whether the restricted scope of the explanations generated by instrumental rationality should constitute a source of worry. It has an obvious attraction in a certain sort of modesty. So, why should we be concerned in economics if other disciplines need to use other rationality assumptions? Why should we be disturbed by the restrictions on the scope of the explanation afforded by instrumental rationality? Why, in particular, should this undermine an exclusive reliance on instrumental rationality in economics?

There are several reasons why we should be worried. Firstly, it ought to cast some doubt on the quality of the explanations we have developed using instrumental rationality alone. After all, it would seem a little strange, a priori, if rational agency took one form in economic qua economic life and some other form in the wider social world. Secondly, there is such a thing as false modesty. We might reasonably have ambitions for economics which stretched beyond the boundaries set by instrumental rationality, particularly when it is realised quite how constraining those boundaries might be. For instance, at first sight, it is not clear that instrumental rationality will explain such obviously economic institutions as firms. To be sure, neoclassical general equilibrium has something called a 'firm', but it does not resemble what most people would recognise as a firm. The 'firm' in general equilibrium theory is really no more than the locus of a large number of market transactions. There is no sense that the firm is an alternative way of co-ordinating agents which is characterised by hierarchical relations between agents rather than market ones (see Coase, 1937). To put it bluntly, should this first impression count for anything, it would seem unfortunate to say the least if economics accepted the kind of restricted scope which meant that it had to draw on other disciplines for a discussion of such a central economic institution as a firm.

There is a further, deeper reason for disquiet. It arises because of the connection between explanation and prescription in economics. There are several ways in which this relationship can be unpackaged, and the precise nature of the disquiet varies with them. In one, explanation establishes what 'is' the case, and then this 'is' becomes the foundation for prescriptive analysis. With this reading, the claim of a welfare economics based exclusively on instrumental rationality is immediately suspect when it does not provide a full account of what 'is' the case. The other types of rationality which are necessary for explaining what 'is' the case might produce very different kinds of welfare propositions.

Alternatively, what 'is' the case can be regarded as largely irrelevant to discussions of what 'ought' to be the case – in other words, the fact that we are not instrumentally rational does not mean we should not be instrumentally rational. With this reading, the problem is that the failure to explain what is the case without recourse to other rationality assumptions translates into an indeterminacy in the prescriptions which are based on that rationality assumption alone. A full discussion of how instrumental rationality fits into welfare economics must be held over until chapter 9. At this stage, it is probably quite intuitive that the gaps in explanation map back as indeterminacies in prescription to blunt the analysis. At a general level, it will make some sense on the basis of the discussion of the last chapter alone. Since one conclusion of that argument was that a strict distinction between positive and normative economics cannot be sustained, one might plausibly suspect that constraints or difficulties with respect to one kind of economics feed into the other.

For the moment, it is sufficient to sound the warning that, whichever way the relation between explanation and prescription in economics is read, a failure of instrumental rationality to contribute exclusively to explanations will circumscribe the relevance of any prescriptive economics which is also based exclusively on this rationality assumption. Hence, in so far as economists are concerned with prescriptions, they have a further reason to be worried if their economics is based exclusively on instrumental rationality, when the explanations in economics need other senses of rationality.

3.5 Conclusion

A variety of examples showing how instrumental rationality has been used to generate explanations in economics have been given in this chapter. Hopefully, they will have conveyed the ubiquity of this assumption, and something of the richness of the explanations built around it. It is not just a matter of explaining an event by reference to the fact that he/she wanted it. There is supra-intentional causal explanation of the invisible hand sort, and there is strategic behaviour of the Ulysses and the Sirens and Lady Windermere varieties.

The comments in the last section are not designed to belittle the explanations which are ground out in those applications of instrumental rationality. Instead, they put a perspective on this contribution which is important when it comes to addressing the question of whether economics can afford to rely on this assumption alone. It will be tempting to think that, in view of the range of explanations already generated by instrumental rationality, this is a fertile vein which it makes sense to continue to exploit, willy-nilly. Against this, it must be recognised that there are grounds for doubting the scope of these intentional explanations in economics; and that economists should be disturbed by such constraints on the scope of their explanations, particularly if they have any aspiration to make policy statements.

The next three chapters assess whether the grounds for doubts about scope, sketched in the previous section, are well founded.

4 INFORMATION

4.1 Introduction

This chapter looks at the informational underpinnings of the intentional explanations sketched in chapter 3. The immediate task is to discover whether the information that agents have about the environment in which they make instrumentally rational decisions can itself be explained by reference to an instrumental account of rationality. If this is possible, then the power of intentional explanations and the claim of instrumental rationality is correspondingly enhanced. The worries about scope on this score, which were raised at the end of the last chapter, will disappear. Alternatively, should there remain aspects of the information sets which need further explanation, then the limits of intentional explanation have been marked and there is support for the idea that an expanded definition of rationality is required for complete explanations in economics.

The next section discusses the rational expectations approach to the question of how agents come to have information about the environment in which they operate. It is based on Hargreaves Heap and Hollis (1987). The rational expectations hypothesis looks promising because it is built on the foundations of instrumental rationality. However, it suffers from a problem, which is going to become quite familiar over the next few pages, of indeterminacy when there are multiple equilibria. In addition, there are special difficulties with learning how to form such expectations in the social world in an instrumentally rational manner.

The third section surveys selectively another part of the economics literature on information, where information is related to institutional context. In some respects, it can be seen as a modern development of a Hayekian theme, as it focuses on the institutional influences which condition how much information agents will reveal about themselves. As such, it does not solve the information problem: it merely diverts it to institutions. Nevertheless, there could not be a better curtain raiser for the next chapter which tackles the instrumental explanation of institutions.

4.2 Rational Expectations

The general question that needs to be answered about information in the standard instrumental description of decision making concerns how agents come to have the information about their environment which services their calculation of the optimal action. One answer is to be found in the 'search theoretic' literature. Here, the instrumental optimiser's eye is turned on the activity of gathering information: information on price vectors, technology and the like is acquired up to the point where marginal benefits equal marginal costs of acquisition. The information becomes an input in the suitably recast problem of optimisation and it is produced in optimum quantities to service the calculation of maximum utility.

This approach appears to fit snugly with the original account of rational decision making because it applies the same instrumental maxim to the activity of information acquisition. However, it also begs an important further question about the origin of information on the marginal benefits of further information, which cannot be answered without begging yet further questions on information. This difficulty occurs because it is impossible to know what the marginal benefits of information acquisition may be, unless the full information set is known. How do you know it is not worth the bother of removing the remaining degree of ignorance unless you know what it is like to be fully informed? To misappropriate the old parable: when you look in the mirror and see a speck in the eye, who is to say this image has not been distorted by the presence of a much larger plank in the eye?

Naturally, it is still possible to make the claim about optimality being purely subjective. The line of argument then becomes that information is acquired up to the point where subjectively perceived marginal benefits equal costs. But this only pushes the question about information one stage further up the chain.

Where does the information come from to service these subjective beliefs about marginal benefits? Can it be explained rationally by recourse to the instrumental paradigm? The obvious move to make is the one which, unfortunately, brings us back to base. Namely, it too was acquired up to the point where subjective beliefs about marginal benefits equalled marginal cost. Well, this is only an answer if the original problem is conveniently ignored. The moment the same question is asked again at this higher level of belief, we continue what will become an infinite regress which leaves any belief as potentially rational. The information set agents work with is to be explained by their beliefs, but there is no explanation of how agents come to hold those beliefs which is not circular. So, neat as the search theoretic approach may seem, it will not avoid ugly questions about what non-instrumental factors are responsible for breaking out of this circularity.

This is the cue for the rational expectations revolution. One crucial move of the rational expectations school is to make beliefs rational because subjective beliefs coincide with objective ones. In effect, the circularity of a purely subjective set of beliefs is broken by the supposition that there are objective beliefs and a rational agent will seek to close the gap between the objective and subjective.

> . . . I should like to suggest that expectations since they are informed predictions of future events, are essentially the same as the predictions of the relevant economic theory. . . . The hypothesis can be rephrased a little more precisely as follows: that expectations of firms (or more generally, the subjective probability distributions of outcomes) tend to be distributed, for the same information set, about the prediction of the theory (or 'objective' probability distribution of outcomes). (Muth, 1961, p. 316)

Although, Muth (1961) makes this clear, it is not always obvious that this is or need be implied because there is a softer way of introducing rational expectations. We begin with the soft-sell.

'The point of departure of rational expectations is that individuals should not make systematic errors' (Begg, 1982, p. 29). This is a typical interpretation of the rational expectations revolution, and it makes the use of rational expectations delightfully simple. The expected value of a variable is set equal to its actual value plus a random error term; and the estimation, or whatever, proceeds apace. Again, the intuition behind this interpretation is the instrumental maximiser's 'eye for the main chance'. You ought to be able to learn about the systematic component of your errors, and there is every incentive to do so since you will profit by removing them. Not unsurprisingly, it is hailed as 'the "natural" hypothesis to use in neoclassical economics' (McCallum, 1980, p. 717) because it keeps faith with the core presumption of instrumental rationality in neoclassical economics.

A slightly different question is begged by the soft-sell. It concerns how agents go about removing systematic errors from their expectations. This is really only unproblematical provided that the Muth version of closing the gap between objective and subjective is taken quite literally. When the 'objective' probability distribution is regarded as objective in the sense of being independent of our beliefs about it, as akin to some feature of the natural world like the landscape, then the forecaster's task is made routine. It is like a person watching a foggy landscape as the fog disappears. Some of it lifts as the future becomes the past, and some is dispelled by better use of available information. The watcher's knowledge varies but the landscape itself does not change with it. Bayesian and Classical statistical theory provide a body of theory which can be readily mobilised to estimate relationships and update predictions based upon them. And indeed, systematic errors might plausibly be regarded as a passing phase.

The trouble is that there are no 'objective' probability distributions in the social world in this sense. The subjective beliefs about probability distributions affect outcomes because action is informed by expectations.

Recognition of this introduces elements of non-stationarity when there is learning, and this makes prediction difficult, unless, that is, some strong form of determinism is true, so that agents are always carrying out a script rather as billiard balls react to the impact of others in a pre-scripted way. As Bray (1983) observes with some irony, because it turns a point made by advocates of rational expectations:

> As Lucas points out so forcibly in his critique of econometric policy evaluation, the reduced form of an econometric model is not stationary if people change the way they form expectations. Lucas considers changes in expectations induced by changes in policy. However, the process of learning also changes the way people form expectations, introducing a non-stationarity into the situation. (p. 124)

It is worth exploring this point in more detail to see exactly what problems are encountered in forming rational expectations in these circumstances.* Frydman (1982) and Frydman and Phelps (1983) provide an extended discussion, but the general points can be appreciated with the use of a simple example. Consider the following relationship between prices, expected prices and exogenous variables in an economy:

$$p = ax + bp^e + u \qquad (4.1)$$

where u is white noise. The rational expectations equilibrium relationship between prices and exogenous variables is given by

$$p^{re} = cx \qquad (4.2)$$

where $c = a/(1 - b)$. This is the relationship agents wish to learn about. However, they start from a position where they do not know the parameter b nor the vector of parameters a.

The problems of learning are obvious once we assume that agents in the past have recognised the general structure of the rational expectations solution and consequently worked with an expectations-generating mechanism like (4.2), but were ignorant with respect to parameter values as in

$$p^e = dx \qquad (4.3)$$

where $d \neq a/(1 - b)$.

Substituting (4.3) into (4.1) reveals that the regression of p on x generated in these circumstances will produce estimates of c ($= a + db$) which depart from their rational expectations equilibrium value. In other words, the very ignorance of agents in the past distorts the relationship between p

---

* It is not always recognised that the standard statistical rules for updating beliefs cannot be applied to non-stationary probability distributions. To illustrate the point consider Bayes's rule and the extreme case where as a result of non-stationarity a previous zero probability event occurs.

and x from which agents are trying to learn the rational expectations equilibrium.

The non-stationarity of the relationship is also clear in the presence of learning because the value of d changes in these circumstances. Nevertheless, it is equally clear that this need not preclude that a process of learning like this reaches a successful conclusion with d being updated as new observations are generated. Whether it does or not depends on the convergence properties of the particular learning procedure. In general, however, the grounds for being sanguine are slight: convergence cannot be guaranteed (see Blume, Bray and Easley, 1982, for a summary, and Bray, 1985, for further discussion). A feeling for this lack of a general result can be gained by considering a simple particular method of updating in this example. Suppose all individuals synchronised their updating of estimates of d at discrete intervals of time $t - 1$, t etc. where the interval of time is sufficiently long for the new estimate of d to be an unbiased estimate of the underlying generating process given by the substitution of (4.3) into (4.1). Then d evolves as

$$d_t = c + b(d_{t-1} - c) \qquad (4.4)$$

Hence, the learning procedure will converge or explode as $b<1$ or $b > 1$.

Nor is this result qualitatively transformed when there are heterogeneous agents, with some who hold rational expectations and some who do not. For example, Bray (1985) considers a situation where convergence on the rational expectation by the non-rational group is not guaranteed by the mere presence of some who already hold it. This closes one potential opening for a rational expectations rejoinder to the problem of learning, namely, that markets might help to aggregate and transmit the information held by the 'rational' agents, thus making learning easier for the non-rational agents.

Likewise, another possible counter in these circumstances is foreclosed in a paper by Haltiwanger and Waldman (1985). If there is important interdependence between the rational and the non-rational agents, then it might be argued that, since the rational agents will have to take account of the behaviour of the non-rational, the actions of the rational agents could compensate for the non-rational, thus producing outcomes which were indistinguishable from a position where everyone held rational expectations. It is 'as if' everyone held rational expectations. Unfortunately, the 'as if' result depends on the particular kind of interdependence and does not hold in all cases.

The basic idea is easy to grasp. When the interdependence is characterised by congestion effects, all is well. Say the rational agents are trying to decide whether to use the minor or the major road when travelling to the same destination as the non-rational agents. The presence of the non-rational agents actually helps the rational ones to form their expectations here, and it will lead them to take actions which minimise the congestion on both sorts of roads. So, when the non-rational believe the major road will be the most congested and consequently use the minor one, the rational agents will take this into account and travel in disproportionate numbers on the major road, thus smoothing the flow of traffic on both roads. By contrast, synergistic interdependence will encourage the rational group to make the same kinds of errors as the non-rational group. When there is synergy it pays to be with the others, and consequently the rational agents do not compensate for the non-rational; instead they compound their mistakes. Hence, the 'as if' argument will not work when there is synergy, while it does for congestion effects.

In other words, there is no guarantee when a rational expectations equilibrium exists that agents, starting from a position of ignorance, will be able to learn it – Muth's closing the gap between the subjective and the objective is not so easy when the 'objective' moves with our subjectivity. This means that we cannot simply explain how agents come to have their information sets by appealing to rational expectations and thereby maintain an explanation which works through instrumental rationality alone. In some circumstances rational expectations cannot be learnt, and in these conditions our explanation of what expectations agents hold will have to appeal to something other than the rational expectation.

There is actually a further problem for instrumental rationality in situations of learning which arises even when there is convergence on the rational expectation. Let us return to the general discussion of learning when everyone is 'ignorant'. Agents are self-consciously using economic theory which tells them that the rational expectations equilibrium is of the form given by (4.3) because it emanates from a reduced form equation like (4.1). Yet they seem strangely unperturbed by the implication of their own learning: individuals who realised that other individuals were using (4.3) would not choose (4.3) as the optimal forecasting rule; they could always do better.

To see this, suppose all agents are using $p^e = d_{t-1}x$ in time t. Then any one agent can always do better by using another forecasting rule. Substituting the rule used by everyone else into (4.1) gives

$$p = (a + bd_{t-1})x \qquad (4.5)$$

This can now be used to generate a superior forecast when agents use the learning procedure sketched above. This follows because $a+bd_{t-1}$ will become d_t with this learning procedure, and d_t can always be anticipated in these circumstances through a reflection on how d evolves under the learning process captured in (4.4). This is given by

$$d_t - d_{t-1} = b(d_{t-1} - d_{t-2}) \qquad (4.6)$$

Observation of how d has evolved in the past provides an estimate of b, which enables the superior forecast rule to be used.

$$p = [(1 + b)d_{t-1} - d_{t-2}]x \qquad (4.7)$$

Of course, if one agent can appreciate that (4.7) is superior, then all agents should be able to draw the same inference and (4.7) again becomes sub-optimal. A further revision is possible for one agent and so on. The process continues and whether it converges on the rational expectations equilibrium will depend critically on the learning process. Should it converge, there will be no learning as such because each agent will zero in on the rational expectation. Should there be no convergence, agents can wistfully watch their expectations spiral away in their own mind as they search for the rational expectation without ever achieving it. Whichever is the case, the important point is that the instrumentally rational learning strategy among agents who recognise each other's instrumental rationality is not well defined when we are actually in a learning situation where agents do not yet hold rational expectations (see Frydman, 1982). Either we could always improve our expectation, or the best option becomes clear, but only because the rational expectation has been achieved (i.e. we are no longer learning). Hence, in so far as we wish to model expectations in situations when agents are learning, we will not be able to rely exclusively on instrumental rationality.

What this example helps to bring out is the game theoretic aspects of forming a rational expectation. What agents realise is that their best expectation depends on the expectation of others, who in turn are also attempting to form the best expectation. The equivalent of a rational expectation is an Nash equilibrium in this expectation game, and it is the stability properties of this Nash equilibrium which are being tested by the learning procedure (see Evans, 1983, for an explicit discussion along these lines). There is more than a hint in this of Keynes's (1936) famous beauty competition:

> . . . each competitor has to pick, not those faces which he himself finds prettiest, but those which he thinks likeliest to catch the fancy of the other competitors, all of whom are looking at the problem from the same point of view. It's not a case of choosing those which, to the best of one's judgement are really the prettiest, nor even those which average opinion genuinely thinks the prettiest. We have reached the third degree where we devote our intelligences to anticipating what average opinion expects average opinion to be. (p. 156)

Keynes's example differs, however, in one significant respect. At least, there is a unique rational expectations equilibrium, or Nash equilibrium, in the problem set out above, whereas it is not difficult to imagine any number of 'conventions' with respect to beauty which could establish themselves as Nash equilibria in the beauty contest game. This makes Keynes's problem of forming a rational expectation doubly difficult because even a full knowledge of the game would not permit Keynes to form a rational expectation by applying the collective consistency/rationality condition implied by a Nash equilibrium. This brings out the final difficulty to be discussed in the formation of rational expectations: the problem of multiple rational expectations equilibria. Forget about problems of learning a rational expectation: how is an agent to decide on the rational expectation to entertain, when there are several expectations which fit the bill of producing non-systematic errors?

To anticipate one possible counter to this particular difficulty, one might query the frequency of such multiple equilibria in the economic world. After all, beauty competitions would seem to have only a passing resemblance to an economy. Against this, one example has already been given in chapter 2: the Hahn (1980) multiple equilibria where 'Keynesian' beliefs produce 'Keynesian' outcomes, while 'monetarist' beliefs generate 'monetarist' outcomes.

There are also further reasons for taking the problem posed by the beauty competition seriously. Keynes used the competition to illustrate a type of difficulty which he believed afflicted financial markets. His point can be appreciated with a simple change in the example which has been developed in this section. Equation (4.1) can be reinterpreted as a reduced form equation for the price of a financial asset, by making current price depend on future price expectations:

$$p_t = ax + bp_{t+1}^e \qquad (4.8)$$

So, the price of an asset depends on current income, which is influenced by a vector of variables x, and the expected resale price of the asset at the end of the income period.

In general, there are an infinite number of rational expectation equilibria in such a market. There is only one stable equilibrium, but there are an infinite number of explosive equilibria. The stable equilibrium when there is a constant x has $p = p^e = a/(1 - b)x$ for all t. But it is always possible to have a larger p_t than this, provided that p_{t+1}^e exceeds p_t, and such a p_{t+1}^e will be rational if it equals p_{t+1}. p_{t+1} can take on this higher value if p_{t+2}^e is expected to be even higher, and so on. All that is required is for the time path of prices to show the necessary rate of acceleration and a rational expectations equilibrium is possible. There will be one for each possible initial jump of prices above the stable equilibrium value. That is, speculation will bid up current prices provided that the expected future price rise is even greater, and it is rational to expect prices to rise by more provided that they do rise by that greater amount, and they will provided that they are expected to rise by even more in the subsequent time period, and so on.

There is a standard argument against including these unstable rational expectations equilibria. It holds that since prices cannot possibly rise for ever without a breakdown of the economic system, these paths should be discounted. This is a superficially attractive argument, but it is not obviously compelling at second sight. Firstly, the threat of a breakdown would only caution agents against holding such expectations if they suffered from the breakdown itself; and it could always be other agents who pick-up the tab. No, replies the critic: this would not be a Nash equilibrium in the expectation game because not all agents can expect other agents to pick up the tab. However, what this counter overlooks is the fact that we do not live for ever: there is always another generation which currently does not participate in the market and which could pick up the bill.

Secondly, the argument has a kind of force because we do not often observe prices accelerating off to infinity. But we often find small speculative bubbles (short periods of acceleration followed by a quick 'correction'), and they too can be shown to be consistent with rational expectations (see Blanchard and Watson, 1982). In general, there will be an infinite number of such rational expectation bubbles which could accompany the unique stable equilibrium: and these multiple equilibria cannot be dismissed so easily because they do not imply a path for prices which accelerates off to infinity. Again, it is possible to give a simple formal demonstration of this possibility. Assume for simplicity that $a = b$ in (4.8): the general solution to (4.8) is now given by:

$$p_t = [a/(1-a)]x + e_t \qquad (4.9)$$

where

$$E(e_{t+1}) = (1/a)e_t \qquad (4.10)$$

The unique stable solution occurs when $e_t = 0$ and the explosive solution occurs when $e_t = e_0(1/a)^t$. Another probabilistic solution which satisfies (4.10) is

$$e_t \begin{cases} = (\pi a)^{-1}e_{t-1} + \mu_t & \text{with probability } \pi \\ = \mu_t & \text{with probability } 1 - \pi \end{cases} \qquad (4.11)$$

With (4.11), there is a rational expectation bubble which has an expected duration of $(1 - \pi)^{-1}$.

Finally, to reinforce the argument about the likelihood of multiple equilibria, it is worth building on the earlier reference to game theory. Recall the concept of a perfect equilibrium from section 3.3. In effect, the perfect equilibrium concept demands that agents should entertain expectations about other agents' behaviour in certain circumstances which would be confirmed by their behaviour if those circumstances arose. To use the language of rational expectations: 'monopolist acquiescence where there is entry' is a rational expectation for the entrant in the chain-store game to entertain. Hence, to all intents and purposes, one can think of the perfect equilibrium concept as involving the formation of rational expectations when the problem of what is uncertain in the decision setting is the behaviour of other agents.

Now, the Folk theorem with respect to repeated games carries an interesting implication for the likelihood of multiple rational expectation equilibria. The Folk theorem states that, in infinitely repeated games, any outcome which leaves no player worse off than he/she would be by not playing is a perfect equilibrium. (This theorem has been extended to cover finitely repeated games by Fudenberg and Maskin, 1986.) So, there are an infinite number of perfect equilibria in these circumstances and, with them, rational expectations for the players to hold. In short, multiple rational expectation equilibria are unlikely to be a theoretical curiosity.

The general difficulty which is posed by such multiple equilibria is obvious. In effect, instrumental rationality, in the guise of rational expectations, may have narrowed down the range of possible expectations which can be entertained but, unless this is reduced to one, the agent is going to have to rely on something other than instrumental rationality when settling on one of these expectations rather than another. Instrumental rationality alone will not do the trick.

Hahn (1987) summarises this message and suggests a direction for the development of economic analysis: 'if you are only interested in equilibrium and not in the dynamic process then you get an answer which is not exactly helpful' (p. 324). The concrete dynamic processes, where agents start from an initial position of ignorance and use particular learning processes, need to be studied and hopefully they may lead agents to converge on one equilibrium. Hahn calls this 'history' and he says we need to get away from the unsatisfactory history-free economics. 'Fair enough', the neoclassical might surmise, but history has radical implications. As we have seen in the earlier discussion of learning, this interest in the dynamic process will not restore the position of instrumental rationality because we cannot describe a learning process in instrumentally rational terms alone either. So, 'history' here stands for something other than what could be rationally reconstructed with the aid of instrumental rationality and some knowledge of agent objectives: it is an acknowledgement that there are processes of decision making which have an alternative logic.

In conclusion to this section, the rational expectations hypothesis seems to offer at first sight a convenient way of plugging the information hole in the instrumental account of rationality, but in the end it appears to leave a large hole which will have to be filled by some other notion of agency.

Firstly, if the emergence of rational expectations is to be explained, then it seems that, in general, the learning procedure will have to rely on some non-instrumentally rational behaviour. Secondly, where there exist multiple rational expectations equilibria, we shall need something other than instrumental rationality if the choice of expectation is to be explained.

4.3 The Institutional Influence on Information

Rational expectations is not the last word in the economics literature on the origin of information sets. Of course, it has a particular relevance to the argument of this book because of its connection with instrumental rationality. But there are other discussions, and this section picks out one fertile area which has particular relevance because it relates information to institutional context. In this way, the issue of explaining how agents come to have particular information sets becomes fused to the other question we wish to explore: how to explain the provenance of institutions.

One strand of this literature focuses on how the institutional context affects how much information agents will reveal about themselves. Suppose a government agency is deciding where to site a shopping centre. It would like to know in cost–benefit style which site will produce the greatest net gain for the community. So, it asks the individuals in the community how much income they would need to be paid or would be willing to pay so as to leave them indifferent between having the shopping centre at a particular site and the status quo. This question is asked of each site. The compensating income variations are summed to discover which site yields the greatest net benefit (this example follows Sugden, 1981).

One can immediately foresee the problems with such an arrangement. There is an incentive for individuals not to reveal their true preferences. It will make sense for an individual to exaggerate the cost of sites he/she does not like and exaggerate the benefits of the sites he/she does like. In short, the institutional structure encourages dissembling. However, it would be possible to design an alternative institutional arrangement which promoted a genuine revelation of preferences, thus demonstrating the importance of institutional context to the revelation of information about oneself. The alternative arrangement involves what is referred to as a Clarke–Groves tax (see Clarke, 1971, and Groves, 1973).

Let c_{ij} be the true compensating income variation of person i for site j. c is the sum you would pay (i.e. is positive) or that would have to be paid (i.e. is negative) to produce indifference between the site and the status quo. Let d_{ij} be the actual sum i announces to the government agency. The site with the largest $\Sigma_i d_{ij}$ is chosen and then each person has to pay a tax. The tax varies across individuals and is calculated in an ingenious way to provide the incentive to individuals to reply honestly to the original question about compensating income variations. It works like this: assume project k is chosen; recalculate the sum of compensating variations excluding individual i; rank the projects again, and we assume that project l comes out on top; the tax paid by individual i is the difference between the excluded sum of income variations on projects l and k:

$$t_i = \sum_{h \neq i} d_{hl} - \sum_{h \neq i} d_{hk} \qquad (4.12)$$

The objective of individual i, when k is chosen, is to maximise his/her true compensating income variation minus the tax:

$$c_{ik} + \sum_{h \neq i} d_{hk} - \sum_{h \neq i} d_{hl} \qquad (4.13)$$

The individual has no influence on the last term in this expression, and so all he/she can hope to influence is the choice of k, thereby maximising the value of the first two terms. But the choice of k is made on the basis of the sum of declared compensating variations:

$$\left\{ k: \max \left(d_{ik} + \sum_{h \neq i} d_{hk} \right) \right\} \qquad (4.14)$$

By comparing this choice rule with the first two terms in the objective function it can be seen that the individual cannot do better than reply honestly in the attempt to influence the choice of k so as to maximise (4.12). To appreciate the logic of this result, imagine an attempt at exaggerating d above c for some project m which is sufficient for m to be chosen rather than k from an initial position of honest reporting. It is matter of simple arithmetic to see that the direct gain to c will be more than outweighed by the increase in the tax when the exaggeration is to be sufficient to cause the switch in choice. To put it slightly differently, it is not worth trying to manipulate a solution because the attempt increases your tax burden under this scheme.

The chain-store game outlined in section 3.3 is a further illustration of how institutional context can influence the information which agents reveal. In particular, in that setting there is a plain incentive for a 'weak' monopolist to mislead potential entrants: and in the sequential equilibrium approach, there are further predictions about how information-revealing behaviour will change as the game progresses. The monopolist is not forced to reveal information until the reputation-building phase of the game has been reached; at this stage there can be misleading behaviour, and the chances of truth-revealing behaviour increase as the game proceeds towards its end.

There are other illustrations from the industrial organisation literature. For instance, the pooling of information by oligopolists may depend on whether there is a co-operative arrangement in place (see Clarke, 1983). Finally, there is a general observation about the influence of numbers on the possibilities for dissembling that comes from general equilibrium theory. It harks back to the original Hayekian concern with the informational characteristics of the market system. The core of the economy shrinks to the competitive equilibrium as the number of traders grows large. In contrast, when the core covers many allocations, there are incentives for agents to dissemble because it could favourably influence the precise allocation within the core.

Another strand from this institutional literature concentrates on how the structure of different institutions leads to different practices in the collection and processing of information. Post-Keynesian economics makes this connection at the cognitive level of the individuals who are affiliated to the institutions. Every institution has an ideology: a set of beliefs and claims which legitimate its own particular organisational form. Since organising the present is not distinct from facing the future, it should not be surprising to find that these beliefs carry with them implications for how the future is to be perceived. By drawing on the anthropological literature which examines the coherence of such webs of belief, it is possible to associate different organisational forms with particular concerns about the future and particular time preferences (see Hargreaves Heap, 1986).

The connection can also be made through a study of the information flows within different forms of organisation. Sah and Stiglitz (1986) characterise hierarchical and polyarchical organisations according to whether they process information (screen projects) serially or in parallel. Information flows to the decision maker in a polyarchy from a number of independent screeners, while the information in a hierarchy has to pass through a series of screens before it reaches the decision maker. The parallel screening of the polyarchy leads to the acceptance of a larger number of projects leading to a higher incidence of type II errors where projects which should have been rejected are accepted. By contrast, a hierarchical method of information processing generates a higher incidence of type I errors, where projects are rejected when they should be accepted.

This section has provided a sample from an important and growing part of the information literature in economics. The details of these analyses are not what is important for the argument here. Rather, it is the general direction of the analysis that is relevant: this is the linkage of information sets to institutional context.

4.4 Conclusion

The rational expectations revolution promised much for the instrumental account of rationality because it seemed to explain the information structure in instrumental terms: instrumentally rational agents should hold rational expectations. However, an analysis of what might be involved in forming a rational expectation, when either there is learning to be done or there are multiple rational expectations equilibria, yields a different conclusion. Instrumental rationality cannot alone provide an explanation of how agents form their expectations.

To put this slightly differently, rational expectations cannot, in some magical flourish, get round the old conundrum about not knowing what is the optimal investment in information acquisition without knowing the full information set. The old conundrum serves to remind us that information in the economy is not just another good. It is quite unlike most commodities and so it is scarcely surprising that it is not amenable to the same treatment which we give to all commodities. What we need is a fresh approach to go with this insight.

The way out of this conundrum, like the matter of how to form expectations when there is learning to be done or when there are multiple rational expectation equilibria, will be to introduce something else into the decision making process. Hahn (1987) offers one candidate, history, and with it issues the challenge of developing a notion of historical agency that will capture those particularities and idiosyncrasies of decision making which cannot be reduced to instrumental calculation. Another candidate addition to the analysis, institutions, was foreshadowed in the last section and this is explored further in the next chapter.

5 INSTITUTIONS

5.1 Introduction

This chapter continues with the assessment of the scope of the intentional explanations afforded by instrumental rationality. It considers whether there is a purely instrumental account of institutions. This question has taken on a double significance as a result of the last chapter. Not only are institutions one of the potentially important constraints on the scope of the intentional explanations sketched in chapter 3, they may also hold the key to the explanation of another important potential constraint, the information sets that agents go to work with. So, should there be purely instrumental accounts of institutions, there would be good grounds for supposing that neither institutions nor information sets constitute a significant constraint on the scope of the explanations generated by instrumental rationality.

Modern analyses of institutions within the instrumental tradition treat them as a feature of a solution to a repeated evolutionary game (see Schotter, 1981, and Sugden, 1986, who both cast Nozick, 1974, in the same way). This is a direct development of the tradition of Hayek, 1973, and Buchanan, 1975, where institutions are examples of the 'spontaneous order' which can emerge in human affairs without any guiding supra-individual hand.* These attempts are discussed in the next three sections.

Unfortunately, the discussion in these three sections makes clear that the repeated game approach to institution creation is not going to provide an exclusively instrumental explanation of institutions. The problem is again one of multiple equilibria. Something else, a particular 'history' of playing the game, in the Hahn (1987) sense discussed in the last chapter, or a particular informational structure must be added to get the explanation of why one rather than another emerges. The latter deflects the problem back to questions of the last chapter, which yielded no satisfactory answers save to bounce the problem on to this chapter or accept the need for 'something else'. So, there seems no escaping the need for an additional notion of historical agency.

---

* It is perhaps worth commenting in passing on a class of explanations of institutions and other sorts of social behaviour which appeal more simply to efficiency i.e. Posner (1977) where the law (especially tort) is thought to reflect economic efficiency considerations and Becker (1968) where criminal behaviour is reduced to a cost–benefit calculation. They are not directly discussed here since they either accept some pre-existing institutional context, and so push the issue one stage further back, or they generate multiple equilibria, and so leave open the matter of how one institutional arrangement rather than another emerges.

This constitutes the final instalment in the argument that some additional conception of rationality is required to avoid the charge that the scope of economic explanations is damagingly constrained by an inability to explain institutions and information sets. It is an argument which justifies in part the procedural sense of rationality in chapter 7. Procedural rationality is the way that the institutional and informational contribution, which cannot itself be reduced to instrumental rationality, is introduced into the explanation at the level of the individual. It is the answer to the challenge of a different sense of 'historical' agency.

Some care, as always, is required not to overlook the contribution of the literature which is being used to generate this conclusion. Like the earlier part of the argument in chapter 4, the economics literature on repeated games is very helpful in establishing precisely where the non-instrumental element needs to be introduced into the analysis. This positive aspect should not be forgotten, even if it is the critical implications which are at the centre of the argument now.

Information features significantly in the repeated game explanation of institutions. This is a more general characteristic of explanations of institutions in economics and the fifth section gives a brief survey of some of these other explanations. Since the last chapter ended on a survey of how the literature contained explanations of information in terms of institutional context, reading this may well feel like chasing your own tail. This is not surprising, and it is no coincidence that much of the first three sections of the chapter bear a close resemblance to the discussion of rational expectations in the last chapter. Institutions and information are two sides of the same coin. They may appear to be separate features of the landscape, but they are closely connected. A definition of institutions will make this clear.

Ordinarily, we think of an institution as some formal arrangement, like a firm, or a market, or a set of property rights established by laws, that constrains the actions which are permitted between the agents who are parties to the arrangement. A system of property rights will define an action called theft and it makes the action illegal. Likewise a market permits a certain kind of 'free' exchange between individuals while firms have hierarchies which enable some individuals to 'command' others. One way of getting at this central aspect of an institution is to define it as a set of rules which govern behaviour. Once so defined, there is no compelling reason for drawing a line between formal institutions of the market, firm, property right variety and the more informal conventions which govern behaviour. There may not be a law or some formal arrangement to which we are party that makes it mandatory to give up a seat to the old and infirm on a bus, or to have lunch between 12 noon and 2 p.m., or indeed to call the meal at midday 'lunch'; but they are rules, nevertheless, which govern our behaviour.

Of course, not everyone respects the informal rules, the conventions, but neither does everyone observe the rules of formal institutions like property rights. What is crucial to both is the existence of rules which enjoy sufficient compliance to impart some regularity to the practices of human action. So, we define an institution as any convention, regular practice or set of rules which influences behaviour. As Wittgenstein remarked: 'A game, a language, a rule is an institution.' This way of defining an institution brings out the relation with information. The great virtue of, say, the lunch between 12 and 2 convention is that it gives predictability to other people's actions: you know that this will not be the best time to phone a person at work. Equally language as a convention enables its users to have reasonable confidence that others will attach the same meaning to utterances. In summary, institutions are information generating devices: they are practices which encode expectations.

The overlap in the argument between this chapter and the last which follows from this relation between institutions and information is justified on two grounds. Firstly, the economics literature typically treats them as separate areas of discussion, and the general point about the inability of instrumental rationality by itself to explain them is sufficiently important to warrant development from a number of angles. Secondly, the sketches of some of the ways that information sets contribute to particular institutional forms and vice versa actually constitute building blocks in the explanations of how institutions reproduce themselves and 'mutate' through the agency of procedural rationality. Again, recognising this puts a useful perspective on this part of economics. This literature both highlights the restricted explanatory power of an exclusively instrumental account of rationality and contributes something more positive: it demonstrates in quite precise ways how other conceptions of rationality can fit into explanations in economics.

5.2   Institutions as Solutions to Repeated Games

The basic idea behind this approach to institution formation is that agents who repeatedly interact in similar circumstances will come to learn efficient ways of handling that interaction. They will develop rules of thumb concerning how best to act in such settings and these rules of thumb become 'institutions'. The interaction is formally handled as a repeated game.

There are a variety of games and ways in which a repeated game can be analysed. I start in this section with a repeated version of a co-ordination game that might plausibly help in a stylised way to explain the emergence of some sorts of property rights. It also lays out clearly the nexus between

B

		I	II
	I	0,0	1,2
A			
	II	2,1	0,0

Figure 5.1   Co-ordination game

information and institutions. In fact, it is a hybrid, formed by collapsing two examples, one from Schotter (1981) and the other from Sugden (1986). There are two pastures (I and II) and two ranchers (A and B). One pasture is superior to the other, and the pay-off to grazing in each pasture also depends on whether it is shared with the other rancher. Figure 5.1 gives the precise matrix of pay-offs: they have been normalised for convenience.

First, take the case of pure strategies, where A is trying to decide between grazing on either I or II. A will prefer I to II if B chooses II, but will prefer II to I if B chooses I. So A's choice depends critically on what B does. But B is in exactly the same position: B's choice will depend equally on what A does; and as we have just seen, what A does depends critically on what B does. So there is no way of predicting what B will do, and so decide what to do, without first having decided what to do. Hence, A cannot rationally choose one strategy or the other on the basis of the game as described so far. Let us suppose, then, that A decides to adopt a strategy of grazing in II with probability p and of grazing in I with probability $1 - p$. In other words, they adopt mixed strategies. Now, there are two ways we can tell the story from here.

Firstly, we could assume that A simply chooses p at random initially and then varies the probability depending on the success of the strategy over repeated plays. A will increase p if it seems that more frequent grazing on II will produce higher expected returns, and conversely reduce p when the expected returns favour I. This can be made more precise. The success of the strategy depends on the probability that B grazes in one place or the other. Analogously, we assume B chooses a probability q of grazing in II, which is updated in a similar manner by experience. Now, when $q < 1/3$, the frequency with which B grazes on II will be observed by A to be q, save for random error. So, the frequency of A observing B on II can also be expected to be less than 1/3, and this will lead A to calculate that the expected return from playing II exceeds that from playing I. Hence, A decides to increase p, the frequency with which II is played. Conversely,

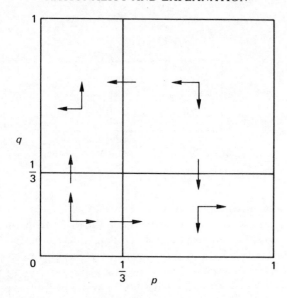

Figure 5.2   Co-ordination game played with a convention

when $q > 1/3$ and this is perceived by A, the expected returns calculation will favour I and p is revised downwards. By similar reasoning q rises or falls as p is less than or greater than 1/3.

Figure 5.2 is a phase diagram with these dynamics. There are three equilibria here for $[p, q]$: [1, 0], [0, 1] and [1/3, 1/3]. The first two are stable, and the last is unstable. Given the lack of any presumed precision in this learning procedure, in the sense that even if one rancher played 1/3 there is no guarantee that the perception will be exactly 1/3, the instability of the last equilibrium would seem to make it exceedingly unlikely to prevail. Hence, the two likely equilibria are [1, 0] and [0, 1]. Either A always uses II and B uses I, or B always uses II and A uses I. In both cases, there is no conflict over this distribution.

This result deserves some comments. Whichever equilibrium holds finally, it will appear to define some clear property rights, and those property rights are encoded in the belief structure of the players which has evolved in the course of the game. The terminal beliefs of each player will be perfectly rational in the sense of rational expectations because, for example, with [1, 0] it is the expectation of A grazing on II that prompts setting q at 0, and this ensures that A will graze on II. However, it should be noted that there is no prediction over what the distribution of property rights to I and II will be between A and B. This can only be given a 'historical' explanation in terms of the evolution of the game and the players' beliefs – i.e. the initial beliefs about $[p, q]$ and the precise updating rules that each player uses.

The second way in which the story can be taken up is through setting a further constraint on the initial choice of p and q by A and B. Since both players recognise the structure of the game and their own interdependence, it might be argued that A will set p in the knowledge that B who is similarly placed will be setting q. So, A is searching for an optimal p knowing that a similarly rational B is looking for an optimal q. Likewise B, and, as similarly placed rational agents should come to the same conclusion, this can be captured by constraining the solutions to $p=q$. This additional constraint singles out a unique equilibrium: $[1/3, 1/3]$.

There might be legitimate worries, given the earlier result concerning instability, over how robust the result would prove under a minor relaxation of the assumptions. Suppose, for example, that there is some doubt in both players' minds about the pay-offs in the game, and so they start with $[p, q] = [1/2, 1/2]$; then the evolution will critically depend on how $[p, q]$ are revised in the light of experience. But, given the instability result, it would be pure serendipity if it jumped to $[1/3, 1/3]$. An alternative way of expressing this worry is that this particular solution to the game will not be very useful when it comes to explaining situations characterised by learning. Nevertheless, should $[1/3, 1/3]$ be achieved, it would define a form of property rights, even if they are only probabilistic. They would merely be much less distinct property rights with conflict occurring with some frequency on both pastures.

There is a deeper disquiet concerning whether this argument for $[1/3, 1/3]$ is really convincing on its own terms. There are three Nash equilibria, given the respective possible rational belief structures which could support them, and it is not obvious why the solution which agents choose should respect some initial symmetry in the game. Why should a person believe the game will end up respecting symmetry just because the players are similarly placed at the start of the game, when other equilibria exist? It would seem instead that there is some other rule which lies behind the construction of this equilibrium as the unique one: namely one prescribing a symmetric outcome. So, even though the earlier considerations may point to the limited applicability of this second way of closing the game, it shares an important feature with the first version. A unique equilibrium can only be supported by invoking some other rule: the specification of initial beliefs and learning procedures was required in the first case, and now a rule requiring a thoroughgoing sort of symmetry is needed.

This is important because it highlights the inability of an instrumental account of rationality alone to provide an explanation of institutions in both ways of telling the story. In the final analysis, a specific institution, like a particular set of property rights here, can only be explained by reference to some other institution or rule which governs learning or admissible beliefs. All that instrumental rationality together with repeated play of the game generates is the prediction of some 'spontaneous order' and not the precise nature of that order.

To be fair, this is well recognised by Sugden (1986) and Schotter (1981) as a problem and they do offer some solutions. But, also to be fair, they are rather half hearted efforts. For example, Sugden (1986) argues for possession and closeness as two salient characteristics which lead to some conventions being picked out rather than others. Hence, it might be argued, rancher A is closer to pasture II and this leads us to expect the [1, 0] solution because everyone tends to recognise closeness as a salient characteristic in such situations. In this form, the answer just pushes the question one further position down the line because we would want to know why closeness is regarded as salient. It is unlikely to be the only difference between the ranchers and so we want to know why this convention with respect to what difference is treated as salient has emerged rather than another. An appeal to its use in other circumstances and an argument which rests on analogy again sidesteps the question: we want to know both why it was originally used and what makes similarity a telling feature in this instance.

There are two further attempts to ground 'salience' in something that is not another convention requiring further explanation, and so on in an infinite regress. One is an argument that some conventions like closeness are much simpler to apply than others, like equality.

It is true as a first impression that there is nothing simpler than measuring the distance between two objects, whereas equality is a very tricky idea. Do we mean strict equality, or have we to take account of needs and opportunities? But a closer examination of the issues reveals that the question has been begged again. Closeness is not an intrinsically simpler concept than equality. Is it closeness as the crow flies, or are we to take account of roads, the rail network and whether there is an air service? Is Paul closer to Mary when they talk on the phone than he is to his neighbour? Is Gibraltar closer to Spain or the UK? It is a convention which singles out the relatively simple version of closeness which is calibrated by a ruler. It is equally easy to think of a simple aspect of equality: equal shares. This is no more complicated to use than the ruler; and it does no less injustice to the underlying concept of equality than does the ruler to that of closeness. So, simplicity cannot explain why closeness in the ruler sense rather than equality in an equal shares sense is the salient solution.

The final argument grounds closeness and possession in our genetic make-up through appeals to evidence from biology. Fortunately, both Schotter (1981) and Sugden (1986) make no strong claim here and so there is no need for an extended comment. For a splendid literary illustration of the difficulties of reading the biological record for such purposes, see Chatwin (1987).

5.3 The Scope of Repeated Game Explanations of Institutions

The implication of the discussion above is important, but it should not blind us to some potentially helpful insights into institutions which this perspective affords. So, while not forgetting the suggestion that instrumental rationality will not suffice, I want to slant the discussion more in the direction of what might be called the positive heuristic of this analysis.

One helpful feature of this approach which has emerged is that it brings out the relationship between institutions and information. A further important insight is taken up in the next section and concerns the prisoner's dilemma game. Another which comes directly from the conclusion of the last section is that any property rights grounded in that type of co-ordination game look rather fragile, not, of course, in the formal game theoretic sense because these are stable equilibria, but in the sense that, if [1, 0] obtains, the [0, 1] would nevertheless be achievable if beliefs could be changed for reasons outside the actual experience of this game. This attempt to step outside the game must be tempting for B if he/she understands the structure of the game. In short, the message of arbitrariness brings with it one of 'revolutionary' fragility, a point which is recognised by Buchanan (1975).

There are also a large variety of contexts where this kind of model of institution formation can be applied, either using the co-ordination games or games with a similar structure. Sugden (1986) and Schotter (1981) provide many applications. Simple amendments, for instance, can be made to the rancher and pasture property rights game. Suppose A and B are a man and woman living together. Many of the features of the arrangement will be the object of formal negotiation. But such negotiations cannot cover every contingency; there will always be new situations arising where the pay-offs look like the co-ordination game and these games have to be played without communication and negotiation. The sequence of these situations constitute a repeated game of the rancher–pasture variety and the same predictions issue from it.

Alternatively, the way in which the game is repeated can be recast. Suppose there is a group of people and in each round each person plays another one from the group. The group is large and so the likelihood of playing the same person again is small, and no attempt is made to remember how an opponent has played before. In other words, each play of the game is completely anonymous. It could be the crossroads game where two drivers are approaching the same intersection on different roads and each must decide whether to slow or speed up; or it could be any essentially anonymous social interaction where there is a premium on a complementary response or more generally a co-ordinated response. Who goes through the open door first? Do you shake hands when you meet or nod? The examples are legion.

Several interesting equilibria are possible in this case. Firstly, let us suppose that nobody sees any asymmetry in the situation. That is to say, there is no reason to place one's self in a role marked A and one's opponent in one marked B. Each person simply decides to use one strategy or the other. We assume that a proportion p decide on II and $1-p$ choose I. Alternatively, each person pursues a mixed strategy with probability p of playing II. Each person then evaluates the frequency with which they come across people playing each strategy and works out the expected returns from following each strategy. Assuming the matrix of pay-offs in figure 5.1 and if they are following the pure strategy approach then the expected return calculation will favour the adoption of II when $p<1/3$, and so p will rise. The reverse is the case when $p>1/3$, and similar considerations apply when agents use mixed strategies. Consequently, an equilibrium will be generated in the population with a third of the people, say, speeding up at the crossroads and two-thirds slowing down. Or if the mixed strategy approach is adopted people will simply speed up one-third of the time and slowdown two-thirds of the time. Whichever way p is interpreted here, there will be crashes and wasted opportunities when both parties speed up and slow down respectively. Indeed, one or the other lost opportunity will occur in rather more than half the encounters.

A second set of equilibria can be distinguished when asymmetries are perceived in the playing of the game. Suppose for example that players notice the following distinctions: their age and their sex. These features combine in a simple way to allocate a role A and a role B to each player of the game. Men get A and women get B in a mixed-sex encounter in the game, while the older person gets A and the younger gets B in a single-sex play of the game. Hence, every pair of players will be assigned to one role or another by this set of distinctions. (So, compared with the original formulation where there was player A and player B, we now have each player being assigned to one role or the other and it need not be the same role in all plays of the game.) Now, the role assignment has nothing to do with the structure of the game since the pay-offs are symmetric. Nevertheless, since agents recognise a difference in roles for these extrinsic reasons, it opens the possibility of playing strategies which are role specific: one strategy when you play role A, another when you play B. Whether this is helpful or not is another matter. First, I explore what would happen in these circumstances. Again, it is possible to conceive of individuals using pure or mixed strategies. A proportion p of the population, say, opt for II when playing A, while a proportion q opt for II when playing role B. These proportions are adjusted in the light of experience in the same manner as before. The dynamics follow those sketched in the rancher–pasture game. There are three equilibria for $[p, q]$: $[0, 1]$,$[1, 0]$ and $[1/3, 1/3]$. Only the first two are stable. Therefore, you could get a male–seniority or a female–youth hierarchy in this anonymous social game. Which actually developed would be a matter of the history of the game, but once one was established it would be stable. It is worth noting in passing that the returns to every player improve when the conventions with respect to A and B role playing are observed and $[1, 0]$ or $[0, 1]$ equilibrium is achieved, compared with when there is no role playing at all because no asymmetries are perceived in the game and $[1/3, 1/3]$ occurs. I return to this result in chapter 7.

The analysis carries through in an almost identical manner for a chicken game which is played anonymously in a population (see Sugden, 1986). This game is illustrated in figure 5.3. The pay-offs here are sometimes thought to capture well a situation where there is a dispute over property. Hence, the repeated play of this game, with a convention arising to assign the roles of A and B to each player, offers another explanation of the emergence of property rights.

These examples probably suffice to give a feel for the range of application and the type of hierarchies associated with property, gender and age which could result from a process of institution creation via repeated games. To restate the earlier point, however, in each of these examples the explanation of the institution creation relies on non-instrumental elements. There is no instrumental explanation here of what becomes the source for distinguishing between A and B players: why should it be age and sex in these examples rather than height or size or any of a number of other bases for distinguishing between players? Nor is there an explanation of why one stable equilibrium rather than the other emerges (i.e. $[0, 1]$ rather than $[1, 0]$): this can only be explained in terms of the history of the games, as the initial beliefs evolve under the influence of particular learning procedures.

There is another potential problem for the instrumental rationality

		B	
		I	II
A	I	1,1	0,2
	II	2,0	−2,−2

Figure 5.3   Chicken game

postulate which can be appreciated in the context of this type of explanation of institutions. It really concerns the other dimension of scope distinguished in section 3.4, that relating to the admissible sorts of preferences. Since this is taken up in detail in the next chapter, it is tempting to delay any discussion until then. But there is also a powerful inducement to trail the argument a little now, as the apparatus for making the point is at hand.

One example of an institution which has been explained in this framework is money (see Schotter, 1981). Money is a convention in a trading game, much like a 'give way to the right' rule is in the crossroads game. Fair enough, it might be thought, this is a formalisation of the kind of explanation any introductory text might give about the origin of money. But it is a pity to leave the story there.

What is missing is a sense of the profound consequences that the institution of money might have which stretch beyond just facilitating exchange. Indeed, they could plausibly have influenced the pay-offs of agents, not only in the 'money' game but also beyond it. For instance, one plausible reading of an emergent property of the convention of money as a medium of exchange is money as a store of value. Put slightly differently, what the convention of money as a medium of exchange has also given us is a new conception of property and capital. Taken one stage further, this could be claimed to contribute to a particular kind of abstraction. Equally, it might be argued that the transformation of personal services and exchanges into impersonal transactions contributes to a particular conception of freedom.

These consequences are potentially damaging for the scope of intentional explanations because the game could be said to have created desires which did not exist before. This is disquieting for intentional explanations because 'desires' have to be plausibly exogenous if they are to do the explaining. The moment they become endogenous, there is a question mark over what is doing the explaining because we need to know what caused agents to hold those preferences. This by itself is not going to be a source of anxiety to the instrumental camp, provided that these unintended preference evolutions can be related back to the preferences which entered the game from which they were created. In this way, it is still an original set of preferences which is in the driving seat. The anxiety sets in when it is further appreciated that the preferences in that original game were not decisive in determining the institutional–conventional solution to that game. Typically, as we have seen, there are multiple equilibria and another institution responding to the same initial preferences could have created a very different set of derivative preferences.

Hence, current preferences may have to be explained by something other than the pre-institutional preferences of the agents in the game. The example of money here is perhaps not the best illustration of the damage which might be done to the scope of intentional explanations because it will not be obvious that any other solution to the trading game would have had significantly different consequences for later preference creation. The force of the point is perhaps plainer when it is made in the context of a game where a gender convention emerges. Suppose 'the female gives way to male' convention arose in some crossroads-like game, and further suppose that this sex distinction helped to create an elaborate gender stratification, one aspect of which was the male treatment of females as sexual objects. In these circumstances, it would not make sense to describe the objectified male sexual desire as simply the derivative of some pre-institutional set of preferences. A different convention, say one with respect to height, might have co-ordinated activity at the crossroads just as well and this could plausibly have had very different consequences for subsequent preference evolution. Thus the power of the intentional explanation is correspondingly diminished.

5.4 The Prisoner's Dilemma

One of the most significant barriers to the construction of an intentional explanation of institutions is the prisoner's dilemma. It is one of the achievements of the 'spontaneous order' theorists that they have gone some way towards overcoming this impediment. The prisoner's dilemma is a game with pay-offs depicted in figure 5.4.

This game would seem to be ubiquitous and it poses obvious difficulties for attempts at co-operation, particularly amongst large numbers of people. Should I attach a pollution control mechanism to my car or not? I would like a reduction in pollution, but there is no point in my attaching a pollution device to may car if others do not, as my effort alone makes no impression on the pollution problem. Equally, there is no point in attaching a device myself if the others do because then I can enjoy the pollution

	B	
	Co-operate	Defect
A Co-operate	1,1	−1,2
A Defect	2,−1	0,0

Figure 5.4   Prisoner's dilemma game

improvement without any cost to myself. Each individual thinking likewise produces the polluted atmosphere. Tragedies of the commons in this vein abound. Take another illustration. Let co-operate stand for wage restraint and defect stand for an inflationary wage claim. An individual work group would prefer to see no inflation, but its wage moderation will not affect the rate of inflation and, if others do not moderate their wage claims, this group not only suffers the inflation it also suffers a fall in relative wages. There is no reason to moderate wages even if all other workers do because a wage increase in these circumstances is the best of all possible worlds: it yields improve relative wages without any inflation. All work groups recognise the logic of this and they press for inflationary wage increases.

These are the classic sorts of case in which Mill argues there is a role for government. Government steps in and legislates on pollution and maybe introduces an incomes policy to co-ordinate non-inflationary wage increases. However, the problem does not really go away by introducing a clever government. We need to know where the government comes from with this mandate. The point can be made from another angle. Prisoner's dilemma situations cry out for a co-operative solution because it is Pareto superior. But this does not guarantee that parties to the decision setting will agree to the co-operative solution once communication and negotiation between them is allowed. The problem is that the prisoner's dilemma can resurface in the co-operative game context.

Would you join a coalition which offered to share the costs of pollution abatement? No. If anyone joins, you get the benefits without any cost; and if you join you get the same benefits because your individual abatement is so small that it makes no difference to the global level of pollution, but you pay the cost. So, there is no reason to join a coalition which shares abatement costs. More generally, with any public good, would you join a coalition that produced a public good by contributing to the cost of its production? If the good is genuinely public in the sense that its 'use' cannot be reserved only for those members of the coalition, then this looks like a prisoner's dilemma.

It is the claim of both Schotter (1981) and Sugden (1986) that a form of co-operation is rationally possible when the prisoner's dilemma game is repeated. Their demonstrations follow different paths. Schotter (1981) builds on Harsanyi (1975), while Sugden (1986) develops Axelrod (1981). I reproduce part of Sugden (1986) to illustrate how the argument works.

The fact that the game is to be repeated an uncertain number of times is captured by the assumption that there is a positive probability π that the game will be repeated in the next time period. No attempt is made to discuss all possible strategies because the number of available strategies rapidly becomes very large when the game is repeated more than a very few times. Instead, four simple strategies are considered. One co-operates in every play (S) and another defects in every round (N). The third strategy is tit for tat (T): a T player co-operates in the first round and thereafter follows the move made by the opponent in the previous round. The final strategy is alternation (A): a player defects in odd numbered rounds and co-operates in even rounds.

It is clear that [S, S] is not a Nash equilibrium because S is not a best reply to itself. It is equally clear that [N, N] is a Nash equilibrium because there is no better response to someone who defects in each round than defection in each round as well. The possibility of [T, T] as another Nash equilibrium is what must be explored.

The demonstration that T can be a best reply to itself exploits the nested structure of the decision problem when you play against someone using T. When you play against someone using T, you know that they will either co-operate in this round or defect because it is a simple response to whatever was played in the last round. Suppose first the opponent will co-operate in this round. (The alternative of a defection by the opponent is covered in due course as part of the discussion of this possibility.) Now, suppose that co-operation is part of the best response strategy in this round; then since that will produce co-operation by your opponent under the tit-for-tat rule next period, the question is then repeated in an identical manner and the answer will be co-operate, and so on in each round. Hence, if your opponent co-operates in this round and co-operation in this round is part of the best response strategy, then co-operation will be the best response in each round.

Now suppose the answer to whether co-operation in this round is part of the best response is no. The only alternative action in this round is to defect. This means that the opponent will defect next round. There are now two possibilities for the next round: either defect is part of the best strategy response or co-operate is part of the best strategy response in this round. (Since the choice of round is arbitrary here, this discussion fills in the general case by covering the play when it is known that the opponent will defect this round rather than co-operate.) First, if defect is part of the best strategy response to defect in this time period, then this will produce defect in the subsequent period and the question of what is part of the best strategy will resurface in an identical manner to before, producing the same answer. Thus, if the opponent is going to defect, and defect this round is part of the best response strategy, then defect will be the best response in each round. In other words, N would be the best response to T in these circumstances.

Alternatively, suppose co-operate is part of the best strategy response to a defect in this round. Then the opponent will co-operate in the next round and the game takes up from where it started because this setting cued the argument that has just been developed. It was because we were considering when defect was part of the best strategy response to co-operate that we have ended up in this position again. Hence, when faced by the same setting again in a subsequent round, it follows that defect must be part of the best response again. Hence, if co-operate is part of the best strategy response in the next round, and co-operate will be part of the best strategy in the subsequent round, and so on. In other words A would be the best response strategy under these conditions.

This exhausts the discussion of possible best response strategies to T. Either it is a strategy involving co-operation in each round – one such strategy is, of course, T– or it is N or A. It is now a simple matter to calculate the expected returns from following each of these possible best response strategies to see which is the actual best response strategy.

$$E(T, T) = 1 (1 + \pi + \pi^2 + \ldots) = \frac{1}{1-\pi} \qquad (5.1)$$

$$E(N, T) = 2 \qquad (5.2)$$

$$E(A, T) = 2 - \pi + 2\pi^2 - \pi^3 + 2\pi^4 \ldots = \frac{2-\pi}{1-\pi^2} \qquad (5.3)$$

It can be seen from this calculation that when $\pi > 1/2$ the best strategy will be T. So, provided there is a reasonable prospect of the game continuing relative to the configuration of pay-offs, [T, T] would be a Nash equilibrium yielding co-operation.

This is a powerful result. It would seem to imply that one of the bugbears of the instrumental account of rationality, the prisoner's dilemma, is well on the way to being defeated. However, it is purchased at a cost which is not often recognised, and which again points to the need for something other than instrumental rationality. Firstly, [T, T] is not the only Nash equilibrium, and so the old problem of multiple equilibria remains to be unravelled here, as elsewhere. Secondly, the assumption that the game will always be repeated with some probability π contains within it the assumption that there is some, albeit very small, probability that the game will go on for ever. Without this assumption we would have a finite repeated game and the backward induction logic would take hold, just as in the chain-store game, to produce cheating in each play of the game (see section 3.3). To be more precise, when the duration of the game is bounded from above, there is always one play of the game for which it would not be correct to say there is a positive probability of the game continuing, and it is necessary to be able to say this is correct for all possible plays of the game to forestall the backward induction process. In other words, the possibility of [T, T] in the repeated version of the prisoner's dilemma game rests on a particular belief structure which itself cannot, in any obvious way, be treated as a consequence of instrumental rationality: namely, there is some small chance of immortality!

Given an apparent similarity here with the chain-store game, it seems that there might be another way of solving the prisoner's dilemma: to follow Kreps and Wilson (1982) and introduce some uncertainty about the motivations of players. Indeed, this has been done (see Kreps et al., 1982). The earlier comments on this solution apply again. This cannot be treated as a wholly instrumental explanation because we need some explanations again of the particular information structure which supports a co-operative solution in the early plays of a sequential equilibrium. Furthermore, as has just been implied, it is not a very satisfactory explanation of co-operation in these games because it is likely to hold in the early stages of the repeated game. Unless the doubt about motives is very large a period will come towards the end of the game when reputation building is required and as this is risky it becomes likely that defection will occur.

What is perhaps worthy of comment is how these two solutions to the repeated prisoner's dilemma depend on two contending and familiar belief structures. In one we combine instrumental rationality with a belief, albeit only in the sense of a small probability, that we live for ever either through our genes or through religious salvation, thus acceding to the existence of some grand design (nature's or God's) of which we are a part. Alternatively we combine instrumental rationality with a belief that there is some small probability of no design whatsoever: we make our own world and consequently anything might be possible, including a 'nutter' who plays tit-for-tat in the prisoner's dilemma game. There is another option, which Kantians would be quick to remind us about. A Kantian finds that an action which can be generalised to good effect by all agents should be undertaken by an individual agent. In effect, this belief structure mixes the two above by allowing that we make our own world aided by a 'grand' design of our own 'reason', which takes this particular form. The Kantian will find some consolation in the Kreps and Wilson result because it suggests that there need only be some small possibility of agents' being Kantian for them to act as if they were Kantian!

5.5 The Informational Influences on Institutions

There is a larger economics literature on institutions, and this section draws attention to the vein of it which connects institutions with the information structure of the activity.

One of the famous papers in oligopoly theory (Stigler, 1964) plots this relation. The difficulty which is faced by an oligopolistic collusive arrangement is how to detect cheating in the form of secret price cuts by the parties to the agreement. The oligopoly game is turned into a prisoner's dilemma when there is not the information to monitor the collusion (see Osborne, 1976), whereas, if the cheats are detectable, then punishment strategies can be developed by the group to deter such behaviour; and the collusive arrangement will prosper.

In Stigler's original model, the sales of firms are observable and what makes detection difficult is a certain degree of random movement of buyers between sellers. This means it is not possible to associate unambiguously a surge in sales with secret price cutting because it could arise from these random variations in purchasing by customers – the firm could just be lucky in that particular period. Using standard confidence intervals to decide whether a surge is due to cheating or random movements, Stigler demonstrates that the incentive towards cheating, in the sense of its not being detected, rises with the degree of random buying. Hence, the greater the random buying, the poorer the information set, and the greater is the likelihood that the collusive arrangement collapses.

Another example of an area of economics which has mapped the influence of information on institutions is the transaction cost literature. It is a modern attempt to flush out the implications of Coase's (1937) famous article on firms and markets. The problem addressed is why economic transactions should be organised in the firm rather than by the market: they constitute two alternative ways of co-ordinating the economic activity of agents and it is important to know why one is chosen rather than the other. Williamson (1975) has argued that the choice of organisation depends on transaction costs: these are the costs of actually co-ordinating economic activity and the primary one is an enforcement cost which arises because agents are opportunistic. It is not possible to write fully contingent agreements between agents; and there are always some agents who cannot be trusted to live by the spirit of an agreement and who will respond in a self-serving manner if the opportunity arises. Hence, the choice of organisation is grounded in the need to minimise the damage of opportunistic behaviour.

Further, it is argued that these transaction costs will differ by organisation according to the different transactional conditions. There are three critical dimensions to the transactional conditions: frequency, uncertainty, and transaction-specific investment. The transactional conditions which favour the use of a firm/hierarchy over the market are those of recurrent exchange, where there is non-trivial uncertainty and where there is transaction-specific investment. The rationale behind this mapping has the following shape: frequency is important because the fixed costs of setting up a firm need to amortised over a large number of transactions; with little uncertainty there are fewer opportunities to respond opportunistically and so the formal structure of the firm, which helps guard against opportunism by making individual rewards depend in part on the performance of the organisation, is less important;* and transaction-specific investments give each party an interest in maintaining a long–term relationship. Hence – to isolate the precise informational strand in the argument–we find that greater uncertainty in the transaction is likely to favour hierarchies over the market.

It was suggested earlier that this plotting of the informational influence on institutions together with the discussion of the reverse in the last chapter had something of the character of chasing your own tail. In a sense, this chasing your own tail is a testament to the force of the general argument that instrumental rationality alone will not suffice. What we have here, instead, and earlier, are examples of the building blocks of non-instrumental theories about how institutions reproduce and mutate over time, in other words, parts of theories which discuss the non-instrumental contribution of institutions.

There are other examples in economics where this non-instrumentality is made quite explicit. It is sometimes termed 'structural' analysis because the accent is on how structures/institutions reproduce themselves or spawn new structures. For instance, the famous Marglin (1974) paper entitled What Do Bosses Do? makes Williamson's 'opportunism' a function of the class antagonist relations between workers and employers. It is the institution of capitalism which gives rise to a particular kind of opportunism and Marglin and later theorists of the 'labour process' (see Friedman,1977) argue that the choice of organisation and technology is often a direct result of the need to contain this opportunism–class antagonism. So, it is one institution/structure (class relations under capitalism) which is responsible for another institution (the organisation at work). For example, the shift from the putting-out to the factory system in the nineteenth century had little to do with any new technologies which were suited to factories and large-scale production; instead it was more 'efficient' because it enabled better surveillance, more reliable supply and better control of 'offcuts', 'waste' materials and the like. Likewise, the production line may or may not have enjoyed purely technical advantages over smaller work groups; what it certainly afforded was a simple way of controlling the efforts expended in the factory.

A final example of this kind of 'institutional' economics, from yet another quarter, is provided by Olson (1982). He argues, on the basis of earlier work, which was concerned with how collective action is generated when there are free rider/prisoner dilemma problems, that institutions tend

---

* This is a version of the Weberian point that the virtue of bureaucracies is that they minimise personal conflicts.

to have built into them the seeds of their own destruction. Collective action in the form of some institutional arrangement or another may initially constitute a successful response to some shared problem. But, inevitably, he argues, it becomes ossified because this is, in part, how the problem of collective action is overcome; and this means that the people who belong to the institution are unable to respond to new conditions demanding new kinds of actions. The institution slides into a backwater. This is the curse of being successful as witnessed by the economic performance of the USA and the UK in the post-war period: well-developed institutions build in rigidities while those economies like France, Germany, Italy and Japan, whose institutions were 'shaken up' by the Second World War have been able to respond much more flexibly to the economic challenges of the post-war period.*

5.6 Conclusion

The instrumental account of rationality has proved a powerful generator of explanations in economics, but explanation in economics never relies exclusively on this conception of rationality. There is always some institutional or informational context which helps orchestrate the intentional explanation; and these props cannot themselves be explained through an exclusive reliance on the instrumental postulate. There is an unavoidable something which is non-instrumental in the explanation, even in those accounts which try hardest to make institutions and information sets the result of actions undertaken by instrumentally rational agents.

This is an important conclusion, and this chapter has provided the institutions' part of the argument. Much of this discussion may seem strangely distant from the institutions we observe in the real world, or from the more complicated events which surround institutional change. This is as it must be. The purpose of this chapter has been to see whether it is possible, in principle, for instrumental rationality alone to provide an intentional explanation of the origin of institutions in a way that does not presuppose some other set of institutions. I am not concerned with difficulties and complications in explanation which occur simply because individuals in the real world are imperfectly instrumentally rational. The point is that, even if they were instrumentally rational in an ideal way, we could not generate a complete explanation of institutions and information sets. As such, this conclusion constitutes a constraint on the scope of the intentional explanations in economics which ought to worry those who work exclusively with instrumental rationality for the reasons sketched in section 3.4.

* I suppose that, with this reading of the post-war period, the election of Maggie Thatcher could be cast as the sensible way of 'losing' the war.

I conclude this chapter by linking the argument so far with others in the social sciences, and by expressing, in a slightly different but perhaps also more familiar way, what it is that has to be added to the economics tool kit to make good the gaps left by instrumental rationality.

One way this idea of gaps is sometimes captured in the social sciences is through the 'action/structure' paradigm. Part of the explanation comes through the purposive actions of individuals, and the other part comes from the 'structural' features of the situation. This carries with it an image of structure as some kind of impediment like a brick wall, which agents bump into every now and then, and which constrains them from taking certain actions. It has been argued by Giddens (1979) that this is not a satisfactory conceptualisation of 'structure'. He advances a theory of 'structuration', which accords much better with the description of the non-instrumental component in explanations in economics developed so far in this book.

There are two key features in the theory of structuration that distinguish it from the action/structure paradigm. Firstly, the structure not only constrains, it also enables: just as, for example, in the co-ordination game discussed earlier in this chapter where one set of property rights constrains the actions of the ranchers but also enables their actions because it offers both ranchers superior pay-offs to the position of conflict where property rights are poorly defined. Secondly, the structure is not something alien to individuals which they bump into: it is implicated in the actions of the individual and it is revealed in those actions. Again, the co-ordination example reveals the same feature because it is the structure of beliefs which sustains the practices of the property rights institutions.

To summarise, at the level of the individual, I am concluding that there are reasons for action which cannot be reduced to the instrumental account of rationality. Hahn (1987) refers to this as an indispensable historical element in economic analysis. When discussing individual motivation, I prefer to capture the idea by referring to agents as procedurally rational. They follow non-instrumental procedures and this is how structure is implicated in action. Thus, procedural rationality at the level of the individual is what allows us to dissolve the action/structure paradigm into Gidden's theory of structuration.

Individuals may or may not recognise their procedural rationality as a reflection of something new and different to instrumental rationality. But it is helpful to reflect on what procedural rationality implies for the individual in more detail, whether recognised or not, because it suggests a tie up with other disputes in economics. So far, it is simply a belief structure or an institution which singles out one equilibrium from the many that are otherwise available. Yet, this has surprising ramifications. One way of putting this is to return to Hann (1987) and note that it is a reminder of how we are historically contingent. Again, go back to the co-ordination game: it is only because we started out with some beliefs and we updated beliefs in a particular way, both of which were arbitrary in the sense of not being reducible to instrumental rationality, that we have ended up with one equilibrium rather than another. Had the history been different, things might have been very different.

As such, procedural rationality is a marker of both a kind of freedom and uncertainty. The freedom and the uncertainty come together. Let us step back to see how this arises.

If we ask, on the basis of a knowledge that we are instrumentally rational, what convention we should expect to emerge to guide behaviours in a co-ordination game, we would have to reply that we simply do not know: there are any number of differences between individuals which could be used to assign roles to each player. *Ex post*, we can see why agents would follow one once it is in place because there is every incentive on instrumental grounds so to do. But, *ex ante*, there is no way of predicting which will emerge if we rely on instrumental rationality alone.

This is the hallmark, to paraphrase Keynes and Knight, of a situation of genuine uncertainty as compared with risk. Uncertainty applies to settings where a probability distribution has no rational foundation; and when rationality is conceived instrumentally, this exactly describes our predicament with respect to predicting a convention in the multiple bootstrap co-ordination game. It is the non-instrumental element of the decision-making process that explains the emergence of one set of institutions rather than another and it is these institutions which help to dissolve the uncertainty. It is the institutions which bring the predictability to social life. However, there is also something illusory about this predictability which relates to the bootstrap quality of any institutional arrangement.

It is the recognition that the particular beliefs stand only with the aid of their own bootstraps, that they are arbitrary and have no foundation in preference satisfaction, that means that there is peculiar type of freedom in the social world. We have a freedom to choose our co-ordinating conventions because, although we inherit from history a particular set of arrangements, they have no special claim to our attention on grounds of preference satisfaction alone. Of course, the corollary of this is that, to the extent that we do entertain that freedom seriously, then the robustness of existing institutions is put in doubt and this enables uncertainty to creep back in some degree.

Hence, I conclude what has been a long argument about instrumental rationality by drawing a counterpoint in the discussion over risk and uncertainty. The recognition of the limits of instrumental rationality sets the stage for non-instrumental features of decision making, and it is at the same time an argument for taking seriously uncertainty as distinct from risk.

6 ARE YOU INSTRUMENTALLY RATIONAL?

6.1 Introduction

This chapter addresses the second possible constraint on the scope of intentional explanations which was distinguished in section 3.4. It examines the restrictions placed on human behaviour and motivation by the need to satisfy the standard axioms of choice theory (see section 3.2) and the need to produce determinant intentional explanations. This second requirement requires no further elaboration after the discussion of the previous two chapters. If instrumental rationality alone is consistent with a number of outcomes, then the intentional explanation lacks determinacy and something else must be added to the analysis for an explanation of how one from the multiple equilibria has arisen.

So, the centre of attention in this chapter is the kind of people who fit the picture of instrumental rationality. Are they recognisably human? Or is there something vital missing?

Section 3.4 has already sketched why an answer to such a question is important because it affects the scope of the explanations generated by instrumental rationality. It is worth recollecting one of those reasons, as it gives an edge to the discussion in this chapter. The scope of the explanation generated by an economic theory matters because it conditions the possibilities for using the economic theory to make prescriptive statements.

The precise nature of this constraint depends on the reading of the relation between 'is' and 'ought'. With one version, the model of rational agency that is helpful in explanation becomes an input into the generation of prescriptive statements – the 'is', so to speak, however imperfectly understood because of the problems with any kind of objectivity in the social sciences (see chapter 2), stands for human nature and this must be taken into account in any prescriptive statement. Under this reading, the problem posed by the explanatory requirement of introducing non-instrumentally rational behaviour is the inconsistency that would then emerge between this and the prescriptive statements which were generated by an exclusively instrumentally based welfare economics.

Alternatively, the insights generated by explanations can be regarded as irrelevant when it comes to prescriptions. Prescriptions are recommendations about the way the world ought to be, and these are not affected by the way we happen to be. In this instance, the reliance on non-instrumental agency in explanation becomes a point about the indeterminacy of any prescription based exclusively on instrumental rationality.

Hence, scope matters because either consistency or determinacy is important in welfare economics. Whichever reading of the relationship is preferred, there is another way of understanding the importance of scope which also connects with normative concerns. With the second reading there is a plain normative question about whether the instrumental vision of rationality is a good recommendation. But, the same question arises indirectly with the first view of the relationship also. This type of straightforward normative question pops up here as well because of the problems with grounding an account of what 'is the case' in anything objective (see chapter 2). Since theory choice cannot always be reduced to some objective method, and since it is now recognised that theory can influence action via the beliefs which agents hold, it becomes appropriate to ask the question whether we actually like the vision of the individual contained within a theory. The plainly normative cannot be cut away to leave a positive economics.

Therefore, scope in explanation matters not only on technical grounds of consistency and determinacy when it comes to prescriptive analysis, it is also important, and unavoidably so, for straightforward normative reasons. We can ask whether we think instrumental rationality alone constitutes a very good metaphor for living; and part of the answer to this question might depend on what it seems to leave out of a recognisably human account of action.

This chapter considers whether two commonly held aspects of human action can be accommodated by instrumental rationality without compromising the quality of the associated intentional explanations. The first is interdependence between individual preferences, and it is examined in sections 6.2 and 6.3. The second concerns preference change, and this is discussed in sections 6.4, 6.5 and 6.6. The last section concludes the chapter by summarising the suggestions, which have emerged in the argument of the chapter, as to what non-instrumental features of human action need to be incorporated in economic theory to remedy the gaps in scope, thus also indicating, I would claim, what is required to make rationality a better metaphor for living.

6.2 Interdependent Preferences

The assumption of instrumental rationality is attractively simple, and at first sight the conditions which are placed on individual preferences (see section 3.2) look minimal. So, it would be surprising to find that some common-sense preferences could not be accommodated within such a scheme. But is this the case? First appearances are notoriously deceptive. Can it cope with altruistic preferences? Or does it only work with selfish individuals? How does it fare with other kinds of interdependence?

I begin with altruism. There is a famous proposition, dating back to Edgeworth, which asserts that it makes no difference whether selfish or unselfish preferences are assumed (see Collard, 1978). The intuition behind this conjecture is that individuals are in a game of exchange with each other, driving hard bargains, and it does not matter what motivates those bargains: it is the fact of hard bargaining and exchange which is crucial to the results. This is a powerful intuition, but does it stand up to a closer inspection?

The proposition can be examined most easily with the aid of a simple example. (It is taken from Green, 1971, and there is an extended discussion of the issues in Collard, 1978.) Suppose there are two individuals A and B and two commodities x_1 and x_2, and each individual has a utility function given by

$$U_A = U_A (x_{A1}, x_{A2}, x_{B1})$$ (6.1)

$$U_B = (x_{B1}, x_{B2}, x_{A1})$$ (6.2)

In other words, the consumption of the first commodity by each individual affects the utility of the other. Nevertheless, the utility function is still well behaved in the usual sense of section 3.2. The equation

$$\frac{dU_A/dx_{A2}}{dU_B/dx_{B2}} = \frac{dU_A/dx_{A1} - dU_A/dx_{B1}}{dU_B/dx_{B1} - dU_B/dx_{A1}}$$ (6.3)

gives the condition which must be satisfied for A's utility maximisation in these circumstances, and a similar expression can be derived for B. There are two ways this can be derived: the simplest sets up the individual's utility maximisation problem in the usual way, and embodies the constraints that the allocation of each commodity sums to its supply and that the utility of the other exceeds some arbitrary value. When equation (6.3) and its analogue for B hold, then there is a Pareto optimum and the allocations satisfying this condition constitute the contract curve for the economy.

When the interdependence between individuals is what is referred to as non-meddlesome, meaning that the allocation of x_1 to B only influences the utility of A through the effect that x_1 has on the utility of B, then

$$\frac{dU_A}{dx_{B1}} = \frac{dU_A}{dU_B} \frac{dU_B}{dx_{B1}}$$ (6.4)

holds. Substitution of (6.4) into (6.3) produces

$$\frac{dU_A/dx_{A2}}{dU_A/dx_{A1}} = \frac{dU_B/dx_{B2}}{dU_B/dx_{B1}}$$ (6.5)

and, if the same non-meddlesome attribute holds for B, then the Edgeworthian proposition has been proved.

Equation (6.5) defines the same contract curve as would exist in an economy where the utility functions of A and B were selfish. This is an important result. It means that a competitive equilibrium in an economy is still (potentially) Pareto optimal even though the preferences of the individuals are interdependent. The point is that, when individuals maximise their utility with respect to the competitive price vector, (6.5) will be satisfied whether preferences are interdependent or not. To appreciate this, consider the case where preferences are interdependent. Under competitive conditions, each individual can only choose their own consumption of x_1 and x_2; they have no control over the consumption of x_1 by the other individual; and so utility maximisation produces the same condition as when preferences are purely self-regarding. It so happens in this case that the contract curve for the 'other-regarding' case is the same as the 'self-regarding' one; and so the contract curve is achieved even though preferences are 'other-regarding'. The invisible hand must be putting in overtime! Even though competitive markets offer no mechanism to take account of 'other-regarding' preferences a (potentially) Pareto-optimal allocation is nevertheless produced with respect to those preferences. In short, the supra-intentional causal explanation of the invisible hand is preserved in conditions of interdependent preferences.

The competitive equilibrium is only potentially Pareto optimal for two reasons. Firstly, the condition of non-meddlesome interdependence must be satisfied. Secondly, it is only 'locally' Pareto optimal. It is Pareto optimal with respect to a given initial distribution of resources, and it may be possible to make both parties better-off relative to this 'locally' Pareto-optimal outcome through a redistribution of the initial resources. Figure 6.1 illustrates the possibility. The indifference curves have been drawn in a 'concentric' fashion to take account of the interdependence between preferences: the 'bliss' points for A and B are a and b respectively. With an initial distribution at c, the competitive equilibrium with prices p would be achieved at d. However, with a simple redistribution of initial resources to e, then a new competitive price vector p' would make both A and B better off at a.

A quick glance and this may not seem to pose any great problem: after all such redistributions look a natural object for government policy. However, the matter is not quite so simple because this imports another institution into the picture and we would need to know where it came from and why it might act in this way, leading us back into the problems of chapter 5. From the purely instrumental point of view, the preservation of the invisible hand result would sit most comfortably with an explanation which generated any of these necessary redistributions through voluntary

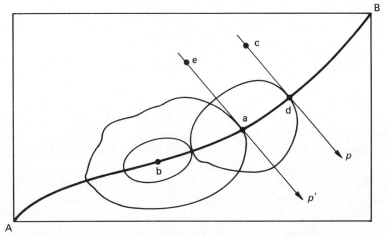

Figure 6.1   Competitive equilibria between altruists

gifts. But difficulties can arise with this voluntarist approach when the economy is complicated to include a large number of agents.

Suppose, for example, that the equivalent interdependence in the large number economy makes the Pareto optimum a position where no one is in poverty. Then, unless each A can be sure that the gift to a B of the requisite amount will be made by each A, then the gift will not realise the desired objective of removing everyone from poverty and hence the motive to make the gift disappears. As Collard (1978) puts it, this kind of assurance becomes possible if agents are Kantian: 'Both A and B perceive the macroscopic effects of their actions as simply the two-person case writ large. Each asks himself in a Kantian fashion, what the effects of his action would be if each A or each B behaved as he did' (p. 26). So, this route for preserving the invisible hand theorem again relies on importing something else into the analysis: this time it is a Kantian kind of reasoning to go with the instrumental postulate (see Hollis, 1983, for an argument that this is not an innocuous addition).

Naturally, the initial distribution may be fortuitously in a spot like e where no redistributions are required. However, the same problems would emerge if the interdependence of preferences was meddlesome. In these circumstances, the Pareto-optimal outcome can only be achieved if A and B face two different prices for x_1. The necessary two price vectors are given by

$$\frac{P_{A1}}{P_2} = \frac{dU_A/dx_{A1}}{dU_A/dx_{A2}} \qquad (6.6)$$

$$\frac{P_{B1}}{P_2} = \frac{dU_B/dx_{B1}}{dU_B/dx_{B2}} \qquad (6.7)$$

(see Green, 1971).

The trouble again is where the 'nice' government comes from to introduce this tax and subsidy scheme for As and Bs respectively on commodity x_1, or how agents come to arrange the same amongst themselves when there are large numbers, without the addition of a Kantian perspective.

Some perspective should be put on these observations. They are scarcely telling criticisms. In fact, they amount to little more than a grumble since the individual analysis of utility maximisation carries over and it is only a question of whether it is still possible to generate the particular supraintentional explanation of Pareto optimality. So, the inclusion of altruistic behaviour would not seem to be precluded by the instrumental picture of rationality – it would be churlish not to acknowledge this, so one up to instrumental rationality!

The same cannot be said, however, of other types of interdependence; and it is not difficult to see why. Veblen and bandwagon effects could easily produce multiple equilibria.

The Veblen effect makes the demand for an item within some relevant range depend positively on price. Higher prices tend to increase demand within limits because higher price signals ability to pay (and possibly quality). The commodity is consumed for conspicuous purposes, in Veblen's terminology, and the high price of the object enables the purchaser to say something to other people about his/her position in society. Since there must be some high price (P_0) at which the commodity is not demanded, the incorporation of this Veblen effect together with any normal price effects could easily produce a demand function like that in figure 6.2, with ample opportunity for multiple equilibria.

The same is true with bandwagon effects. Let the demand for commodity x_i by individual i depend on price and the total expected consumption of x $(x^e)^*$

$$x_i = a - bp + c\,(x^e) \qquad (6.8)$$

where $c' > 0$ to capture the bandwagon effect. When this demand is

---

* It is well known that existence can be demonstrated in neoclassical general equilibrium theory when there is interdependence and when price affects the perception of quality (see Arrow and Hahn, 1971). The significance of these effects is not here; it is in their contribution to the possibility of multiple equilibria and the difficulty this poses in explaining why one in particular occurs. Indeed, it is perhaps worth recalling that uniqueness proofs are not in the same category as existence proofs in general equilibrium theory. Like stability analysis, we have only sufficient conditions. For example, gross substitutability is a sufficient condition. That is when all cross price effects are positive and the own price effect is negative. It is not difficult to think of cases where this would be violated, namely, when there are Veblen effects.

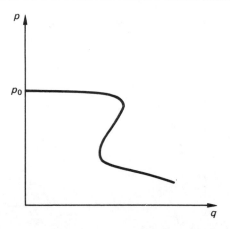

Figure 6.2   Veblen effects

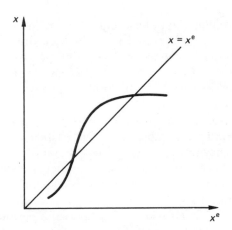

Figure 6.3   Bandwagon effects

summed over all individuals for a given price, the relation between x and x^e will be positive because of the bandwagon effect. The precise shape will depend on the c function but it could look like figure 6.3. Through inspection of the equilibrium points where $x = x^e$, it can be seen there are multiple quantities which could be demanded at this price. The demand curve in these circumstances would look like figure 6.4, again yielding plenty of opportunities for multiple equilibria. Of course, stability here might favour one equilibrium over another, but more complicated c functions could yield multiple stable equilibria.

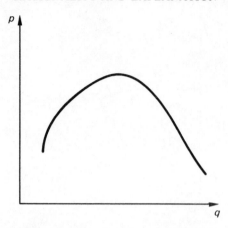

Figure 6.4   Bandwagon effects

One way of avoiding the awkward question occasioned by the prospect
of multiple equilibria here would be to make a firm marriage between
individualism and instrumentalism. For this purpose, individualism is
taken in the Hobbesian sense to mean that agents are motivated by a set of
self-regarding preferences. Thus the problems introduced by interdependence are removed at a stroke.

But how much of life would be lost by such a move? To what extent
would this undermine the impression from chapter 3, that a remarkably
thin notion of agency was generating an extraordinary mileage of explanation, by making those explanations work through atypical preferences? In
short, how significant are Veblen and bandwagon effects?

A quick response to these questions might note that there is a sort of
Veblen effect at work in Hirsch's (1976) analysis of positional goods. These
are goods which derive their value because others do not have them. This
attribute is a consequence of the property of the good rather than individual preferences. Nevertheless, it is likely to have the same effect and
Hirsch (1976) argues that these positional goods assume an ever greater
importance as the economy grows: in fact, they are a root of the social
limits to growth. Likewise, the growing contemporary literature on efficiency wages in the labour market revolves around a Veblenian association
between quality and price.

These are only quick impressions. But they should serve to caution
against immediate acceptance of the verdict we find in the standard text,
where Veblen effects feature as curiosities. Indeed, in the next section, it
will be argued that these interdependences are quite the opposite: they are
central to consumer choice.

6.3 Rules and Meaning Again

We are told that when John Birt left London Weekend Television to become deputy Director General at the BBC he stopped wearing Katherine Hamnett suits and began to sport a blue blazer instead. How might this change in behaviour be explained?

The features of the instrumentally rational answer spring to mind: a preference change, perhaps; a cut in salary; a change in relative price. The first would be slightly disturbing as preferences are supposed to be in the driving seat, and yet there is no evidence to support either of the others.

Consider another puzzle. Why does it make sense to distinguish between the market for leisure trousers and that for work trousers? And why, if you work in the City, are pin-stripes allocated to one category while blue jeans are allocated to the other? In principle, an answer might be found by following Lancaster (1966) in dissecting the physical attributes of pin-stripes and blue jeans and matching these to the requirements of work and leisure. It is the characteristics of trousers over which we have state contingent preferences and trousers differ in the technology used to produce these characteristics. But this is soon going to run up against some uncomfortable evidence in the form of people who wear blue jeans to work, and the work of, say, a 'creative' person wearing blue jeans at an advertising agency which does not seem any more physically demanding than the work of his/her counterpart in the agency who manages the accounts attired in pin-stripes.

Here is a final teaser. Why do I not wear those flared trousers that languish at the bottom of the chest of drawers and which are still in a pristine state, despite the years of neglect? Again, the Lancaster move will be obvious, but scarcely compelling. There is simply very little evidence to support the idea that an increase in low level updraughts has made the smaller trouser leg diameter a technically better solution to the problem of satisfying my various desires for warmth, comfort etc.

What is missing from each of these responses, and which once introduced opens the way to an explanation, is the idea that clothing is a vehicle of non-verbal communication. We use clothes to say things about ourselves, and we decode the messages of other people's clothing. And like all languages the meaning of the trousers (the word) is not to be found in some intrinsic property of garment (or through its correspondence to a concept). Instead, the meaning of a pair of trousers depends upon a social convention and like all conventions it works through compliance. Hence, when numbers or even expected numbers of followers of a convention change, so does the convention, the meaning of the trouser and with it the demand for its use.

The analogy with language and the reference back to Wittgenstein on language (see section 2.5) should give the argument some shape. In effect, what is being suggested is that just as there are rules of language which create meanings for words, so there are the broader rules of behaviour that constitute the cultural context and which give meaning to a whole range of non-verbal actions. To continue with the dress example if you doubt the general point about the role of conventions in enabling communication: imagine how else you would explain the confidence you are likely to attach to the advice received on when to cross the road from a man on a boiling hot day dressed in a heavy blue cloth with silver buttons and a strange shaped helmet.

We need to be clear on what this recognition of cultural context implies for instrumental rationality. Firstly, there is nothing special about clothing in this regard: the same points could be made with almost any item of consumer expenditure. Secondly, minimally, it means that even if we start with some preferences over warmth, convenience and the like which are relevant to the choice of clothing, we cannot thereby deduce what the demand for particular items of clothing will be because clothing fulfils another function. It serves as a medium of communication and we are sensitive to the message which is imparted in this medium. So, if we wish to plot the actual demand for goods, we will have to explore how the communicative property of goods is constructed. And without developing this analysis in any detail, it is plain that compliance with a convention by specific groups in society is crucial to the communicative properties of a commodity rather than any physical, intrinsic property of the good itself. Hence, this builds in a root and branch interdependence between the demands for goods by different individuals; and bandwagon affects within groups will abound.

This point can be summarised in a slightly different way. We can start with preferences over warmth, comfort and the like, which are obviously relevant to our demand for goods, but this will not explain our demand for particular goods. Our demand for actual goods and services, which is what we want to study in economics, also depends on a 'preference' we have for communicating certain sorts of messages (for instance, see Becker and Stigler (1977) later in this chapter who refer to a preference for 'style'). The communicative dimension of a commodity is socially constructed by compliance with conventions; and consequently the preferences which count in the demand for actual commodities have interdependence of the bandwagon variety built into them from the beginning.

Thirdly, the insight could have further ramifications for instrumental rationality depending on how the 'preference' for communication is interpreted. There can be several reasons behind the sensitivity of our demand for clothing to its message. One is plausibly purely instrumental and it can be related back to those primary desires for warmth, comfort and the like.

The city-slicker treats his/her pin-stripe simply as a means to an end; he/she has no particular desire for pin-stripes *per se*, or for recognition as a good 'city-type'. But he/she realises that it would be foolish not to send the message of good 'city-type' to prospective customers because this would undermine his/her capacity to do the business which supports the primary preference satisfaction of warmth, comfort etc. So, the 'preference' for communication is not really a new sort of preference which ranks on a par with the more familiar sort. This interpretation leaves the damage done to instrumental rationality at bandwagon effects, multiple equilibria and the charge of indeterminacy.

Alternatively, the 'preference' for communication could be regarded as more fundamental. It could be the case that we derive pleasure from 'saying things to other people about ourselves' with the consumer goods we purchase, quite independently of how these statements smooth our passage through the world and aid the satisfaction of those preferences for warmth, comfort and the like. We just like to do things which express features of our selves. For instance, it might be argued that the purchase of Levis 501 is as much about simply saying something about yourself which is an end in itself as it is a manoeuvre to expedite business. One way of capturing this idea is to say that we have a 'preference' for self-respect that is satisfied through expressively rational action of this kind. Two things should be noted about this interpretation, in passing. It makes self-respect a funda-mental preference not reducible to those other primary preferences, so interdependence has been built in at a much more basic level with respect to the preferences in the instrumental account. Furthermore, it is not obvious that the language of preference satisfaction is appropriate to this 'preference' for self-respect. Another model of rational agency may be called for (see chapter 8).

Finally, it is possible to construe this 'preference' for communication as the generator of many of those primary preferences like warmth, comfort etc, thus inverting the relation between what is plausibly individual and what is social in origin, making the former depend on the latter rather than the other way round. The idea here is that the cultural conventions which enable the de-coding of consumption choices might also provide com-pletely internal reasons for action (see also section 2.5). Individuals take these to be motives for action, but they can hardly be cast as individual in origin. It is the same as the meaning of words being internal to a language game rather than reflecting some prior set of concepts. Once you embark on the cultural game, then you may find reasons for playing which are internal to that game, just as the meaning of the movement of chess pieces is internal to the game of chess.

Consider the activity of playing a game of cricket. It consists of a certain amount of 'leather on willow', some running about, and a bit of throwing.

Yet cricket is certainly more than the sum of its basic parts in this sense, and it would be absurd to describe our preference for the game in terms of how these constituent activities satisfy some basic desires we have for running and hitting. The satisfaction found in playing cricket owes much to the construction of meaning and value which is internal to the rules defining the game of cricket: a brilliant catch in the slips off a no-ball is not just another dive to connect with a fast moving piece of leather. The feeling associated with hitting a cover drive owes almost everything to the rules which make up the game of cricket. And yet, it is the feeling of hitting a cover drive or catching the ball in the slips which is part of what we play cricket for, and that feeling is constituted within the game rather than being decomposable into feelings which are prior to all games.

This threatens to weaken the standard instrumental account of rationality by making what stands at the pinnacle of intentional explanation, agent preferences, depend in important ways on cultural context rather than the individual qua individual. Of course, it would be possible to relate the various preferences which are created and satisfied in the game of cricket to some generalised desire for pleasure or happiness. But this move would undermine the whole explanatory enterprise because our interest in the demand for trousers or playing cricket is much more finely focused. Appeals to a generalised desire for happiness say everything and nothing. Why trousers and not skirts? Or why Levis 501s? Or why cricket and not horse racing?

Alternatively, it might be argued that there were originally a simple set of quite specific desires which were satisfied by the game of cricket, and that the subsequent development of other reasons for playing cricket which are internal to that game are merely unintended consequences of those original preferences. In this way, some original set of specific preferences still rule the roost. The more discriminating preferences we now enjoy can be related back to those preferences, thus ceasing to be some alien intrusion in the instrumental account. But this wrinkle is not without problems. There are questions which concern the relevance of such a historical account to the actions of contemporary agents. More importantly, this tracing procedure is unlikely to explain completely the origin of our contemporary desires for the reasons of indeterminacy outlined in sections 5.2 5.3 and 5.4. There is likely to be more than one convention which could emerge to satisfy some basic set of preferences, and which actually emerges will owe something to a non-instrumentally rational component of decision making.

A rather good illustration of this problem is again provided by cricket. A common historical reading of the origins of modern cricket relate it to an aristocratic desire for gambling. In this way one might treat the later reasons for playing cricket which have emerged through playing the game to be the unintended consequence of those original preferences for gambling. However, the appeal to the preference for gambling cannot do all the work because we have another example of a game which developed in response to this same desire, horse racing, where the subsequent internal reasons for play are very different from those of cricket. The fact that we have historically seen multiple solutions developing in tandem to the problem of satisfying the desire for gambling, so that one solution did not preclude another, is not the real point here. Rather, it is that the historical record confirms the impression from section 5.3 that there are multiple solutions to such problems and the explanation of why one emerges cannot rest exclusively on a reference to the original preferences which were satisfied by the arrangement.

There is no need to press the subversive line of argument about the autonomy of individual preferences. Once the communicative dimension of consumer actions is recognised in the weakest way above, there is a root and branch bandwagons interdependence which makes the problem of multiple equilibria a real one for instrumental rationality. The possibility of interpreting this communicative dimension in other more radical ways merely contributes additional support to the general conclusion that the scope of intentional explanations is compromised by this communicative impulse.

6.4 Preference Change

Another possible worry about the range of intentional explanation surfaces with the prospect of preference change. If preferences do change, then intentions as such no longer seem to be doing all the explaining: much of the explanation would seem to be contained in the causes of this preference evolution.

In this section and the next, I shall be exploring the grounds for taking the phenomenon of preference change seriously, and delving into how the picture of the individual might be altered to incorporate such change.

Let us begin with one reason why we might expect to encounter preference change: the existence of multiple selves. Schelling (1984) draws attention to the woman who asks the obstetrician not to make anaesthetics available during delivery. She anticipates asking for an anaesthetic because a transient period of pain will make her usual values and preferences inaccessible. There are lots of activities involving pain and/or substances like alcohol and nicotine which are known to produce changes in brain chemistry; and it is plausible to think of such changes being responsible for temporary preference changes. Indeed, classical literature reminds us of the point by telling of the celebrated powers of the Sirens' voices to produce this effect; and modern research has discovered that physical exercise can increase the production of endorphins in the brain. So, these preference changes are plausibly more than pathological curiosities.

Schelling uses the term 'self-command' to describe the woman's instruction; and likewise Ulysses' order to his crew to tie him to the mast. It is the deliberate constraining of future actions because you recognise that your preferences at a later date will be different from those prevailing currently and that those preferences will lead you to do something your current preferences do not favour. Schelling (1980) insists that self-command should be understood as a management skill. In contrast, it is argued here that self-command cannot be treated so simply. It cannot just be a device which helps satisfy preferences better: it must stand above and outside the normal idea of preference.

It helps, in making this argument, to recognise self-command as a response to the time inconsistency of optimal plans. This enables self-command to be discussed using the insights of the literature based on the difficulty of making credible commitments when there is time inconsistency.

Take a simple instance, the choice over drinking in the early and the late parts of the evening. Here are some plausible preferences. Self 1 in the early evening likes best to drink (d) in the early evening and then stop (nd) in the late evening. He/she rates drinking in both parts of the evening as the worst outcome because the next day will be a 'write-off' and there will be all the regrets about things which were done the night before. No drinking is better than this, but drinking in one part of the evening is better still. The reason for preferring the early to the late drinking session is simply that less of the 'relaxation' induced by alcohol is 'lost' in sleep. The difficulty encountered by self 1 in executing the optimal plan of drinking only in the early evening is that his/her preferences change with alcohol. Self 2 takes over after a session of drinking, and this self prefers to continue drinking in the late part of the evening. A normalised set of pay-offs capturing these orderings in the game between self 1 and the late evening self is given by figure 6.5. The late evening self will be self 1 if there has been no drinking in the early evening, but self 2 appears if there has been drinking.

Self 1's optimal plan [n, nd] is inaccessible because it is time inconsistent: d would be followed by d. The best time consistent plan for self 1 is [nd, d]. The problem of settling for the second best can be expressed as a difficulty of forming a credible commitment not to drink in the late evening. The problem and purpose of taking 'self-command' is precisely that of forming a credible commitment in such circumstances. If only such a commitment could be made and enforced, then the superior [d, nd] solution would become available.

Self 1

		d	nd
Late evening self	d	2,–1	1,1
	nd	1,2	0,0

Figure 6.5   Dynamic multiple selves

This is a familiar problem in the economics literature: the decision for self 1 has exactly the same features as the chain-store paradox game in chapter 3, or the inflation reputation game played between the government and the private sector (see Barro and Gordon, 1983 and Backus and Driffill, 1985). The only twist in the game is that it is played with oneself. It is this feature, however, which is at the nub of the argument.

Consider either of the solutions offered to the chain-store paradox game (section 3.3): neither will work here in the same way. Firstly, suppose that self 1 attempts some type of pre-commitment (see Thaler and Shefrin 1981). What would be required is a contract which specifies the forfeiture of at least 1 utile in this normalised pay-off scheme when you are caught drinking. This does not seem a viable solution for two reasons. It would be extremely costly to make such contracts if there was to be any attempt to build in contingencies which would permit a drink when something unforeseen happened requiring celebration. In addition, such contracts have proved to be of dubious legal standing. As an alternative to formal contracts, there is a range of possible informal strategies which might be adopted, e.g. leaving the house with only enough money for early evening drinking. But these require the complicity of others, and this merely throws the problem of inconsistency onto them. Should your friend at the pub believe the protestations of self 1 and ignore the request of self 2 when he/she requests a loan? What reason has the friend for prioritising self 1, when the person requesting the loan clearly does not have the same priorities? If you do not appear to know which is your true self, why assume a friend will decide for you? And if he/she should decide, why assume that it will be the correct decision?

Alternatively, we could inject some doubt into a repeated version of the game. Self 1 might have some doubt about the preference orderings of self 2. Furthermore, self 2 might be willing to fuel those doubts by not drinking in the second period, because it is only through not drinking that self 1 contemplates a drink in the early evening and so creates the conditions where self 2 comes alive. The Kreps and Wilson (1982) analysis of sequential equilibrium goes through perfectly. In fact, the structure of the problem is almost identical with the inflation reputation game (see Backus and Driffill, 1985, for a detailed derivation of the sequential equilibrium). It produces the somewhat paradoxical, and possibly dismal, result of self-command in the early plays of the game, yielding to an increased likelihood of the sub-optimal [nd, d] outcome in older age.

However, this is not a very plausible information structure to assume. Firstly, it is not obvious that self 1 can have doubts about self 2, since self 2 is actually a part of the same person as self 1. The case of the monopolist and the potential entrant are very different in this regard. Secondly, even if such doubts were conceded, there is no good reason for assuming that they attach only to self 2's motives. Why should not self 2 entertain doubt over self 1's motives? For example, self 2 might believe that there is some chance of self 1 coming to prefer [d, d] if there is a prolonged experience of drinking. Consequently, self 2 will not yield the stage to self 1 by stopping drinking at the end of the evening. The boot is now on the other foot: it is self 1 which would have to fuel a reputation for being like self 2 in order to make an appearance at the beginning of each evening. The point is really that unless there is a reason for privileging one self over the other, by making the doubt (or the greater doubt) attach only to the other, then there is no way of predicting which self takes self-command. But why do this? What is it about a person that would enable us to privilege one self over the other in this fashion? As it stands, each self has a set of preference orderings and if this is all that defines an individual, if there is nothing more to a person than such a set of orderings, then there is no reason to choose between the two selves.

The simple fact of the matter is that there is a battle between two selves and we have no reason for presuming that one self will command the other. Injecting doubt just gives the battle some new twists and turns; it will only prove decisive when it is asymmetrically introduced: and that begs the question about what it is that prioritises one self over the other in this manner. Whatever it is, it cannot be related to the individual when the individual is just a set of preferences because, if this were the case, there would be no reason for distinguishing between the two selves. Each self can contend equally for the title of the individual, if individuals are only a set of preference orderings. Instead, an explanation of the phenomenon of self-command requires a conception of the individual which has something other than preference orderings. Individuals must be allowed a reflective capacity, something which stands in judgement over ordinary preference orderings and thus enables the privileging of one self over the other. How this reflective capacity sets about the task of prioritising one self is a another matter. What the chain-store paradox literature usefully suggests is that it might work through differential doubts. Or to put it slightly differently, it involves a kind of self-deception because, assuming self 1 takes command, beliefs about self 2 are entertained at the same time as they are also known to be false.

Returning to Schelling's original suggestion, this means that self-command cannot be conceptualised as some management skill that simply serves to satisfy preferences better. To make the point again, this begs the question of which preferences are to be served by the device. If the 'reflective capacity' which we have associated with self-command were to become just an instrumental device for satisfying one set of preferences, then why should not the other self also use a 'reflective capacity'? Once the reflective capacity becomes subordinated to preferences, it will become a move in the game between preferences, part of the strategy in the battle. What is required is not more weaponry for each side in the battle; rather it is a reason for giving weaponry to one side rather than the other. Such a reason will not be found in preferences alone because both selves are equally placed on this score.

The argument about the damage that such preference changes do to the instrumental account can be put in a more formal way. Hammond (1976) shows that when choices reveal this type of inconsistency between time periods, then the underlying preference structure is not consistent with the standard axioms of consumer theory and the agent cannot be construed as maximizing a well-behaved intertemporal utility function. This same in-coherence in the observed behaviour of an individual can arise because the agent has multiple selves at a moment in time (a problem of static multiple selves). In these instances, you always feel like several people and some reflective capacity is required to integrate the competing voices.

'Being in two minds' may not be a problem for Debreu's agents, but it is also a recognisably human predicament. Indeed, it often seems that more than two selves struggle within a single person. As Bismark observed: 'Faust complained that he had two souls in his breast. I have a whole squabbling crowd. It goes on as in a republic.' (Steedman and Krause, 1986, p. 107) Steedman and Krause (1986) use the Bismark quote in a recent survey of the static multiple self. There, they consider under what circumstances such multifaceted individuals might behave in a fashion which was consistent with the behaviour of our singular individuals driven by well-ordered preferences. One interesting example of multiple selves that falls foul of the Steedman and Krause conditions and which commands some empirical support is Loomes and Sugden's (1982) regret theory. Let me give some background here.

There is a notorious decision-making problem under uncertainty which is called the Allais paradox. It can be illustrated by the following prospects (i.e. outcome and probability pairs, so prospect x is an outcome of £2500 with probability 0.33):

$$x = [£2500, 0.33]; \ y = [£2400, 0.34]; \ z = [£2400, 0.66]$$

When people are offered the choice of $\{x, y\}$ in experiments, typically the majority reveal a preference ordering of xPy. However, when the same group is offered the choice $\{x+z, y+z\}$, they reveal $(y+z)$P$(x+z)$. In other words, although the second choice differs from the first by the addition of the same prospect z to both options, there is an inversion of the ordering which is inconsistent with expected utility theory (see section 3.2). A number of explanations have been advanced to account for this paradox. One that has received strong support from the experimental evidence is regret theory. The origins of this theory can be found in Savage (1951) and it has been developed and tested recently by Loomes and Sugden (1982) and Starmer and Sugden (1987).

In effect, regret theory posits two selves.* There is the 'regular' self from neoclassical decision theory who has a well-behaved utility function c_{ij} which assigns a value to each possible outcome x_{ij} associated with all actions i in all states of the world j. Out of respect for the 'rationality' of the neoclassical person, we call this the Promethean self. In addition, there is an Epimethean (meaning after thought) self who values an action by the regret or rejoice which comes through comparing the outcome c_{ij} of an action i with what might have been the outcome (c_{kj}) in that state of the world had another action k been undertaken (i.e. regret/rejoice = R$(c_{ij} - c_{kj})$). Recall that in Greek mythology Prometheus had a brother Epimetheus who came to regret his acceptance of the gift of Pandora from Zeus. So, an Epimethean spirit has as much claim to motivate on the basis of classical mythology as does the Promethean spirit.

Finally, there is 'something' (an integrative or reflective capacity) which stands above these two selves which weighs the claims of the two selves. This is represented through a modified utility function given by

$$m_{ijk} = c_{ij} + R(c_{ij} - c_{kj}) \qquad (6.9)$$

The choice of action is then made on the basis of maximising this expected modified utility function:

$$E_{ik} = \sum_j p_j m_{ijk} = \sum_j p_j Q(c_{ij} - c_{kj})$$

When Q is convex, it can be shown that the Allais paradox is predicted, as well as a variety of other 'perverse' results from the experimental evidence

* This is not the interpretation which is offered by Loomes and Sugden, but it seems a natural one to make.

(see Loomes and Sugden, 1982). So it would seem that the idea of multiple selves at a moment in time not only fits with common sense, it receives support from the new literature on decision making under uncertainty, thus further undermining the range of the instrumental account in chapter 3.

Against this, it should be noted Becker and Stigler (1977) offer a spirited defence of the instrumental approach by arguing that many of the behaviours which are taken as illustrations of preference change actually can be understood as emanating from a stable set of preferences. For example, advertising produces a change in behaviour, but this does not reveal a change in preferences: the advertising merely provides more information and it is the additional information which leads agents to choose differently.* Likewise, 'fashionable' changes in behaviour can be related to a constant preference for 'style'. Both observations are useful reminders not to get carried away by the idea that we are always changing our preferences. But neither touches on the multiple self problems discussed above, and both these counters are likely to reinforce in different ways the points in the previous section about interdependence and its effects on the instrumental model.

Another interesting example they give concerns addiction and this seems closer to the multiple self mark. Prima facie, the addicts preferences would seem to change in the course of becoming an addict: the more music you hear the greater becomes your desire for music. This looks very much like the example of inconsistent choices induced by alcohol; but, they argue, this is a misleading way of putting things. These behavioural changes are consistent with stable preferences for music appreciation; what changes over time is the productivity of time spent listening to music in the production of music appreciation.

As they put it: 'On this interpretation, the relative consumption of music appreciation rises with exposure not because tastes shift in favor of music, but because its shadow price falls as skill and experience in the appreciation of music are acquired with exposure.' (p. 79)

Again, this looks a useful defence of the generality of the instrumental approach. However, it needs to be made clear what they have done. They have solved the dynamic inconsistency problem by positing that there is a

---

* There is an interesting twist to the discussion linking information with the appearance of preference change in Axelrod and Cohen (1984). They argue that when agents are learning about the environment in which they operate, it will actually pay to build in routines for changing the objective function which guides action because this enables the agent to learn more about the environment. The trick is to make the changes sensitive to changes in utility, and in this way you maximise your utility. The paradox, of course, is that this means that, in choosing your objective function to maximise, and change, you are deliberately not choosing to maximise utility. Maximising utility in these circumstances is a state which cannot be attained if you pursue it. As Elster (1983b) puts it, maximising utility becomes a 'state that is essentially a by-product' because it cannot be willed.

supervening self that arbitrates between the music lover and the musical dolt by deciding how much 'music appreciation' is going to feature in that person's utility function. Two things should be borne in mind about this move. Firstly, the discussion above indicates that music appreciation as the integrating factor has to be something which is importantly different from preferences over time spent listening to music. So, the shift from a utility function in goods to a utility function in the attributes of goods is not an insignificant move. Secondly, there is no sense in which Becker and Stigler's music addict feels a conflict within the soul. There are not two selves. This is fair enough. But, it means that it is not so much a solution to the problem of multiple selves and dynamic inconsistency as a denial that it is an important one: it is as if agents were born with self-command.

The question then becomes whether the predicament of multiple selves is a real one. If it is, then the argument about the diminished scope still stands. Alternatively, if it is not, then the 'preference changes' which we observe are really nothing of the sort according to Becker and Stigler; rather they form part of an optimal intertemporal plan of a person who suffers from none of these conflicts.

6.5   Contradictory Desires

This section and the next offer some argument and evidence in support of the idea that preferences do genuinely change in ways which should worry the instrumental account of rationality. This comes in two forms. Firstly, people do seem to suffer from the sorts of conflicts which are captured by the idea of multiple selves. Indeed, there is a literary-cum-philosophical tradition which makes the grappling with these conflicts an important part of what it is to be human. Secondly, there is important psychological evidence that points to some preference changes which cannot be construed as part of some plan for intertemporal utility maximisation. Instead, they belong to a category of sub-intentional causal explanations.

Elster (1978) has an interesting discussion of the concept of contradictory desires, which is akin to that of multiple selves. He begins with an analysis of the Hegel contradiction between the master and the slave, and casts this as a contradiction within the mind of the master. 'The master would like to have both the satisfaction derived from the recognition accorded to him by the slave and the satisfaction deriving from his absolute power over the slave.' (p. 72) The problem is that having absolute power over the slave turns the slave into a thing, an object which is incapable of recognising the worth of the master. The slave as an object cannot respect the master. If the master wants respect, then some autonomy must be conceded to the slave and the power is not absolute.

There is a nice line from Donne which Elster quotes in support of the thought that this is a predicament which was well recognised before Hegel.

> Take heed of hating me,
> Or too much triumph in the victory
> Not that I shall be mine own officer,
> And hate with hate again retaliate;
> But thou wilt lose the style of conqueror,
> If I, thy conquest, perish by thy hate.
> Then, lest my being nothing lessens thee,
> If thou hate me, take heed of hating me. (*The Prohibition*)

Consider some of his arguments.

What is at stake here is some kind of conceptual contradiction or inconsistency. The person is motivated by contradictory desires and the project cannot be realised. You cannot have a little bit more of one and less of the other; such trading at the margin is impossible. You either have absolute power or you do not. It falls within the category of what Hintikka (1967) calls existential inconsistency. It can also be found in Sartre's discussion of love. Elster (1978) summarises: 'The lover does not want the total subjection of the beloved person nor a free and voluntary engagement; he wants the impossible, 'to possess a liberty'. . . . Love requires the impossible 'synthesis of the assimilation and the maintained integrity of the assimilated object.' (p. 75)

Of course, ordinarily love is categorised as an emotion and held distinct from the desires which motivate our preference orderings. So it might be thought to hold little interest for an analysis of economic behaviour. But our lives are not so neatly compartmentalised. Much economic activity is affected by non-economic desires, whether they go under the separate label of emotions or not. A moment's reflection will suggest that buying roses is the tip of an iceberg here. Furthermore, even if it does make sense to separate emotions from desires, and even if we are no longer faced by the problem of the master and the slave, who is to say that these problems do not reflect something deep about human motivation which afflicts desires of all sorts?

Sartre certainly makes the claim that the formation and pursuit of contradictory concepts, like love, is a central feature of the human condition. And there is a familiar ring to this analysis, echoes of Groucho Marx's old quip about not wanting to belong to a club which had him as a member and Heller's ubiquitous Catch 22. Enough to suggest that Sartre's claim is not completely off-the-wall!

The philosophical-cum-literary tradition, which begins from contradictory desires, is opening a space for a new kind of activism in the definition of the individual.* The individual is engaged in a project of trying to make sense of these contradictions. It is in that project that individuality is defined. Put more prosaically in the language of neoclassical preferences, the individual is found in the 'reflective' capacity that tries to make sense of and integrate the competing preference orderings which were sketched earlier.

This kind of activism in the concept of what it is to be an individual seems to make being an individual much more exciting and rewarding – after all, at least it would banish the ennui of fixed preferences! Furthermore, as Rorty (1986) has argued, it provides a way of understanding our fear of death. He illustrates the argument with a Larkin poem, *Continuing to Live*. The poem revolves around a very personal sense of what it is that is extinguished by death. The 'I' is something distinctive that we partially recognise and which has evolved over time: 'we half identify the blind impress', the 'contingencies which make each of us "I"', as Rorty (1986) suggests, 'rather than a copy or replica of someone else'. By contrast, if the 'I' was just a set of preferences which came with our genes at birth, or was just a copy of someone else's, death would not matter: nothing special would be extinguished, nothing that was unique to me. Instead, what makes death especially feared is the extinction of an active 'I' that has been responsible for something unique.

This discussion is erring on the literary side and a philosophical-cum-literary treatment was promised. Two quick comments attempt to rectify the balance. Firstly, freedom is an important concept in the modern world, but is its appeal going to be intelligible if it merely makes us a slave to our passions? We can leave this as a query at this stage because we return to the issue of freedom in chapters 8 and 9. Secondly, it is a mark of all philosophy to reflect on the obvious and the common sense. What is being suggested here is that reflective capacity is deeply bedded in all individuals, but it is missing in the individual who is captured by only a set of well-behaved preference orderings.

6.6 Sub-Intentional Causal Explanation

Elster (1983a) employs the term sub-intentional causal explanation to describe cases where there may be 'causal processes which shape beliefs and desires in terms of which actions can be explained intentionally' (p. 84). There are a variety of models of socialisation which exhibit this

---

* There is also a sociological tradition that healthy individuals compartmentalise these multiple selves. The conflicting bits are kept apart by living in different boxes. I shall not want to deny that this does happen, but I shall also want to claim that this often happens as a result of unsuccessful attempts to produce coherence from these conflicts.

property with respect to desires. They range from simple models of imitative behaviour driven by a process of conformism, to models of acquiring desires through a process of habituation, to more complicated models which rely on processes like wishful thinking and cognitive dissonance removal or indeed the various mechanisms sketched by Freud.

Elster (1983a) calls these hot mechanisms because they 'explain the formation and change of preferences through the drives and pleasure wirings of the individual' (p. 86). They are motivationally based mechanisms. This contrasts with another group of cold mechanisms that rest purely on biases; they are unrelated to any motivational spring and act in a way which is akin to optical illusions. A simple example of such a cold mechanism can be found in Kahneman and Tversky's (1979) discussion of the anomalous experimental results of decision making under uncertainty, when they argue that there are biases in the perception of probability distributions.

The importance of these mechanisms is that their existence points to preference changes which cannot be thought to be part of some conscious plan of the agent. They work behind the back of the individual to cut the scope of the explanation afforded by intentions.

For instance, a central message from Freud makes the actions of an individual unintelligible with reference only to the conscious intentions of agents. There are unconscious motives which are expressed in actions in convoluted, concealed and complicated ways. So, however admiring we may be of the instrumental vision, at best we can only order the conscious motives we have, and there will always remain the rarely accessible world of the unconscious. The shape of the unconscious in Freud can only be understood developmentally. What ends up there depends on the early history of infancy and childhood. So, the sense in which the person is in command of his/her actions through having autonomous preferences is quite slim in Freud – at least without the benefits of psychoanalysis because it is the project of psychoanalysis to move in this direction by revealing the unconscious roots of action.*

---

* Freud's model of the development of the unconscious offers one reading of the relation between society and the individual. The unconscious is the depository for the instincts which society, broadly understood, does not permit explicit expression. However, there are other ways of reading the relation which come from different models of the 'unconscious'. A frequent sociological ploy is to turn the 'unconscious' into the social rules of section 6.3. So, the social rules become the 'unconscious' orchestrator of our desires. A variant on this theme is to locate the source of mental disorders with a poor match between the private and the social construct systems (see Kelly, 1955). Again, it is easy to see the line of the argument: when such mismatches arise communication becomes extremely difficult, with impoverishing effect for the individual. At this stage, these references are nothing more than markers for later developments. However, they do indicate that, at least, there may be a coherent picture of something other than instrumental rationality in the social sciences for economics to bite on. This is not just an isolated set of observations on the difficulties with the instrumental vision.

The mechanism of cognitive dissonance reduction is probably less familiar to economists. Its origins lie in the work of Festinger and it is usefully surveyed in Aronson (1972). The basic idea is that we tend to rearrange our desires and our beliefs so as to remove cognitive dissonance. So, for example, we do a lot of research about the relative merits of different cars. We weigh up speed and comfort against cost, and so on and so forth, for different models and finally come to a decision: we are to become the proud owner of a Citroen 2CV. Once the acquisition has been made there is a familiar pattern that takes hold, which amounts to *ex post* rationalisa-. tion of the decision. All the evidence which points to the lack of safety and speed in the 2CV is filtered out, while evidence that reinforces the choice by emphasising the strong features in the 2CV, its economy, its contribution to the problem of depleting fossil fuels and so on, gets filtered in. This is to be explained by the tension, the cognitive dissonance, that any evidence which shows the 2CV in poor light sets up once we have become the proud 2CV owners. Such tension is psychologically disturbing and so we develop ways of removing it, in this case by selecting out the adverse aspects because the decision itself cannot be reversed. It is as if our preferences shift between safety and economy.

There is a large psychological literature which has found cognitive dissonance theory a revealing guide to individual behaviour (see Aronson, 1972). It has even surfaced in economic analysis. For instance, Marx makes copious use of these mechanisms in his explanations. Elster (1985, chapter 8) offers a detailed review. One example is the use of a kind of cognitive dissonance mechanism in the analysis of religion. It is only through a Feubachian act of creation and projection onto a spiritual world of all that is absent in the material world that the inconsistencies of the material world can be made tolerable. Religion is the vehicle for reducing dissonance.

> Man makes religion, religion does not make man. Religion is the self consciousness and self esteem of man who has either not yet found himself or has already lost himself again. . . . (Religion) is the fantastic realisation of human essence because the human essence has no true reality. The struggle against religion is therefore indirectly a fight against the world of which religion is the spiritual aroma. . . . Religion is the sigh of the oppressed creature, the heart of a heartless world. . . . It is the opium of the people. (Marx, 1975, p. 175)

In a similar fashion it is a species of self deception in Marx which allows the bourgeoisie to present their own sectional interest as the interest of society as a whole. 'Deliberate deception on the part of some, self deception on the part of others, who give out the world transformed according to their own needs as the best world for all . . .' (Marx, 1978, p. 126).

There are even examples where economists within the neoclassical tradition have modelled these sub-intentional causal processes (see Akerlof and Dickens, 1982, on cognitive dissonance theory and Pollak, 1970, on habit formation). So it does not appear to be a feature of human behaviour which can be lightly dismissed – *pace* Becker and Stigler.

6.7 Conclusion

This chapter contains a mixture of arguments to support the views that individuals are interestingly more complicated than the instrumental picture will allow, and that these complications matter for explanations in economics. They are not just observations about life in general, and taken seriously they reveal gaps in the instrumentally driven intentional explanations in economics.

Interdependent and changing preferences pose different problems for intentional explanations, but they constitute a significant combination of difficulties which warrant further doubts about the scope of the explanations which can be generated by instrumental rationality alone. Scope matters and the argument need not be repeated here (see sections 3.4 and 6.1).

However, to return to the purely normative aspects of the question, I doubt that an exclusively instrumental account of rational agency could provide anyone with a flattering metaphor for living. There does not seem to be a lot that is human about the instrumentally rational person which would commend it as a model of how to be in the world. Indeed, there is no real difference between the individual who is just instrumentally rational and a relatively simple piece of software. As Pareto remarked: 'Once we have a picture of his tastes, the individual can disappear.' To put it bluntly, 'individuals as computers' or 'individuals who disappear' is not a very flattering metaphor for living. Or to return to the question in the title of the chapter, if the answer is exclusively yes, then my verdict is, hard luck!

What seems to be missing on the basis of the discussion in this chapter is a sense of social (and historical) location (to borrow a thought from chapters 4 and 5) which speaks to our interdependence; and a sense of individuals struggling and reflecting on who they are, a kind of self-consciousness if you like, which is manifested in preference changes. The recognition of these missing ingredients would also seem, to me at least, to have the virtue of being the first steps towards the construction of a reasonable metaphor for living.

7 PROCEDURAL RATIONALITY

7.1 Introduction

Procedural behaviour is defined as action which emanates from the use of procedures or rules of thumb. These rules cannot be reduced to, or explained in terms of, instrumental rationality alone; and they are often shared by several agents. I describe the use of such procedures or rules as procedural rationality, thus preserving the idea that these actions are rationally motivated.

Defined in this way, procedural rationality fills some of the gaps in the intentional explanations which have been detected in the last three chapters. In particular, through being shared in some degree, they are a source of co-ordination and communication in the social world; and as such, they constitute the building blocks for our shared institutions and culture. They are the irreducible institutional underpinnings and the cultural context for our instrumentally rational actions. So, when the instrumental accounts of the last three chapters run up against the problems of scope, procedural rationality can be invoked. It is the following of procedures which provides the missing ingredient. This will not avoid all difficulties, but it will help in those cases of indeterminacy to single out one course of action when many might satisfy the canon of instrumental rationality.

For instance, to take a trivial example, one might refer to the use of the procedure/rule of 'give way to the right' in a crossroads game to explain the behaviour of agents. 'Give way to the right' has become an institution in that society, and it has become a part of the cultural context which would enable us, together with other procedures, to explain the complicated meanings and expectations which agents in that society would attach to the following/transgression of such rules. Of course, in saying that the use of the rule is procedurally rational, it is not being denied that the use of the rule is also supported by instrumental considerations. Rather, the term procedural rationality is being employed to signal that something other than instrumental rationality is at work in the following of this precise rule. Instrumental considerations will typically explain why agents will want a convention, because there are gains from communication and co-ordination in the social world. But it will not explain why one convention emerges as the institution of that society rather than any of a number which would satisfy the instrumental desire for co-ordination and communication.

To explain why one particular convention has gained widespread use, it is necessary to look at the procedures which agents used in the evolution of the game to generate initial expectations about what others were likely to do, and the procedures which they used to update these expectations in the light of experience. It is the specific history of following actual learning rules which needs to be studied, rather than a broad appeal to instrumental considerations. Hence, the statement that following the 'give way to the right' rule is procedurally rational is really a shorthand for the compendium of procedural influences which have been responsible in the actual history of a society for the emergence of this particular rule.

In short, procedural rationality is a response to the need which was discerned at the end of the last chapter to give a social and historical location for individuals. The following of procedures is an intrinsically social activity because these procedures will only function as conventions in co-ordination and communication when they are shared; and their exist-ence can only be explained in a historical way – where what is meant by 'historical' is the specific history of actual rule following that becomes necessary once it is recognised that the contemporary use of particular rules cannot be rationally reconstructed by appeals to instrumental ration-ality alone.

At the outset, it will be helpful to draw attention to the way this definition of procedural rationality differs from that of Simon (1976). The term procedural rationality owes its currency to Simon (1976) and his definition differs slightly from that used here: his procedural action is any action which is guided by a rule of thumb rather than an optimising calculation. This much is the same. However, for Simon, agents become procedural when the task of optimising comes up against limited computa-tional power: they are forced to rely on procedures instead.

> A theory of rational behaviour must be quite as much concerned with the characteristics of the rational actor – the means they use to cope with uncertainty and cognitive complexity – as with the characteristics of the objective environment in which they make their decisions. In such a world we must give an account not only of substantive rationality – the extent to which appropriate actions are chosen – but also procedural rationality – the effectiveness, in light of human cognitive powers and limitations, of the procedures used to choose actions. As economics moves out towards situa-tions of increasing cognitive complexity, it becomes increasingly concerned . . . with procedural rationality. (Simon, 1978, pp. 8–9)

The accent in Simon's work is on the matter of limited computational power and the directions for research which are set by procedural ration-ality are those of artificial intelligence and cognitive psychology. The concern is with discovering the most effective rules of thumb, those which economise on the scarce resource of the mind. The presumption in this tends to be that there will be unambiguously good and bad ways for going about things; and that procedural rationality is some kind of second best optimising. It is optimising subject to the constraint of limited computational capacity. Indeed, this seems to be exactly what Simon has in mind when he also uses the term 'satisficing' and talks about 'bounded rationality'. If this were all there was to procedural rationality, then there would be no rhyme nor reason for elevating this behaviour to a new kind of rationality, let alone for hanging out the flags of freedom and uncertainty in the way that I did at the end of chapter 5.

The argument introducing procedural rationality in the last few chapters was built around the same impossibility of calculating the optimal course of action – that is why it is appropriate to use the same term as Simon – but, and this is the crucial issue, the impossibility was a consequence of there being no optimal course of action defined in terms of instrumental rationality. It was not a problem of limited computational power. No amount of growth in our computational power would enable the instrumentally rational agent in the co-ordination game of chapter 5 to decide on the basis of instrumental rationality alone between the beliefs supporting the [0, 1] equilibrium rather than the [1, 0] equilibrium. Something more must be added to the account of human agency. It must be given a historical and social location; and this is what is achieved by my definition of procedural rationality.

Put in this way, it may be tempting to think of custom or habit as the additional ingredients provided by procedural rationality. In one sense, this would be true. Custom and habit would give the rules of thumb the crucial shared characteristic that they do not have in Simon's account and which enables them to function as co-ordinating and communicating devices and not just short-cut calculating devices. But, in another sense, it would be deeply misleading for much the same reasons, as Simon's use of the term has connotations I wish to avoid. Talk of custom and habit is liable to conjure a vision of an ersatz individual who cannot make up his or her own mind and who relies instead on the opinions of others, just as Simon's agent is an imperfect version of the perfect calculator. Yet, this misses the point: procedural rationality is not a testament to imperfection of one sort or another. It is a recognition that people are something more than instrumentally rational and not something less.

The something more concerns the peculiarly social sort of choice which we face with respect to these shared procedures (see section 5.6). In a nutshell, this choice presents us with a kind of freedom. We may inherit a particular set of procedures, courtesy of history, but we are not bound by them on instrumental grounds. Exactly how we might consider exercising this choice when instrumental considerations do not yield guidance is really the topic of later chapters. For the moment, the point is that procedural rationality does not foreclose on these choices as talk of custom and habit might imply: rather it signals a potential area of choice.

The difference with Simon now becomes clearer. It can be traced to the shared nature of some procedures in my definition. Unless they were shared they could not act as co-ordinating and communicating devices, whereas it is neither here nor there in Simon's world whether my short-cut coincides with yours. They are a response to a different kind of indeterminacy: social and historical location is not the same as deficient computing power.

To tease out what is at stake here from a different angle, it may be helpful to reflect on the use of the term uncertainty. It involves some repetition, but the points are worth making again.

For Simon, the problem is that we do not have the computational power to track down the objective probability distribution governing events. But there seems to be no doubt in his analysis that there is an objective probability distribution. Otherwise, it is difficult to see how he can conceive of procedural rationality in terms of effectiveness – effectiveness in terms of what, if it is not anchored in cost-effective movements towards an objective probability distribution?

In contrast, the uncertainty in chapter 5 was more radical: it was characterised by the absence of an objective probability distribution. There is an unavoidable indeterminacy with respect to the choice of institutional arrangements. We cannot say what we should expect from a situation where we know the preferences of agents and that they are instrumentally rational. There are literally thousands of differences between individuals which could serve as the linchpin for the development of a convention, and in the abstract, none can command the special attention of the instrumental agent. What actually brings determinacy is procedural rationality. So, it is not that procedural rationality gropes towards the discovery of the objective probability distribution à la Simon, it actually creates the determinacy which enables us to form expectations.

Once the role of procedures is conceptualised in this way, it still has little to do with objective probability distributions. Procedures help to create the order which enables expectation formation but this is scarcely the creation of an objective probability distribution over what we can expect. There is nothing objective about the procedures in the sense of being grounded in preferences and instrumental rationality alone. They are in place partially because of the historical use of other procedures. This self-referential, bootstrapping character of procedures makes them arbitrary in some degree with respect to the canon of instrumental rationality. In fact, it makes the probability distribution, at best, historically contingent. It is worth reiterating, in passing, that even then some uncertainty with respect to action, that is not captured by such probability distributions, can remain for two reasons. Firstly, there need be no presumption that history determines completely the use of procedures: self-conscious agents who realise the arbitrary character of any set of procedures may decide to alter them. Secondly, the following of rules of this sort never provides an exhaustive prescription for action. Rules are never fully extensive. Consider, for example, the rules governing serving in tennis, and the lack of any prescription with respect to the height of the initial toss of the ball (see section 2.5).

Therefore, one way of understanding the existence of genuine uncertainty as opposed to risk is through the recognition that procedures in general are doing something more than Simon allows.

Nevertheless, it would be foolish not to acknowledge that people also follow procedures for Simon-like reasons. Simon is plainly correct when he identifies limited computational capacity as another reason why agents are forced to rely on procedures. Indeed, although we take the argument no further here, the Simon observation is acute. And it greatly expands the number of settings where procedural rationality becomes the appropriate explanatory canon. The purpose of these remarks has been to make clear that this is not the only reason why the optimal calculation is not possible; and consequently procedural rationality stands for much more than is often supposed.

This has been a long introduction to the topic of procedural rationality. Having cleared the ground in this way, let me give a quick outline of the rest of the chapter. The purpose of this chapter, much like chapter 3, is to survey the use of the procedural rationality postulate in economics and to isolate the type of explanations which are generated by it. I begin in the next section with a survey of the use of procedural rationality in economics. This is followed by a short section on procedural rationality in everyday life.

The fourth section introduces and discusses a new type of explanation. I have already considered intentional and causal explanations and combinations of the two in previous chapters. I now introduce functional explanations. They are an important, but controversial, kind of explanation in the social sciences. Elster (1979, 1982, 1983a) has launched a major attack on this form of explanation and it has spawned a debate which is reviewed in this section. There is nothing which necessarily ties functional explanation exclusively to procedural rationality. Functional explanations can combine with instrumental rationality. However, the association with procedural rationality is a natural one to make.

I pursue the theme of historical location in the fifth section with a discussion of some approaches to explanations of the present which pay particular attention to the role of history. These do not constitute any 'new' or further type of explanation as such. And their connection with procedural rationality should not be overstated. Some degree of procedural rationality is inescapable. But, once procedures are in place, history also matters for instrumental accounts of rationality, and the ideas which are surveyed in this section, like cumulative causation, hysteresis, emergent properties and latent conflicts, can combine quite easily with this canon of rationality. Nevertheless, they can be given a straightforward interpretation once procedural rationality is in place: they are simply ways of describing different ensembles of procedures which yield various dynamic properties.

The sixth section develops some of the connections, first mentioned in section 5.6, between this discussion and wider debates in the social sciences. I believe that procedural rationality is one of the pivotal concepts in the reintegration of the social sciences; and this section, while brief, is designed to give some substance to this claim with two illustrations. It is not usually important for much of the remainder of this chapter to distinguish between whether recourse to procedural rationality arises from the deep kind of interdependence which occurs through sharing procedures or through Simon's limited computational power – in the survey side of the chapter, I am mostly interested in how procedural rationality contributes to explanation in economics, and not in why agents in particular cases come to follow rules. However, in this last section, it is through recognising that procedural rationality is wider than Simon's definition that the connections with other social sciences can be made.

7.2 Procedural Rationality in Economics

It is a corollary of the earlier argument that we have already given a large number of examples of procedural rationality in economics. There is an irreducible procedural element in all the intentional explanations given in chapters 3, 4, and 5. Rather than excavate the precise procedural element in those earlier examples, I focus on three new examples where the procedural element is usually more explicitly recognised. They are Keynes's analysis of unemployment, Nelson and Winter's work in industrial economics, and Binmore's recent discussion of rationality in game theory.

Keynes is well known for his argument in chapter 12 of *The General Theory* that agents, when confronted by uncertainty, rely on conventions which are in some degree arbitrary. However, it is also possible to detect a more persistent procedural vein in the literature which has grown up around *The General Theory*. One way of understanding the industry of interpreting of Keynes is to see it as a dialogue between those who wish to reduce Keynes to instrumental rationality and those who deny that this is possible. Naturally, there is no necessity to view the reappraisal of Keynes literature in this way, nor is there any implication that this is the way participants would describe their positions and motives. Nevertheless, it is one way of placing an order on the debate; and as such, it does bring to the fore Keynes's more general reliance on procedural rationality.

It is probably accepted by most parties to this debate that unemployment is a consequence of trading with a vector of false prices. Granted this, the discussion gravitates towards the question of why prices fail to adjust to their Walrasian levels; in particular, with whether price stickiness can be explained rationally – whether a gradual price adjustment scheme, which followed Walrasian excess demands, would help is another matter (see Hahn and Solow, 1986). There is a large literature which has grown around this issue and I will consider some parts of it.

Leijonhufvud (1968) has the trouble starting in bond markets, with the failure of interest rates to adjust to a new Walrasian equilibrium value. The failure of interest rates to adjust to, say, a decline in investment is what transmits intertemporal disturbances to the goods market as a general decline in demand rather than a redistribution of demand between investment and consumer good industries. The story goes something like this. Speculators in bond markets hold inelastic expectations with respect to what they regard as the 'normal' interest rate. Consequently, when interest rates move there is little change in the expected 'normal' interest rate. This means that any tendency of interest rates to move down from their perceived 'normal' level as investment declines is checked by the large speculative interventions which such a movement would induce. The excess flow demand for bonds is satisfied by speculative portfolio adjustments in favour of money. With interest rates stuck in this way at their old levels, the re-equilibration of savings and investment is thrown onto goods markets.

Once the disturbance is transmitted to the goods market in the form of a decline in aggregate demand, there is a process of quantity adjustments because final commodity prices are also sticky. These quantity adjustments are, in turn, transmitted to the labour market as a contraction in the demand for labour; and quantity adjustments occur there to produce unemployment because wages are sticky. Leijonhufvud's explanation of these later price and wage rigidities relies on Alchian's (1971) search theoretic model (developed further by Okun, 1975, 1981). In both instances there is a problem of extracting information from a signal. Workers do not know whether the contraction in demand is local or general. They believe there are jobs elsewhere in the economy at the old prevailing equilibrium wage and so reject the wage cut at the current place of employment and become unemployed as the most efficient way of conducting search for those job offers at the old wage rate. Firms likewise have difficulty in deciding whether the contraction in final demand is temporary or permanent. Price adjustments are not part of the most efficient strategy of finding out, and consequently we observe price stickiness.

It is not difficult to dig out the procedural and institutional underpinnings of these 'instrumentally' rational explanations of wage and price stickiness. Why, for instance, do workers assume that there are still jobs on offer elsewhere in the economy at the old prevailing wage? And why should the perceived most effective way of conducting search be via unemployment? It is difficult to make these beliefs any more instrumentally rational than their opposites; yet the analysis relies heavily upon them. It seems that we just have to assume that workers also have inelastic expectations and so discount the relevance of local evidence in assessing general prospects in the economy.

Gordon (1982) gives some reason for rationally discounting local evidence; and indeed, this line of argument might help to explain more generally why the whole problem is not short circuited by the introduction of fully contingent contracts. The explanation revolves around the incentive incompatibility in the provision of information to service a fully contingent contract. Employers are responsible for giving information about contractions in final demand, and they suffer from a problem of moral hazard because it is in their interest to claim contractions when none have occurred. Workers recognising this may doubt the veracity and hence relevance of the local evidence on the state of demand. Faced by a reduced wage offer locally, they may reasonably think to themselves: 'employers would say that wouldn't they!'.

This places the burden of the explanation on the moral hazard problem, but this arises in the form that it does because of the particular set of property rights. For instance, it would not arise in the same degree if there was a system of profit sharing; the element of profit sharing becomes like a tax on dissembling because it gives back to workers some of the profit gains from feeding false information into the wage contract (not quite a Clarke–Groves one, but at least it would act as discouragement).

Institutional context also matters in other explanations of wage stickiness. For example the implicit contracts approach requires something like the institution of unemployment benefits for the optimal response to a contraction in demand to be a constant wage and employment variation (see Sargent, 1978). Likewise, once the existence of unions is recognised, an explanation in terms of union politics can be constructed (see Freeman and Medoff, 1979). The problem with all the explanations which rely on institutional context is the one we have come across in the discussion of institutions. It is often very difficult to give a purely instrumental account of institutions: several institutional arrangements are potentially consistent solutions to a particular problem of social interaction and it necessitates some procedural element to explain why one occurs rather than another.

These same difficulties are evident in the cases mentioned here. The moral hazard explanation is likely to contain a procedural element because it will be difficult to explain why one set of property rights, which gives rise to these problems, should be in place without an appeal to procedural rationality. Similarly, the seniority rule for firing is likely to command a majority in the union and lead that majority to prefer lay-offs to wage cuts, but so might any rule such as, first in, first out, which identified who got laid off. To explain why the seniority system should operate either will directly require a procedural element or, indirectly, is likely to require such an element through a further appeal to some other institutional context for the rule itself.

To return to our speculators in bond markets: what can be said to justify their inelastic expectations? Well, one thought is that at least they are proved correct. Once output has declined, and with it savings, the re-equilibration of savings with investment no longer requires a fall in interest rates below their perceived 'normal' levels. The difficulty with this rational expectations approach is again the old one. Equally, a set of expectations which allowed the 'normal' interest to move in line with the Walrasian equilibrium value would also satisfy the condition of being proved correct by subsequent developments in the economy. How, then, are we to explain why one set of beliefs comes to be held rather than the other? It looks very much like a procedural element of the sort suggested by Keynes. It is convention pure and simple, and a number of conventions might do the job. The choice of one now is simply procedural; it is a procedure which is currently followed that can only be explained historically in a self-referential manner because it has no ultimate foundations in instrumental rationality alone.

Nelson and Winter (1975, 1978, 1982) have developed several explicitly procedural models. I use Nelson and Winter (1978) to pick out some of the insights afforded by explicitly modelling procedural rationality. This paper focuses on the Schumpeterian sense of dynamic competition. It is a sense of competition which is almost completely absent from standard texts, yet it probably corresponds more closely to the common-sense notion of competition than does the standard definition. Market power in terms of the capacity to set prices is the usual index of competition in textbooks, or the lack thereof. It is a structural, static state that an industry finds itself in, and it usually depends on the number of firms and their respective sizes. In contrast, Schumpeterian competition is concerned with the active process of competing: the cut and thrust of move and counter move, with firms innovating to gain a temporary advantage as other firms attempt to follow suit or go to the wall. It is a process of 'creative destruction', in Schumpeter's immortal words, and the kind of tally of winners and losers at a moment in time which is found in standard treatments of market power bears little relation to this rich process.

To probe how some of the elements of Schumpeterian competition combine, Nelson and Winter (1978) simulate a model where firms have three major decision rules which they employ:

> Firstly, given the techniques they have (characterised in terms of output per unit of capital and constant returns to scale) firms produce at capacity levels regardless of prices. . . . Secondly, investment is triggered if the product price is such that firms earn more than a target markup over production costs. The target markup is higher for large firms than for small ones, reflecting their appraisal of their market power. . . . Thirdly, the amount firms spend on R & D, which involves both exploring new technological opportunities and scanning what other firms are doing, is proportional to their size (capital stock). pp. 527–8)

The simulations are conducted under various different assumptions concerning four important features of the competitive process. These are the aggressiveness of investment policies (i.e. the extent to which firms reinvest profits); the ease/difficulty of imitation; the rate of latent productivity growth (i.e. the rate at which best potential practice improves); and the variance of research outcomes.

There is a wealth of detail in these simulations. They lead us to expect that industries which start from the same position but which are characterised by aggressive investment policies, and/or where imitation is difficult, and/or where the rate of latent productivity growth is high, and/or where there is a high variability of research outcomes will be much more concentrated than industries where the reverse conditions hold. Each factor here is an independent and apparently statistically significant contributor to concentration in the simulations; and the simulations yield predictions for distributions of firm size, and correlations between firm size and growth, and firm size and productivity levels which are consonant with a number of studies in industrial economics.

Perhaps one of the simplest ways of gauging how this approach produces insights which are not expected from the standard static view of competition is by reflecting on the following paradox, which Nelson and Winter (1978) isolate: 'The actual exercise of market power by the larger firms in an industry may be an important factor tending to limit the growth of concentration in the industry.' (p. 542)

It ceases to be paradoxical when one appreciates the Schumpeterian perspective and realises that high market power will be associated with less aggressive investment policies. The reason is that when there is high market power firms are aware that changing output has a negative effect on price and so, *ceteris paribus*, they will decide to invest less than a firm which is less aware of the feedback. Since aggressive investment policies accelerate the concentration of an industry, this means that the recognition of market power actually constitutes a check on concentration in an industry.

The final illustration of procedural rationality comes from game theory. Binmore (1987, 1988) has argued that the analysis of games with a dynamic structure often necessitates a procedural sense of rationality rather than the conventional instrumental version.

The first part of the argument goes back to Binmore and Dasgupta (1986) and, before that, Bernheim (1984) and Luce and Raiffa (1957). It concerns the necessity for a Nash equilibrium of an assumption of common knowledge that players are rational. Following Binmore and Dasgupta (1986), consider a non-Nash equilibrium pair of strategies, say [*a, b*] where *a* is not the best reply to *b* in a two-person game with common knowledge. For *a* to have been chosen, it must be the case that player 1 believed player 2 was going to play something other than *b*; otherwise 1 would not have chosen *a* since it is not the best reply to *b*. Hence, 1's beliefs are mistaken. But this cannot be the case if it is assumed that rational players can duplicate the reasoning of other rational players provided that they have the same information, and it is common knowledge that players are rational.

In the words of Binmore and Dasgupta, the role of the common knowledge of rationality assumption is not immediately transparent. But without it, the ability of rational players to duplicate the reasoning of other rational players would have nothing to bite on. The point is that player 1 is not playing Nash, and so it is tempting to call him/her irrational, but without the common rationality assumption it would have to be acknowledged that 2 might be irrational in which case it could be rational for 1 to play irrationally.

Binmore (1987) goes on to argue that in dynamic games, where a one-shot version of a game is repeated or where the game itself potentially involves a series of sequential moves, this common rationality assumption runs into a difficulty because equilibrium strategies rely on an inconsistent counterfactual.

> . . . 'it is common knowledge that all players are perfectly rational'. This implicit axiom confronts the analyst with the necessity of dealing with counterfactuals of the type: Suppose a perfectly rational player carried out the following irrational sequence of acts. . . . Such considerations are unavoidable. A perfectly rational player will not deviate from his equilibrium strategy. But a profile of strategies is in equilibrium because of what would happen if a player were to deviate. (1987, p. 181)

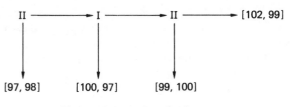

Figure 7.1   Centipede game

To bring out this difficulty, consider a truncated version of the centipede game captured by figure 7.1

Each player must decide whether to play across or down when their turn occurs. The perfect equilibrium of this game has player II playing down at the first decision node. The logic works backwards from the third decision node. If this was reached then II would play down, and this would yield a worse outcome for I than if I chose to play down at the second decision node. So, if the second decision node is reached I will play down rather than let the game continue. But, as down from the second decision node yields a worse return for II than down at the first decision node, II will play down at the first decision node. In other words, the equilibrium strategy of playing down at the first decision node emerges from a consideration of what would happen should agents not follow this strategy and find themselves at the second and third decision nodes. The issue for Binmore, then, is simply whether there is a deep inconsistency between the supposition of rationality which has agents playing down and the counterfactual that supports this standard of behaviour which involves agents playing across.

To put it slightly differently, is there a way of explaining how agents might reach later decision nodes that does not undermine the assumption of common rationality which has agents not proceeding beyond the first node?

Selten (1975) introduces the idea of a trembling hand to remove such paradoxical counterfactuals: the trembling hand permits an irrational act to be attributed to a blunder on the part of the rational player. Thus, consideration of out of equilibrium behaviour at later decision nodes need not undermine the presumption of common rationality. However, Binmore disputes that trembling hands can always do the trick of removing the conundrum. Instead, he argues that in some environments a better approach is to recognise that agents are procedurally rational. His justification of procedural rationality follows Simon closely and is based on Godel's incompleteness theorem: 'this tells us that all reasoning systems are necessarily imperfect in the sense that any such system can be fitted inside a bigger and better system' (p. 182).

This loosens the concept of rationality because all individuals, if they are not to go on calculating for ever what is the best prediction of the opponents play on which to base their own best play, must introduce arbitrary stopping rules. Different agents can have different stopping rules and so a deviation from anticipated play need not pose a problem for rationality; it can be attributed to what have become necessarily faulty reasoning processes under this procedural perspective, thus opening the way to a different response to unanticipated moves, which is more in the spirit of Kreps and Wilson (1982). Such moves now become the basis for revising opinions about the type of opponent you are playing and hence the predictions of their future play.

> There are an infinite number of types of models which can justifiably be described as 'rational'. This leaves open the possibility of explaining deviations from predicted play without the necessity of abandoning the hypothesis that the opponent is rational. He or she may not be of a type to which high probability was attached originally but such probabilities can be updated as the game proceeds. (Binmore, 1988, p. 12)

The only difference with Kreps and Wilson is that whereas they have a clear conception of rationality and irrationality with doubt creeping in about which category your opponent fits into, Binmore has doubt creeping in at an earlier stage to produce a range of rationalities. There is no perfect conception of rationality. This is the message of Godel's theorem. Instead, there is a range of procedurally rational types of play, where the procedural element comes from the arbitrary stopping rule employed by the player in deciding what to expect of the opponent.*

7.3 Procedural Rationality in Everyday Life

It is always difficult in a short space to convey the possible importance of something through a list of the cases where it features. I hope to have provided a few 'key' examples in the previous section to add to those implicit uses of procedural rationality noted in earlier chapters. I conclude with a final reference, which is drawn from everyday life. The reference has more than a passing interest. After all, it would be very surprising if we were procedural in our daily life and something significantly different in the 'economy'.

---

* The precise argument about counterfactuals might be thought controversial since there are two rather different ways in which counterfactuals have been construed philosophically (see Elster, 1978). However, this does not matter for this illustration because a similar appeal to procedural rationality can be found in Harsanyi's (1975) tracing procedure for isolating one from multiple equilibria in games.

Imagine a world without stereotypes. Consider how difficult it would be to understand and act in strange and novel situations without the use of stereotypes. Suppose you meet a stranger: you do not ask an exhaustive set of questions to illicit exactly what person you are dealing with before deciding whether to do x, y or z. Instead you ask a few 'strategic' questions, the answers to which enable you to plug into an array of stereotypes and thus establish what kind of stereotypical person you are dealing with. You then decide on x, y or z on the basis of this stereotypical assessment.

Or, even better, consider watching a movie. The movies offer a paradigm case where we encounter novelty. We do not know the people in films, we do not have their histories, we do not know what they are really like, and we cannot ask the actors any direct questions. Yet the director is expecting us to get involved with these 'strangers' in a script which is usually highly synoptic and rarely lasts more than two hours. What audacious presumption!

Yet, the director gets away with it: we do get involved. We have no difficulty understanding what is going on even though the action is between complete strangers. We know to be worried when Indians appear on the horizon in a Western. We know there is a conflict between cattlemen and townsfolk. We know the tradesman cannot be relied on to defend himself and his town against rampaging cow-pokes. There are 'good' women and 'bad' women in Westerns, just as there 'good' men and 'bad' men: and we know which is which almost from the moment we first see them. For example 'bad' women run saloons and 'good' men have few friends or relations with the warring parties; instead, they plot a course which transcends existing social institutions.

There is so much we know about the strangers in westerns because we come to the theatre armed with a powerful range of stereotypes. They are our guides. Of course, like every procedurally rational device, they are sometimes arbitrary and they sometimes lead us astray. Indeed, it is precisely this attribute which directors often deliberately exploit to create dramatic tension in the movie. It is the confusion and uncertainty in the playing of a role which conflicts with the stereotypes for the genre that provides a classic kind of entertainment. Westerns are a good source for illustrations of the point.

One of the things that makes *Shane* such a good Western is Allan Ladd's struggle with being a gunslinger. For most of the film, he does not carry a gun and does not act like a gunslinger. But we know that he is a gunslinger, and we watch the battle between personal history and a desire to escape that history develop in the context of a social setting that gives the whip hand to history. The same is true of Doc Halliday in *My Darling Clementine*. Victor Mature is the centre of the dramatic action in this film, despite the fine performance from Henry Fonda as Wyatt Earp. Likewise, there is

Joan Crawford in *Johnny Guitar*: she is another stereotypically 'bad' woman struggling with that stereotype in a pointedly McCarthyite town, where guilt by association is threatening to turn the 'badness' of running a saloon into a conviction for robbery and murder.

The list is endless, and the point once made need not be laboured: stereotypes are perfect examples of procedural rationality; and stereotypes make life go round just as they make 90 minutes of synoptic shots of strangers on celluloid dramatically engaging.

However, lest these examples from everyday life seem removed from an economic context, there is a rather obvious one closer to home: advertising. Take a very simple advertisement: the picture of a woman (Catherine Deneuve) with a picture of Chanel Number 5 in the corner of the image. As Williamson (1978) and Leiss, Kline and Jhally (1986) observe the meaning of this advertisement is something like 'Chanel Number 5 is chic, sophisticated and elegant; by wearing it we would be adding something to our character that is the epitome of "Frenchness", specifically glamour, beauty and sophistication'. This is not stated explicitly in the advertisement. Yet it will be a common inference. Indeed, it would be difficult to believe that the French perfume company would be paying large sums for this advertisement unless this was a common inference. So, how is this understanding of the image achieved? The viewer makes sense of the image by using a variety of rules of thumb, procedures for decoding the message; and the advertiser, recognising this, is able with great economy to convey complicated messages in a single image.

In short, it would be difficult to understand why this was the 'era of the 30 second advertisement' unless consumers made dextrous use of a multitude of procedures for decoding images: that is to say, the contemporary advertising industry would be quite improbable if we were not procedurally rational.

7.4   Functional Explanation

One new type of explanation which can be associated with procedural rationality is functional explanation. The basic idea is that we might explain an action by its function rather than its intention. Thus, the direction of cause and effect is inverted relative to what is found with intentional explanations. It is a controversial form of explanation because it seems to require a kind of teleology which is often difficult to swallow. If actions are to be explained by their function, it suggests that there is some grander purpose or direction that is served by individual action but which goes unrecognised by the agent; and it is only through contributing to this grander aim that the individual finds himself or herself in a position to take the action in the first place. So, it is the grand aim which accounts for the action. The difficulty is simply where this grand purpose comes from. Societies do not obviously have purposes which are distinct from those of the individuals who comprise them; and invoking God's design is no less problematic.

Before considering this controversy, I want to fill in some of the details of functional explanation and provide illustrations of its use in economics. We can approach the discussion of this form of explanation more formally through Elster (1983a). He gives the following five-part definition of it. A behaviourial pattern X is explained by its function Y for group Z if and only if

1 Y is an effect of X,
2 Y is beneficial for Z,
3 Y is unintended by actors producing X,
4 Y – or at least the causal relation between X and Y – is unrecognised by the actors in Z,
5 Y maintains X by a causal feedback loop passing through Z.

It will be clear from this definition that there is nothing to preclude action X being an instrumentally rational calculation. It might be a little strange to make this association because it seems that instrumentally rational agents ought to spot that it is actually the attribute Y which is responsible for the success and so perform Y directly, especially since this more direct performance of Y will probably be less costly. Nevertheless, there is nothing to prevent functional explanations working with an instrumental conception of rationality. However, there are two reasons why this form of explanation is more naturally allied with procedural rationality.

Firstly, when X is undertaken for procedural reasons, then it is plausible that there are unintended consequences Y which do not attract the attention of the procedurally rational agent. As long as the performance of X appears to yield success, in terms set by other procedures, there is no reason to expect the agent to seek out the causal feedback loop. Hence, even though such unintended consequences are also a feature of instrumentally rational action, they are likely to abound by comparison in the procedural world because there is no backdrop of optimality which might be expected to pick up on the unintended consequences. Secondly, the causal connection in (5) usually involves an institutional setting (or a particular rule for processing information) and, as we have seen, such institutions cannot be explained with exclusive reference to instrumentally rational agents. Institutions are in some degree self-standing and the reference to procedural rationality is a mark of that self-standing characteristic. Hence, again, it is natural to associate functional explanations with procedural rationality, even though the same kind of explanation can also be found when actions are driven in part by instrumental considerations.

There are several explanations in economics which fit this pattern. Paradoxically, some were developed to support the relevance of the instrumental rationality postulate!* For example Alchian (1951) and Friedman (1953) both used functional explanations in their argument that the evidence of firms apparently pursuing objectives which differ from profit maximisation should be discounted. Firms often seem to be guided in their actions by simple rules of thumb, procedures. But this evidence should not be taken to undermine the hypothesis of profit maximisation. Whatever the actual motives and reasons for action, so the argument goes, competitive market pressures will ensure that only those firms which behave in a way that is consistent with profit maximisation will survive. So, even if firms follow some behaviourial rules of thumb which bear no obvious relation to profit maximisation, they will only survive in the marketplace if the rules amount to the same thing as profit maximisation. Hence, the analysis of firm behaviour can legitimately presume profit maximisation as an objective. The argument works in exactly the same way as biological arguments which use the principle of natural selection. It is the competitive process of markets that ensures the survival of firms which profit maximise, just as natural selection favours mutations which increase 'reproductive fitness'. This is the origin of the feedback causal loop in (5) which helps explain the occurrence of X, the apparently non-profit- maximising behaviour: it is the unintended consequence Y, profit maximisation, which ensures the survival of the particular procedures X used by firm Z.

Nelson and Winter (1982) have shown that this particular argument actually requires a rather stronger set of conditions than is perhaps implied by the intuitive appeal to the analogy with natural selection. Nevertheless, it can be rigorously demonstrated. Indeed, they extend the scope of this type of functional explanation by considering what happens in a procedural model of firm behaviour when factor prices change, and they generate precisely the same conclusion of factor substitution as is predicted by the instrumental model with profit maximising firms. Again, what produces the

---

* It is perhaps just worth heading off once more a general line of attack on procedural rationality which might be triggered by this functional argument, namely, that procedural rationality can be discounted because arguments like this demonstrate that it is 'as if' we were instrumentally rational. In a similar vein, when procedural rationality is construed as some imperfect version of the instrumentally rational agent, it may be tempting to deal with the limiting case of instrumental rationality and allow for these imperfections to add some white noise around the limiting case, in practice. As observed above, in general, procedural rationality is not an imperfect case of instrumental rationality; and as Radner (1980) demonstrates in the particular context of this kind of industry behaviour it would be grossly misleading to take the procedural outcomes as white noise around the limiting case associated with instrumental rationality.

result is a process of natural selection in the market together with a procedural assumption that firms constantly search for techniques with lower unit costs.

Functional explanation has also been at the heart of economists' discussions of non-economic factors which impinge on the economy. For instance, the Becker (1965) analysis of racism revolves around the same argument as that of Friedman and Alchian above. He models racism by assuming that some employers suffer psychic costs when they employ blacks: this leads to a sub-optimal employment of blacks by racist employers compared with non-racist employers (and to lower wages for black workers). Hence, non-racist employers enjoy a profitability advantage over the racist ones, and will eventually drive them out of the market. In effect, the psychic costs impose real costs on the racist employer by leading him/her to choose an inappropriate combination of black and white workers, and the competitive market mechanism punishes him/her for this racist psychology.

In contrast, Marxists have used the functional argument to explain the perpetuation of racism. Racist attitudes constitute the X behaviours above. They have the unintended consequence Y of dividing the working class. In particular, when a firm has a mixed workforce with racist attitudes, that workforce becomes divided and, in consequence, has reduced bargaining power because whites are reluctant to bargain and form coalitions with blacks. This lowers the average wage paid to workers, thus increasing the profitability of firms which operate in racist areas and employ both blacks and white (see Roemer, 1979). The market then provides the selection procedure which accounts for the perpetuation of racist attitudes by favouring the most profitable firms. The most profitable firms are those in racist areas and they will be those which have internal procedures and practices that heighten racial tensions. Here, it is the market mechanism which rewards racism.

More generally, Marxists have often used functional argument to explain the emergence of particular social institutions. The source for this is Marx himself. Marx distinguishes between the forces and the social relations of production in a society. The forces of production are the machines, the knowledge, the skills of the workforce etc. used in production, while the relations of production comprise those social institutions like property rights, labour markets, corporations, trades unions etc. which constitute the way the economy is organised. Marx (1950) is the canonical basis for a functional argument which links these two economic aspects with the legal and political superstructure in a society:

In the social production of their life men enter into definite relations that are indispensible and independent of their will, relations of production which correspond to a definite stage of development of their productive forces. The sum total of these relations constitutes the economic structure of society, the real basis, on which arises a legal and political superstructure. . . . (pp. 328–9)

Cohen's (1978) defence of Marx's historical materialism revolves around making an explicit functional argument to connect the forces, relations and superstructure. It is the contribution of the social relations of production and the superstructure to the promotion of the forces of production which explains the emergence of those institutions in a society:

> . . . history is, fundamentally, the growth of human productive power and the forms of society rise and fall according as they enable and promote, or prevent and discourage that growth. . . . The content of a legal system is explained by its function. . . . Legal structures rise and fall according as they sustain or frustrate forms of the economy that . . . are favoured by the productive forces. [This] implies an explanation why whatever economic structure obtains at a given time does obtain at that time. Once more the explanation is a functional one: the prevailing production relations prevail because they are relations that advance the development of the productive forces. (pp. 483 and 487)

The causal loop in (5) is provided by a presumption that societies rise and fall according to the development of their productive forces. The societies with highly developed forces of production expand while those with poorly developed forces contract and wither away. (For a contrary view, see Giddens, 1979, 1982). This mechanism is the equivalent of the selection procedure provided by the competitive market in the earlier examples, with the development of the forces of production signalling success and failure in the same way as profitability. So, to fill in the five steps of the functional argument, we may choose our institutions, legal, political and economic, because we intend them to be just and moral or to enrich our own bank accounts or whatever (X), but the unintended consequences (Y) are the contributions these institutions make to the promotion of the forces of production and it is success here which explains the occurrence of these institutions and not our intentions (X). We can go on pedalling our notions of justice, morality and the like, and we can pass these ideas down to later generations in the form of institutions which embody those principles, but the acid test of whether those institutions survive is their contribution to the forces of production, as this is what ensures the survival of the society in which those institutions are embedded.

Elster (1979, 1983a, 1985) has been extremely critical of functional argument in the social sciences in general, and in Marxism in particular. His complaint is primarily concerned with the failure of many functional arguments to specify the causal loop feedback mechanisms in (5), which are necessary to complete the analysis. In effect, this is another way of getting at the apparent presumption of a teleology, because if there was some grand purpose then the causal loop feedback would be provided by the satisfaction of that objective. Too often, Elster argues, functional arguments rest, having merely identified that a particular action has unintended beneficial consequences. These benefits cannot be said to explain the action unless there is the addition of stage (5). To be blunt, there is a difference between functional explanation and the discovery of unintended consequences.

Undoubtedly, Elster has drawn attention to a problem. There are all too many analyses of the sort which explain, say, the State in capitalist society because it is beneficial for capitalists' interests. The delineation of benefit is somehow regarded as sufficient explanation for its occurrence. This is bad social science; and it is a point which appears to have been taken on board even in those areas of the social sciences, like anthropology, which have hitherto made liberal use of functional arguments (see Douglas, 1986). However, Elster goes somewhat further in his criticism. He doubts that functional explanation could (or should) ever be important in the social sciences because there is no general principle like natural selection in biology which can be appealed to to provide the causal feedback mechanism. In so far as functional explanations are legitimate, they will always have to use particular feedback mechanisms.

Van Parijs (1981, 1982) has argued against this view, suggesting that 'reinforcement' in the social world provides a general feedback mechanism for functional explanations. (Cohen, 1982, has also defended the use of functional argument on epistemological grounds. This aspect of the debate takes us back to the issues of chapter 2, and so we do not pursue it here.) What van Parijs appears to mean by this is that agents in the social world 'learn'. Agents in the social world adjust their behaviour according to whether they succeed in their objectives: success 'reinforces' behaviour while failure leads to behaviour adaptation. Thus, he argues, we have a general mechanism to supply the crucial stage (5) of the argument.

At first sight, it is not obvious that such learning could qualify as a feedback mechanism for a functional argument. It is certainly a feedback mechanism, but it seems to restore intentionality to a crucial position because it is the agents who must want to learn here. However, van Parijs has argued, and Elster 1983a, 1982) seems to accept this, that this is importantly different because the learning takes place with respect to actual consequences of action and not the intended consequences of action. The point is sometimes made with reference to 'absorbing' Markov chains (see Elster, 1983a, and van Parijs, 1982).

Suppose agents follow a set of procedures that give guides for action, specifying, at least stochastically, how they interact with other agents and which establish routines for revising behaviour when it fails to reach satisfactory levels. We say that the agent behaves in a particular way (agents are in state i) when they follow a particular set of procedures. The rules of interaction generate some probability distribution over the events to which the agent responds and the consequences that will follow from the use of the particular guides to actions in these circumstances. This probability distribution over consequences will, in turn, given the rules governing what is satisfactory, map onto a probability distribution for learning. Finally, the procedures for learning will translate this probability distribution into a probability distribution over the agent taking on a new type of behaviour (state j associated with a different set of procedures) in the next time period. So, each agent in state i has a vector p_i where each element p_{ij} gives the probability that the agent moves from state i to state j ($\Sigma p_{ij}=1$). This way of describing individual behaviour follows exactly that of Nelson and Winter, 1975, 1978, 1982.)

When each type of behaviour has a transitional probability vector associated with it in this fashion and these probabilities are independent of the time period when the agent is in the 'state' (behaves like that type), then we have a stationary Markov chain. If the matrix of these transitional probabilities is indecomposable, then there will exist an 'absorbing' state. That is to say, as the number of time periods increases, the process of interaction and learning will tend to a fixed vector of probabilities governing the likelihood of an agent's being in each state, independently of where the agent starts. This fixed vector is given by the eigenvector corresponding to the eigenvalue 1 of this transitional probability matrix.

To take a trivial case, Figure 7.2 gives three possible types of behaviour with their respective transitional probabilities of moving to another behaviour after interaction and learning. The absorbing state is given by the vector of probabilities [0,0,1]. In other words, it does not matter where you start here, you will end behaving like type 3.

In this example, the interaction and learning rules give a very clear purpose, namely becoming like type 3. But it is only implicit in the application of the rules; it need not be an explicit purpose of those using the rules. The rules would then provide a feedback mechanism that was not acknowledged by the agents themselves and which encouraged behaviours of type 3. To put it slightly differently, the procedures, when aggregated in this fashion, amount to a selection process which goes on behind the backs of individuals. The explanation of why agents behave like type 3 would be a functional one: it is because it is 'beneficial' to agents in this economy to behave like type 3 agents.

It is quite important to notice that a Markov chain of this sort can be derived by procedures which govern interaction and random learning; there is no necessity for explicit learning procedures. In other words, van

State in $t+1$

		1	2	3
State in t	1	$\frac{1}{3}$	$\frac{1}{2}$	0
	2	$\frac{1}{3}$	$\frac{1}{4}$	0
	3	$\frac{1}{3}$	$\frac{1}{4}$	1

Figure 7.2   Teleonymy as an absorbing state

Parijs sells the functional argument somewhat short by focusing on explicit learning mechanisms because the emergence of a selection principle does not depend on learning alone. Another illustration will help to ground this remark, and complete the discussion of functional explanations.

Consider the co-ordination game from chapter 5: imagine this applies to some set of tasks within a firm where there are no explicit rules governing which person does I and which does II. The pay-offs now refer to the earnings of the firm generated by each player. Some firms develop conventions, $[p, q]$ vectors, for assigning role A and role B to each person with the probabilities $[p, q]$. These $[p, q]$ pairs are randomly distributed across all firms and each $[p, q]$ evolves randomly within the firm because there is no explicit learning mechanism.

There is also a set of procedures in the economy in which these firms operate that governs interaction between firms. We focus on one aspect of this interaction: that which is mediated through capital markets. Firms apply to capital markets for funds and there is a simple set of procedures which imply that funds are allocated according to existing profitability. This means that firms which have solved the co-ordination problem better by having $[p, q]$ pairs which approach $[0, 1]$ or $[1, 0]$ will prosper compared with those firms which are still tending towards interior $[p, q]$s.

The procedures within the economy governing who gets funds for expansion provides the selection process, and this is sufficient to generate a functional explanation. The conventions which emerge, $[0, 1]$ or $[1, 0]$, say, for the example of the age/gender convention sketched in chapter 5, are explained because they are beneficial in solving the co-ordination game and the procedures governing the disbursement of loanable funds in the economy select firms which solve the co-ordination problem. In fact, a moment's reflection will suggest that most of the game theoretic accounts of institution formation in the previous chapter could be functional. Again it is worth stating that there is nothing to prevent instrumental elements appearing in functional explanations: functional explanations are being discussed here rather than before simply because the procedures which provide the causal feedback loop are in some degree self-standing from instrumental rationality and the introduction of procedural rationality is an explicit recognition of this feature of the social world.

Of course, this process of selection might be reinforced or could be replaced by a simple learning procedure within the firm, along the lines of van Parijs. Suppose there are procedures within the firm that make individual wages depend on company earnings and individuals learn in a simple adaptive manner by changing the convention in the direction which has proved successful in terms of earnings in the past. This process corresponds to our earlier discussion of evolution through learning in this game. Consequently, in these circumstances, we will also see the convention $[0, 1]$ or $[1, 0]$ emerging. Again, the explanation of the emergence of, say, the gender/age convention will be functional. Nobody wishes to distinguish between people according to their age or sex, but the convention arises because it is functional: it is beneficial in the solution of the co-ordination game.

To summarise, the argument can be put in a slightly different way. What seems to be rather disturbing about functional arguments is the idea that societies have some kind of purpose, a teleology. If they had such a purpose then it would be easy to see why actions and behaviours were selected according to how well they helped satisfy that purpose. But societies do not have purposes in that sense; only individuals have such purposes. From this perspective what is wrong with functional explanation is that it seems to rest on an inappropriate projection of the individual with his/her motives onto a society with the suggestion that it too has objectives. However, functional arguments work perfectly well when there is tele-onomy, i.e. processes guided by patterned selection compared with processes governed by a purpose, as in teleology. And it is relatively easy to see, either via repeated play of something like a co-ordination game under certain procedural rules or through the analysis of social processes governed by rules as Markov chains, how a teleonomy can be generated as a result of the procedures followed by procedurally rational agents.

Whilst Elster seems to accept the argument about deriving a teleonomy from a set of procedures, he seems loathe to grant the insight much force. Let us return to the Markov chain approach. He doubts that it will have much relevance to modern industrial societies because too much is changing for any particular 'absorbing' state to command our attention: ' . . . it seems clear to me that in modern societies too much is changing for equilibria to have the time to work themselves out. . . . The association between social anthropology and functional explanation, therefore, may not be accidental.' . . . (Elster, 1983a, p. 64)

The observation is an important one, but it is misdirected. Undoubtedly, stationary Markov chains are poor descriptions in many social contexts because the transitional probabilities change with time, as does the range of 'states'. However, this does not mean that Markov processes which more realistically capture the modern social world, with its hustle and bustle for change, do not share the same property of selection which is crucial for functional arguments to work. For example, with non-stationary Markov processes (i.e. the transitional probabilities change over time), it is still possible to generate strong and weakly ergodic behaviour (see Isaacson and Madsen, 1976), i.e. behaviour which respectively either still converges to a fixed vector of probabilities or follows a particular pattern independently of where you start. In the former, there is a fixed vector of probabilities to which the system is still tending and in the latter the vector of probabilities is time dependent.

Furthermore, in non-ergodic processes it is still possible to develop 'state'-dependent 'absorption' probabilities (see Isaacson and Madsen, 1976). A non-ergodic process exists either when there is no 'absorption' state or where there is more than one such state and the probability of moving towards one or another depends critically on the starting position. An illustration of a non-ergodic process is provided by the co-ordination game. With suitable assumptions concerning the procedures for learning and/or funding expansion, this game could be transposed into a Markov chain. It could be a stationary chain, but it would definitely be non-ergodic because there are two 'absorbing' states, [0, 1] and [1,0]. Which state a firm ended up in would depend on where it started and the precise formulation for selection and learning. The phase diagrams in chapter 5 provide the obvious insight as to why there is this initial state dependence and this is responsible for making the process non-ergodic. Nevertheless, one could still develop state-dependent probabilistic assessments concerning which state a firm will move towards.

Elster's observation has an important implication. It is not, however, that the idea of an unintended direction to evolution through the use of procedures should be jettisoned. More complicated Markov processes still have this unintended directional quality imparted by the procedures: it has simply become more complicated than the idea of a single 'absorbing' state. The important difference between the single absorbing state and more complex Markov chains for our purposes is that history does not matter in the former. In the simple case it does not matter where you start and which state you next visit; you still terminate in the same 'absorbing' state. By contrast in the more complicated cases history, in the form of what moves you make when and where, does matter. This is plain in the non-ergodic example of the co-ordination game. The same applies to the non-ergodic behaviours which can be generated by non-stationary Markov chains. Likewise, history also matters in a more attenuated form in the non-stationary, but still ergodic processes. Firstly, history is important in the sense that the evolution of transitional probabilities influences the absorbing state in strong ergodicity, and the actual state is time dependent in the case of weak ergodicity.

7.5 The Legacy of History

It was suggested in the last section that one way of modelling the operation of procedural rationality was through the theory of Markov chains. The last section also concluded with the thought that the real force of Elster's observations is that history matters. It is a feature of much economic analysis that the outcomes in the present bear a heavy imprint from the past. Sometimes this is uncontentious, but sometimes it is a special feature of explanations offered by the 'fringe' of the discipline and is regarded as so much 'waffle' by the mainstream. The purpose of this section is to show how some of these ideas can be given a quite precise formulation within the theory of Markov chains.

There is no necessity to associate Markov chains and their attributes in this 'historical' sense with procedural rationality alone: instrumental rationality could also feature in the behaviour summarised by Markov chains. But, once again, it is a natural connection to make for the reasons which have already been sketched. Furthermore, it makes sense to underline that connection now because procedural rationality is frequently assumed to pose insuperable analytical barriers, but actually there is a well-established analytical approach which can be used to study the operation of procedural rationality. In other words, this section really has a dual purpose: one is to show how certain ideas can be made quite precise with the aid of Markov chains, so rigour need not be dumped; and the other is to reinforce the claim of procedural rationality by noting how with the aid of Markov chains it could be tied in with ideas like cumulative causation, hysteresis etc.

History influences the present quite uncontentiously when the decisions of the past leave us with a certain distribution of resources and options in the present. This is the kind of connection between history and the present which surfaces in much economic analysis because it is inescapably dynamic. I am not concerned to enumerate instances of this sort of influence. Rather, I begin by discussing two broad patterns to this dynamic influence that are often deployed in actual economic explanations. They are captured by the ideas of cumulative causation and hysteresis.

The idea of cumulative causation is what lies behind vicious and virtuous circles and the oft proclaimed inertia of the status quo. For example, when it is conjectured that high output growth leads to high productivity growth, which in turn improves international competitiveness and this feeds back to prime the original high growth, we have a virtuous circle where past performance lays the seeds for its perpetuation in the present (see Cornwall, 1978, and Beckerman, 1965). Likewise, Olson (1982) and Kuran (1987) provide a variety of explanations concerning how a bias towards the status quo emerges. They revolve around the awareness that parties to collective decisions have of their interdependence. In Kuran (1987) it is bandwagon effects that feature in collective decisions which are responsible for this inertia. In such settings, outcomes depend on the expected outcomes and this can insulate outcomes from changes in actual opinions about what is good and bad (see chapter 6). In Olson, it is precisely the difficulty of overcoming the free-rider problem in collective decisions which makes institutions that solve this problem inflexible.

Cumulative causation captures the thought that there are some situations where whatever agents try to do over time they are locked into either a particular trajectory or a particular stationary state. What they actually do or are capable of doing seems to make no difference to what happens eventually. Now, this idea can be expressed quite simply. If we conceptualise a set of procedures in terms of a Markov chain, where the procedures establish a particular matrix of transition probabilities, then cumulative causation can be associated with the existence of an 'absorbing' state. It is precisely the characteristic of a conjuncture of procedures which generates an absorbing state that, once in that state, whatever you do seems to make no difference: you always return to that state.

The absorbing state may be a singular one from an ergodic process or one of many from a non-ergodic process. This would depend on the actual conjuncture of procedures and their associated transitional probabilities. In the former, the precise history would make no difference – a particular destiny is inescapable. In the latter, however, history will have mattered by nudging us towards one absorbing state rather than another. But, once in that state, outcomes will seem to bear the stamp of cumulative causation.

Likewise, it is easy to place the phenomenon of hysteresis. Hysteresis refers to cases where the time path of a variable influences its destination. So, for example, in recent studies of unemployment, it has been argued that a history of high unemployment tends to raise the actual level of unemployment through increases in the 'natural' rate of unemployment (see Hargreaves Heap, 1980, and Blanchard and Summers, 1986, for a survey). Periods of high unemployment have this effect on the 'natural' rate because on-the-job training falls, skills atrophy and the numbers who are structurally unemployed rises: similarly, insider–outsider problems develop within unions and they become more concerned with the wage of their members in employment than the prospects for employment of their currently unemployed members; and so on. This time dependence is precisely the hallmark of a non-ergodic process. So, there is nothing mysterious about the phenomenon of hysteresis: it can arise whenever the combination of procedures generates a non-ergodic process.

A phenomenon of 'emergent properties' is sometimes distinguished by social scientists. Again, there is nothing very mysterious here from the vantage point of the previous section. An absorption state would be a good example of an 'emergent property' of a set of procedures. It is really just an application of the idea of unintended consequence to the domain of procedural action. Emergent properties are sometimes regarded as something completely new, but as long as the original Markov chain contained the state as one of its dimensions, then this interpretation of an emergent property still holds. If one wants to make it recognisably new, then the absorption state can simply be made one from among many in a non-ergodic conjuncture of procedures. This would mean that only societies with particular histories would achieve certain absorption states, and when those states were achieved they could be 'new' relative to that history.

This would turn emergent properties into an example of hysteresis. For instance, a co-ordination game may evolve with the use of the sex and age convention. The sex and age convention in general terms can be explained functionally, but once in place it can have further repercussions. If there are further conventions in a society which single out candidate conventions from those in existing use, then other games may adopt the same age/sex convention, now that it has achieved prominence in one game. In this way the convention develops into something which is more than a simple device for achieving co-ordination. Its widespread use turns it into an instance of a much broader gender and age stratification of society with implications and effects which stretch beyond problems of co-ordination. Age/gender stratification has become an emergent property of the set of conventions in play in that society. Where the timing of the original use of the age/sex convention is crucial to its subsequent adoption in other games and transformation into a system-wide source of stratification, then we have a hysteresis effect.

While cumulative causation is concerned with understanding historical continuity, hysteresis and emergent properties give some insight into historical change. There is another feature of procedures which also helps explain historical change: this is latent conflict. Latent conflict exists whenever the procedures define a non-ergodic process.

This can be illustrated most clearly with reference again to the co-ordination game where there are two absorbing states. Here, which convention gets established is genuinely arbitrary in the sense that any number of differences between agents could have been used as the linchpin for the development of a convention. It could be age/gender or any of a number of possible ways of distinguishing between two agents when they meet.

Equally, the hierarchy established by the convention could work one way or the other: role A to males and the old, or males and the young, or females and the old, or females and the young. There are four different ways of reading the age/gender distinction as a convention. Indeed, many of these possible conventions may have been tried by the players of the game, with history determining which becomes the dominant one (see Sugden, 1986). Once established, however, this essentially arbitrary convention will be maintained by a self-fulfilling set of beliefs.

The latent conflict arises because, while the convention may be arbitrary, its distribution of the benefits of co-ordination is not random: change the convention and you change the distribution predictably. This implies that the essentially arbitrary convention produces an equally arbitrary distribution of the rewards from co-ordination. Since these reward distributions are often not equal, as in the original version of the co-ordination game or other games in the same mould, this arbitrariness is a source of potential conflict. Agents playing the game may reflect that, since arbitrary procedures carry no moral sanction, there will be reasons for seeking to change the procedures and with them the distribution of rewards. In short, the perception of latent conflict as a source of discontinuous change is based on the insight that, if history is arbitrary in its rewards, then there is no good reason to be a prisoner of its processes. It is the complementary notion to the earlier thought in sections 5.6 and 7.1 on freedom.

7.6 Discourse within the Social Sciences

It is one of the features of contemporary social science that it is fractured into separate disciplines. This has, I believe, had unfortunate consequences for all. I also believe that procedural rationality is a pivotal concept in the reintegration of the social sciences. I believe this partially because, once the concept has been severed from its narrow Simon definition and becomes a source of interdependence locating the individual socially and historically, it corresponds to some of Wittgenstein's idea of rule-governed behaviour. I also believe this because the concept constitutes a natural bridge between economics and specific debates within the social sciences that tend to be ignored by economists. One example of this has been given with the action–structure debate mentioned in section 5.6. There is not the space here to make good this claim in any serious sense. But, it is possible to indicate in this section further areas where the concept of procedural rationality might help repair some of the damage which has been caused by the false separation in the social sciences.

Heilbroner (1988) in reviewing the *New Palgrave Dictionary of Economic Thought* has lamented that there is no mention of power. He does not take this as a comment on the encyclopaedia – it is actually a reflection of the state of our discipline. In fact, it really is extraordinary when you consider how power struggles seem to slice through so much of our lives that there is no economics of power.

Of course, it would be foolish to suppose that those social sciences which address power seriously have a settled understanding of the concept. Power is one of those notoriously slippery concepts in social theory. There is a minefield of issues which require careful treatment if they are not to blow up in your face. However, this is not the place to chart a measured course and I intend to make only two partial and episodic references to the power debate because they have an obvious bearing on the procedural side of life.

Firstly, two different senses of power are often distinguished. One is the power that one agent or a group of agents has over others, and the other is the power that a group of agents has when they combine compared with when they act individually. The co-ordination game and others like it constitute obvious examples of how the two aspects come together. The conventions which evolve create both a collective sense of power and a distributive sense of power. The players of the game both prosper through the use of a convention rather than no convention, thus demonstrating the feature of collective power. The convention also establishes a particular distribution of the rewards from co-operation. Role A players enjoy a capacity to do things in society which B players do not because the distribution of the rewards favours A players. A's capacity is a direct result of B's incapacity and that is why this aspect qualifies as a power relation between groups: A has power over B as a result of the convention. Hence, it might be said that the power relations of a society are a way of describing certain attributes of the ensemble of procedures in a society, just as the ideas of cumulative causation and hysteresis were ways of describing other attributes of those procedures.

Secondly, three dimensions of power relations between individuals and groups are often distinguished (see Lukes, 1974). The first is the common-sense notion of power which has been used above. People have power by virtue of the resources they command. Agents with more resources have a greater capacity to influence events than those who have less. When the interests of two individuals collide, this gives greater power to the one with more resources. Secondly, there is power which comes from the ability to manipulate agendas. Thirdly, there is power which comes from the capacity to influence the interests which agents perceive as their own. The second and third dimensions are the controversial ones from a pluralist perspective. I leave all comment on the third dimension until the next chapter. The second dimension, however, is clearly present in the earlier discussion of procedures and this should worry pluralists.

The agenda-setting dimension of power is well captured in the co-ordination game. Different procedures would have generated different results. More generally different procedures might turn an ergodic ensemble into non-ergodic ones yielding a wider and different range of outcomes. This connection suggests that this aspect of power is a dynamic aspect of the power relations in a society while the first dimension is a static representation of those power relations. Again, we can think of these as two further ways of describing the attributes of a particular conjuncture of procedures.

In other words, procedural rationality could constitute a bridge to the richer discussion of power which is found in the other social sciences. And this not only would help endow economics with a crucial concept, it might also help to clarify some of the power debates in the other social sciences.

The second illustration is concerned more with what an economics which recognises procedural rationality might do for the other social sciences rather than the other way round. In a sense, it is a return to the theme that has been brewing throughout the last four chapters, because it relates to the irreducible nature of procedures, so it need not be laboured again. The point is that economics ought to be telling the other social sciences that instrumental rationality is not enough. Instrumental rationality by itself will not do. Instead, most of the social sciences are probably getting exactly the opposite message. As we export more and more 'economic' (meaning instrumentally rational) analyses of this, that and the other part of social life, we appear to be telling the social sciences that there is no limit to the explanatory scope of this instrumental brand of economic analysis.*

This is unfortunate because it adds fuel to a position in the social sciences broadly understood as methodological individualism at a time when economics ought to be undermining this view. Again, this is a controversial area in social theory and it would be foolish not to recognise that a brief intervention can only hope to blunder about. But again, this is not the time for caution, and I make no apology for hand waving because this section is only designed to interest the reader in the idea rather than persuade him/her that procedural rationality is a useful bridging concept for the social sciences. In a broad sense, methodological individualism can be associated with the attempt to reduce all social outcomes to the participating individuals and their intentions. Chapters 3, 4 and 5 constitute rather a long argument about why this has not proved possible in a discipline which has probably, more than any other, taken this picture of agency to the limit (see Elster, 1985, and Levine, Sober and Olin Wright, 1987, for further discussion).

---

* Of course, there will be those who will not be in the least surprised to discover that disciplines with imperial ambitions, much like countries in the same position, do not always export their best goods.

To conclude this section with an implication that this holds for economics, it might be argued that a position of methodological individualism has informed the search for the microfoundations of macroeconomics. This search is plainly important because it is individuals who act in the world and not aggregates. However, the terminology used to describe this search can be misleading because microfoundations in economics tend to be equated with instrumentally rational behaviour, especially when the search is inspired by methodological individualism. By contrast, once the microfoundations also contain procedural rationality, then it is no longer clear that they warrant the term microfoundations. Procedural rationality often rests on procedures that are shared in some degree and which cannot be reduced to individuals and their intentions. Hence, it would be as accurate to describe the process of explaining social outcomes through the constituent individual behaviours as establishing the macrofoundations of micro behaviour as the reverse.

7.7 Conclusion

This chapter has provided a survey of the use of procedural rationality in economics and it has suggested that functional explanations are a coherent and new type of explanation which can be plausibly associated with this canon of rationality.

Procedural rationality adds considerably to the scope of the explanations offered by economics because it has been defined more widely than is the case in the pioneering work of Simon. Not only do people use procedures for quick calculation to save on the scarce computational capacities of the brain, they also use shared procedures to communicate and co-ordinate their actions with each other. In this way, procedural rationality fills some of the gaps, discerned in chapters 4, 5 and 6, in the scope of the instrumentally driven explanations. Procedural rationality becomes a building block in our explanation of institutions and information sets; and it helps make intelligible a distinct concept of uncertainty and the peculiar freedom individuals have collectively to choose their procedures. In short, the wider definition of procedural rationality expands the explanatory power of economics by bringing institutions into the domain of economics and by licensing concepts like uncertainty and freedom.

Functional explanations need not be exclusively associated with procedural rationality. Nevertheless, it is a natural link to make because once procedural rationality is in place it becomes much easier to answer the objections levelled against this type of explanation by Elster. Procedures can generate a teleonymy and thus avoid the controversial presumption of a teleology which is sometimes found in functional arguments. Nor is procedural rationality exclusively associated with functional explanations; it is also possible to see how different ensembles of procedures create broad patterns of historical influence on the present which correspond to such ideas, often used in explanation, as cumulative causation and hysteresis. Finally, nor does the introduction of procedural rationality spell the demise of analytical rigour because the consequences of procedural rationality can be plotted with the aid of Markov chains.

At root, procedural rationality adds greatly to the explanatory scope of economics and is a crucial bridging concept with the other social sciences because it reflects the historical and social location of an individual. The failure of instrumental rationality to capture this dimension of action was one of the summary complaints to the discussion in chapters 4, 5 and 6. The other summary complaint focused on the need for a self-reflective individual, and this is addressed in the next chapter.

8 EXPRESSIVE RATIONALITY

8.1 Introduction

Instrumental and procedural rationality pick out two important attributes of what it is to be human: we are purposive and we are socially and historically located creatures. This picture, however, is incomplete. We are not just a slave to our passions or a prisoner of history or convention, however loose those chains may be. In particular, there are at least two aspects of human behaviour that have been noted in chapter 6 and which remain unaccounted for. One is our use of actions to say things about ourselves and the other is an active sense of self-management.

The purpose of this chapter is to tie these and other behaviours into a concept of expressive rationality, and to illustrate how this notion of rationality has been used, typically implicitly, to generate explanations in economics.

I want to claim that expressive rationality stands for a universal human concern with understanding the world in which we live. It is precisely because we are purposive that we wish to make sense of the world: the world must be rendered intelligible if we are to act in it. I take this need for a cosmology, which gives answers to questions about the meaning of this, the foundation for that, the relation of the individual to society etc., to be one of the few areas of agreement about the human species which comes from anthropology. I also take it to be a lesson of anthropology that there are a variety of cosmologies which have at different times and in different parts of the world satisfied this need. Finally, I take it that in contemporary industrialised societies the individual sits at the centre of our cosmology in a way that would be quite alien to 'traditional' and 'religious' societies. It is the individual whom we celebrate. In contrast, 'traditional' societies are liable to attach value to the group, with the individual enjoying a status only because of his/her relation to the group, whilst religious societies find meaning in the plans of gods and the individual is valued as an instrument of those plans. (See Douglas, 1982, for a more detailed classification of the webs of belief found in different cultures.)

In broad brush terms, I doubt that this characterisation is controversial and I shall focus on 'modern' individualist societies in this chapter. By making the individual so central, 'modern' societies have placed an enormous burden on the individual. It is not enough for an individual to have a set of preferences; it is important that those desires be his or hers in a more active sense. They should belong to the individual because he/she has come through reflection to hold them as his/her own.

I am not alone in distinguishing something like this as a feature of our age and linking it to a concept of rationality. Elster (1983b) labels it the quest for autonomy, and likens it to a 'thick' notion of rationality. Likewise, Berlin (1958) in a famous essay appeals to the same idea when defining a second and positive sense of freedom. This is to be distinguished from the negative sense of freedom which applies to the absence of coercion and the ability to satisfy given preferences. He makes the point most elegantly and again allies it with the concept of rationality:

> The 'positive' sense of the word 'liberty' derives from the wish on the part of the individual to be his own master. . . . I wish to be a subject, not an object; to be moved by reasons, by conscious purposes, which are my own, not by causes which affect me, as it were from outside. I wish to be a somebody, not nobody; a doer – deciding, not being decided for, self directed and not acted upon by external nature or by other men as if I were a thing, or an animal, or a slave incapable of playing a human role, that is, of conceiving goals and policies of my own and realising them. This is at least part of what I mean when I say that I am rational and that it is my reason which distinguishes me as a human being from the rest of the world. I wish, above all, to be conscious of myself as a thinking, willing, active being, bearing responsibility for my choices and able to explain them by references to my own ideas and purposes. I feel free to the degree that I believe this is true, and enslaved to the degree that I am made to realise that it is not. (p. 131)

The idea receives further support from the psychological literature, where it is frequently referred to as a regard for self-esteem or self-respect. These terms broadly capture the idea that people need to stand back from their selves and value them. And, in the hands of someone like Kelly (1955), this feeling good about your self is explicitly related to what I have defined as expressive rationality because it comes from your ability to make sense of the world.

However, I want to suggest something further than this. The quest for intelligibility is beset by the epistemological problems which were encapsulated in chapter 2 by the idea that we are forced to inhabit an epistemic world located between objectivity and relativism, where the claims of both are recognised. Magritte's painting, the frontispiece of this book, entitled the 'human condition', expresses the predicament. The canvas on the easel stands in relation to a landscape which suggests strongly that the picture like life is not arbitrary. In this case, the picture encourages the idea that it corresponds to the bit of the landscape which is hidden by the easel. But there is no way we can check whether the picture captures what is true in this world because the picture obscures the landscape it appears to portray.

At one and the same time we are encouraged to hold beliefs in an objective world which we also know we cannot hope to validate.

It might be thought that the recognition of this predicament reveals a fatal weakness in the project of the social sciences. But I think this is very wrong – it tells us something about the human condition which the social sciences can build on. Rather than a weakness, it should be regarded as a strength. Put prosaically, it means that our beliefs which make the world intelligible to us are bound to suffer from incoherences and inconsistencies. (Anthropologists make the observation that all cultures have strengths and weaknesses, or blindnesses of one kind of another which are contained or hedged about with taboos, the sacred and the profane.) In turn, this sets an agenda for a part of human action: there is a concern with unravelling those inconsistencies and incoherences. Action becomes dynamic and process oriented in a manner that is lost on the instrumental account. (See also Wiggins, 1976, who draws a similar contrast between a temple building style of life where meaning consists in the finished work with a Sisyphus style where meaning comes from the doing; likewise Taylor, 1983.)

In 'modern' individualist societies, the general problem with making sense of the world is focused on the individual. It is revealed as a kind of existential problem of how to judge your worth. What conditions and criteria are to be applied in deciding to hold one set of desires rather than another? What is it that informs Berlin's self-mastery and Elster's autonomy?

In the next section, I discuss two 'modern' approaches to this problem of establishing self-respect. It is designed to demonstrate more concretely that both run into difficulties which can be roughly understood as inconsistencies of the sort mentioned above. The third section considers the implications for behaviour which follow from a recognition of these inconsistencies. Three characteristics are distinguished: behaviour is communicative; it involves the exercise of a special quality, 'judgement'; and it necessarily relies on procedures of the mind which are arbitrary in some degree. The following five sections provide illustrations of how the concept of self-respect and these associated behaviourial attributes have featured in economics explanations.

It will be clear from this brief description that there is nothing in the idea of expressive rationality which makes it incompatible with instrumental and procedural rationality. Just as procedural rationality did not undermine instrumental rationality – it simply opened up another dimension of human motivation – so expressive rationality adds to the picture of human agency without subtracting any of the previous elements.

Indeed, it might be tempting to go further than this and suggest that expressive rationality is really reducible to instrumental rationality. It merely involves specifying another goal or objective which action is designed to satisfy: the goal of self-respect. There is a sense in which this is an accurate description of what is involved in recognising expressive considerations in modern societies. But enough has been said for the moment on the dynamic and open-ended nature of the quest for self-respect to caution against fitting it in a means-to-given-ends framework and thereby reducing it to a species of instrumental rationality. This issue is taken up in more detail in the penultimate section where the relationship between the three sorts of rationality is more fully discussed. This section can be read as a brief summary of the argument in part II of the book.

8.2   Strategies for Self-Respect

This section is concerned with trying to pin down what is involved in recognising that people sit in judgement over their desires and that they derive a sense of individuality from this activity. We will all be aware of this aspect of life, but what exactly does it amount to?

At a general level, it seems that we would like there to be good reason for the desires that we hold, and the activity of reflection for an individual is really about establishing what constitutes good reason for that person. So, one way of answering this question and unpackaging the notion of expressive rationality in the 'modern' world is to focus on different approaches to the issue of what is good reason for holding some preferences or objectives rather than others.

Two traditional treatments of good reason find the source of good reason in a match between the individual's project and that of some external authority. One looks to God and the other looks to nature. Unfortunately, for reasons which are familiar from chapter 2, the mere commitment to one external authority or another is not going to make the attribution of good reason a simple exercise. Neither God nor nature's project is self-evident. Clues to both might be thought to exist in the world for those who have faith in the existence of one or other project, but putting these clues together to form some kind of theory about this project is not simply an act of adjusting theory to the facts as an empiricist methodology might seem to imply. Rather than merely 'discovering' the world, social science helps to create it. We cannot avoid our own ideas about what constitutes the project of life from affecting what we believe to be God or nature's project, and so we cannot subordinate the former to the latter.

It is precisely because we cannot escape responsibility for the meaning we attach to life, even if we do have faith in the existence of God (or a natural project), that it makes sense to hold the 'death of god' as a slogan for 'modernity'. As Rorty (1987) suggests in reviewing Habermas: 'Habermas's question of modernity is: how can we live with the thought that we create our own nature, our own values, our own purposes? Modernity, as he puts it, "has to create its normativity out of itself".' (p. 11)

Two approaches to the problem of 'modernity' are discussed here. In effect, each prioritises a different side of the objectivity–relativism dilemma. The first attempts to build a secularly based ethics. It does not allow the absence of a manifest objective criterion to undermine the character of the human project. It remains a project which would be intelligible to God: the meaning and purpose of human existence is still to be found in an ethical system which establishes what is good and bad. The only difference is that God cannot be relied upon to 'pop down' and validate the 'correct' ideas about what is good and bad; instead, the ethical system must have secular foundations. By contrast, the other, existential, approach sees this as just another attempt to recreate a god, whereas the real point is to do without a god altogether. The 'modern' task is not to decide on what is good and bad in the absence of god; rather it is to decide whether to think in terms like good and bad.

This is not the place to launch into a survey of ethics. But there is one aspect of this part of philosophy that I do want to bring out with an example taken from economics. It is that there seems in practice to be an unavoidable conflict between ethical principles, which it is very difficult to resolve because each of the ethical principles involved seems to command our attention in equal measure.* Consider, for instance, two ethical principles, paretianism and liberalism. Both seem reasonable principles to entertain and yet they will often collide. Sen (1970) gives a famous example.

I update his example of Lady Chatterley's Lover by supposing that a 'feminist' and a 'chauvinist', travelling on a train, are sitting at the same table on which is deposited a pornographic magazine. There are three possible outcomes 0, c, f: either nobody reads it, or the 'chauvinist' reads it of the 'feminist' reads it. I further suppose that the initial preference orderings of the 'feminist' and the 'chauvinist' upon which they wish to reflect ethically are given by the following:

'feminist': [0, f, c]
'chauvinist': [f, c, 0]

These orderings might be regarded as plausibly fitting the types. The 'feminist' prefers that nobody reads the magazine, but if someone is to read it, he/she prefers it not to be the 'chauvinist' because this will only reinforce the 'chauvinist's' tendency to treat women as objects. The 'chauvinist' finds that the worst outcome is when nobody reads the magazine, but ranks the

---

* This is why the concern with self-respect, understood as an ethical concern, cannot be reduced to individuals, having 'ethical' preferences. Conflicts of the sort discussed here do not produce well-behaved preference orderings.

'feminist' reading the magazine most highly because he/she believes it will help the 'feminist loosen up'.

Now, let us allow for paretianism and liberalism to guide the reflections on these initial preference orderings. To tell the full story: in pursuit of expressive rationality, the two railway travellers consult these ethical principles to decide on what would be a 'good' set of preference orderings to hold in these circumstances. Both principles are potentially relevant here as they propose ways of mediating between two individuals when their preferences conflict. The first offers a consequentialist kind of consideration and says simply that if both prefer x to y, then it is appropriate to rank x more highly than y. The second is a rights principle, and says only that an individual's preference should hold sway when the action involves only that individual: the individual knows best what is in his or her own interest in these circumstances. It is, in effect, an argument about the rights of consenting adults to do what they like in private.

Both principles seem quite unobjectionable at first glance, and they are probably widely held. However, they are also in conflict. Take the liberal line of argument: in the choice between $\{0, c,\}$ the 'chauvinist', as the only interested party, should know what is best for him/her and so decides cP0; in the choice between $\{0, f,\}$ the 'feminist' is the only interested party and so decides 0Pf; combining these two liberal ideas we produce a ranking of cPf. By contrast, the paretian principle notes that both rank fPc, and consequently presses the opposite ordering to the liberal argument. In short, to hold both principles produces an inconsistency because they are in conflict.

The existential approach to the modern dilemma of establishing meaning and purpose, when there is no objective external basis for such meaning, focuses on the latter aspect of the predicament. Its ruthless reflection on the implications of accepting this absence of an objective basis leads to a rejection of the presumption that the project of meaning should be conceived in terms which would remain intelligible to God. The problem is that, by putting the matter in terms of building a secular ethics, as the earlier approach does, God is simply reinvented in another guise: and as such too much is accepted from the *ancien régime*.

Nietzsche is the famous source for this line of reasoning, and much might be said about how his 'superman' and the various prescriptions for 'authenticity' can be built on such a view. They deny any role for ethics, and treat any moral disposition as an affliction of the 'weak'. But there is not much in this for economics, or indeed life, we might suspect. However, there are other strands of the existential literature which are worth drawing out. Two, in particular, combine in the recent work of Rorty (1986).

Rorty (1986) continues to take seriously the idea of meaning and purpose, but it has to be grounded in a recognition that there is no truth as such: it has to be a theory of meaning which makes chance rather than truth 'worthy of determining our fate'. As a first step he sides with Nietzsche in finding that when faced by a world where there is only chance and contingency, with their accompanying arbitrary descriptions, there is only one meaningful thing an individual can do. Since the individual cannot triumph by discovering some enduring truth about morality, the only boundary which can be crossed is between the old and the new. The human life emerges as triumphant 'just insofar as it escapes from inherited descriptions of the contingencies of its existence and finds new descriptions' (p. 12).

However, whereas the Nietzschean emphasis on self-creation leads to the celebration of the poet/superman as one of a small band of people in society capable of transcending their inheritance by making descriptions of their own, Rorty (1986) democratises this creativity by introducing Freud. (For an alternative to Freud which also democratises creativity, see Hobson, 1988.) The virtue of Freud for Rorty is that he starts from the premise that there is only chance and contingency – 'moral consciousness itself develops from repressions which are the product of countless contingencies that never enter experience' – and he offers a different reading of human creativity. This alternative reading makes the Nietzschean type of creativity a part of every individual and, interestingly, also preserves a bridge to the 'old' moral philosophical debate by allowing for this to be an arena in which such creativity might occur (see MacIntyre, 1981, for an example of the use of this bridge).

The first step in the argument is to see how Freud makes self-definition a matter of weaving an idiosyncratic story which connects the contingencies of a personal history.

> The Platonic and Kantian idea of rationality centres on the idea that we need to bring actions under general principles if we are to be moral. Freud, by contrast, suggests that we need to return to the particular: to see particular present situations and options as similar to or different from particular past actions or events. He thinks that only by catching hold of crucial idiosyncratic contingencies in our past are we able to make something worthwhile out of ourselves, to create present selves whom we can respect. . . . He suggested that we praise ourselves by weaving idiosyncratic narratives – case histories, as it were – of our success in self creation, our ability to break free from an idiosyncratic past. He suggests we condemn ourselves for the failure to break free of that past rather than for a failure to live up to universal standards. (p. 12)

The next part of the argument comes from noticing that Freud does not ask us to choose between Kant and Nietzsche, between the moralist and the poet/superman. Neither is a more accurate or correct description of what it is to be human. Both visions provide a vocabulary for adapting one contingency of life to another, for spinning case histories. Of course, they are but two, albeit prominent, vocabularies from many which are the stock of inherited descriptions; to which, incidentally, we must now add Freud. What is important for both (and for Freudian analysis) is the ability to create new descriptions of each life with the vocabulary: to create metaphors in the Davidson sense of new meanings. Of course, we paradigmatically think of the poet as creative in this sense, but it is precisely Freud's point that 'if we look inside the bien-pensant conformist, if we get him on the couch, we will find that he was only dull on the surface'. All of us have the equipment for, and make good use of, fantasy, which is the faculty used in redescribing the contingencies of one's life.

> Seen from this angle, the poet, the person who uses words for this purpose, is just a special case – just somebody who does with inscriptions what other people do with spouses and children, their fellow workers, the tools of their trade . . . the music they listen to, the sports they play or watch. . . . Anything from the sound of a word to the colour of a leaf to the feel of a piece of skin can, as Freud showed us, serve to dramatise and crystallise a human being's sense of identity. (p. 13)

Of course, this capacity for self creation is relatively limited – although one might add that Rorty seems to have done quite a good job on 'reweaving' Freud! The contingencies of our life are what they are; we have only certain vocabularies with which to work. Nor can we stray too far from these vocabularies because every innovation relies on a lot of standard descriptions of the past to gain a purchase. There is necessarily a lot of stage setting in the conventional descriptions of the past from which an innovation draws its contrast. Furthermore, much of this redescription is idiosyncratic. It is a personal fantasy. Some redescriptions catch on, just as some metaphors do in language. Freud's analysis is just such an example; his innovations have become a part of the stock descriptions we use to weave a personal case history. This is perhaps the most a person can make of meaning; for the most part life is 'only a web of relations to be rewoven . . . [and] we shall be content to think of any human life as the always incomplete, yet heroic reweaving of such a web' (p. 15).

There is another way of expressing the constraints on innovation which serves the argument later. The fact that innovation paradoxically requires a good deal of conformity in the form of shared vocabulary if it is to gain a purchase and stand out as something different might be phrased as a conflict which the individual feels between the need for belonging to a group and the need to stick out. It is only through belonging, through sharing a vocabulary with others, that you can define an individuality through innovative individual behaviour but this paradoxically actually sets you apart from the group. This may seem an obvious way to restate the point about innovation, and it will become apparent why we should want to state it in this way when we turn to some of the examples of expressive rationality in economic explanations. But there is a deeper reason why it is not just convenient but it also makes sense to state the point about innovation in this way, which can be found in the argument of the previous chapter. It was suggested there that it was through the inheritance of practices, procedures and institutions that history makes itself felt in the present. Consequently, as these institutions help to define different groups in society, it is possible to express the sense of individuality which comes from breaking with history in terms of the individual need to stick out from groups with which he/she otherwise identifies.

I have spent rather longer on this version of the existential response to the modern dilemma because it is probably less familiar to economists. But by way of a conclusion, I want to draw out a rather similar implication because the prescription of innovation often involves an assessment of conflicting positions. There is frequently more than one way that one might innovate and the choice cannot always be dissolved into the normal instrumental calculus. The problem is that in choosing to be a particular way you are often at the same time choosing the values with which to judge that way of being. (Take, for instance, the multiple self problem from section 6.4. This can be recast as a choice between two different ways of experimenting: self 1 and self 2 are two candidates for experimentation and the problem is that once either has been adopted it will seem from the perspective of that decision to have been the correct choice.) The existential person faces the same difficulty as the ethical: he/she can see the merits of two (or more) positions, but they cannot always be entertained simultaneously and the individual is forced to choose between them with very little to go on. In fact, we might summarise by saying that the expressively rational individual often acts from a position of uncertainty with respect to what values they wish to entertain.

Of course, it should not be forgotten that the vocabulary of the conflict is different and there is an underlying difference in expectation about conflict resolution which is related to those vocabularies. Rorty believes there is only innovation with this kind of destruction and reconstruction, whereas the ethical approach still inclines to the belief that these adjustments represent, on balance, improvements, movements which get us closer to the secular version of heaven on earth, even if that passage is not always smooth or linear.

8.3 Responses to 'modernity'

It is the argument of the previous section that being expressively rational in the 'modern' age makes conflict and uncertainty within the individual a central problem. How, then, do we respond to this conflict, to this uncertainty within the soul (whether it be ethical or experimental)? There are several places that one might go for answers to this question, and what is perhaps surprising is that there is actually a large measure of agreement across a variety of disciplines about what we do in these circumstances.

For instance, from the philosophy of Heidegger to the cultural anthropology of Douglas (1982) to the evidence from cognitive psychology (see Steinbruner 1974), we find that a response to this sort of uncertainty is often bound up with a reliance on shared norms or procedures, ways of doing and valuing things. The precise understanding for why this should be the case varies across disciplines. Heidegger might describe the shift as a move to 'conformity': it avoids 'anxiety' even if it courts a danger of 'inauthenticity'. The cognitive psychologist might talk about 'social corroboration'; and Mary Douglas would discuss the matter in terms of 'fixing meanings through appeals to numbers'. At a purely common-sense level, I suppose the matter can be put quite simply: there is some comfort, if there seems no good way of deciding between the value of this or that, when your actual choice is shared by others.

This description of the role of shared procedures is liable, though, not to do full justice to their contribution. It may seem as if these shared conventions are a contrivance for avoiding facing the uncertainty we all suffer from. Certainly, this is why Heidegger might warn against 'inauthenticity'. But the shared procedures of society surface also with respect to how one might innovate, how one might do something different from the norm. This is perhaps the implicit point which Rorty makes when describing the limits to innovation. And we know from a cursory glance at other cultures that there are shared accepted ways of experimenting and innovating: for example, the drive across the USA and the aboriginal walkabout. Dreyfus (1987) describes a similar view in Heidegger:

> So you probably go on doing the same thing that you did but how you do it changes. You no longer expect to get any deep and final meaning out of life or find any rational grounding for anything. . . . In this authentic activity, Heidegger says, you no longer respond to what he calls the general situation. You respond to the unique situation. . . . Take the carpenter Heidegger talks about. When he puts down his hammer at lunchtime, he could just eat his sausages and sauerkraut, but if there are beautiful flowers blooming outdoors and he is authentic, he does not have to conform with what a respectable carpenter normally does. He can skip lunch and go wander in the flowers. But, it is important to remember that he can do only what one does. He can't take off all those clothes and roll in the flowers. One doesn't do that. (pp. 267–8)

So, a shared set of procedures, a cultural web of beliefs about what is the source of worth, is one aspect of the response to 'modernity'. Of course, there is nothing in this which is particular to 'modernity', Douglas would be quick to remind us. What is special to 'modernity' is the rapid change introduced by making innovation and experimentation *de rigueur*. It is actually very difficult for the 'modern' individual to keep abreast with what ought to be his/her cultural supports.

Procedures are also important at the level of the individual. There are procedures of the mind which arbitrarily fix what is taken to be valuable when conflicts arise. To be specific, there are the sub-intentional causal mechanisms sketched in section 6.6. To this list might be added the box of rhetorical tricks discussed by McCloskey (1983) (see section 2.6), with a special emphasis from the anthropologists on the power of analogies with nature to fix one set of beliefs rather than another.

It is difficult in making these observations not to leave an impression that the 'modern' concern with self-respect turns us into zombies following either shared rules of thumb or individual psychological rules of thumb. But I think this would be the wrong impression for two sorts of reasons. Firstly, if one is self-conscious in the use of procedures of this sort, their use is an acknowledgement of the modern predicament. They only seem to turn us into zombies if we posit some alternative way of resolving these deep conflicts. It is when we make this move that the use of procedures appears as a distorting arrangement. But, if the modern predicament is taken seriously, we live in a world where we do not know what that alternative is, even if it does exist, so this is not the right comparison to be making. Instead, we should think of the use of these shared procedures as the basis for a continuing dialogue about the 'modernist' predicament which we undertake because there is some value in reaching agreement amongst ourselves. In other words, the use of these shared procedures should be seen as part of a communicative response to the 'modern' predicament: we use a shared language and culture to express and debate with others who we are and what we value (see Habermas, 1985–6). It is when we deny their provisional nature and treat them as solutions rather than stepping stones that we suffer from zombie-like inauthenticity.

Secondly, the following of rules of thumb does not provide an exhaustive guide to action. It is a point which has been made before, and it repays making again. The rules never give us the full script for life! There is still scope for individual creativity in the application of a rule, be it a socially shared one or an individual psychological one. Wittgenstein would put this as a point about rules never being fully extensive or exhaustive. But it is perhaps more natural in the context of the development of the argument here to see this as a direct consequence of the artificial way that these procedures contain the conflict. The procedures do not actually reconcile the conflict; they are a means of abatement and this necessarily means that there will be circumstances where the conflict cannot be contained by simply following the rule. They are not solutions to the conflict, otherwise there would not be a state of conflict within the individual: they are a way of proceeding in the world in the presence of conflict. So, new situations are bound to arise which call for amendment to the procedure or the creation of a new procedure if the conflict is to remain abated.

The introduction of judgement is another way of making this vision less zombie like. We often talk about the exercise of judgement when we are faced by apparently irreconcilable conflicts like those of the 'modern' predicament (see Bernstein, 1983, and Hollis, 1987). It is the faculty we use when instrumental calculation can gain no handle on the problem; and we actually respect its use by referring to wisdom rather than knowledge. Wisdom is usually conceived as the attribute of a life's experience of rearranging procedures, of experimenting in the art of constructing self-respect. It is not something that can be reduced to a formula.

Legal decision is often taken as a paradigm of judgement. Again, it brings out the curious kind of resolution which is involved in the exercise of judgement and its historical location, which makes it seem an appropriate skill to associate with the 'modern' predicament. MacIntyre (1981) makes the point nicely when commenting on the Bakke decision of the Supreme Court:

> So the Supreme Court in Bakke both forbade precise ethnic quotas for admission to colleges and universities, but allowed discrimination in favour of previously deprived minority groups. Try to conjure up a set of consistent principles behind such a decision and ingenuity may or may not allow you to find the court not guilty of formal inconsistency. But even to make such an attempt is to miss the point. The Supreme Court in Bakke . . . played the role of a peacemaking or truce-keeping body by negotiating its way through an impasse of conflict, not by invoking our shared moral first principles. For our society as a whole has none. (pp. 235–6)

If the Bakke decision makes any kind of sense, it will be found in a historical understanding of the nature of the conflict at the time of the decision. It represents precisely the kind of updating, in the light of historical experience, of a juggling act between incommensurable positions which I have associated with the 'modern' predicament.

Finally, if these references have not been sufficient to dispel the image of an expressively rational zombie, consider the natural scientist, the model for Kelly's (1955) view of the human concern to make sense of the world. In Kuhn's (1970) analysis of the practice of science, he distinguishes two sorts of scientific activity. The one is 'normal' science, a kind of application of the rules or procedures of a particular research programme or paradigm. The other is science involving new paradigms and paradigm displacement. This is much rarer in the natural sciences than 'normal' science: it involves a choice between incommensurable views and requires the type of art of decision making which we associate with the exercise of judgement. In short, Kuhn's picture of the natural scientist corresponds closely to the image of the expressively rational person that I have been developing. He/she finds meaning in his/her work through following procedures, because these procedures enable among other things communication with a community of scholars which establishes a shared standard about what is worthy, and through the creative exercise of judgement when the procedures do not offer specific guidance.

8.4 Consumption Behaviour

A typical economist's reaction to the discussion of the previous three sections might be that, while it touches on something which is very human, it is not the kind of thing that need detain the economist. We may ponder about meaning and purpose now and then, and indeed we may skirt around the issues in odd dinner conversations or over a drink in a pub. We may have ethical preferences which summarise some of these beliefs, but they are only expressed in these odd discussions or periodically via the ballot box. Most of the time, when people are acting in the economy, it is 'business as usual' and that is where economics with its instrumental and procedural rationality comes into play: we can leave the expressive to the philosophers.

There is a certain appeal to this prospective division of labour with the philosophers, but it would be a mistaken attitude for economics to adopt. Whilst it is true that there are few occasions for debating modernism and dinners and pubs are not the hub of the economy, existential concerns remain central to life and this is why we actually use other, non-linguistic, forms for expressing what we regard as worthy about ourselves. And as these feelings about ourselves are part of a more general cosmology, we also express ideas about what we think is important, what is good and bad and so on. In particular, and this is why economics cannot set expressive rationality on one side, we use goods and services symbolically. Commodities stand for and mean something which stretches beyond their literal or physical properties. As was hinted at in section 6.3, and in the earlier quotation from Rorty, and as Douglas and Isherwood (1980) suggest most powerfully, goods are used for communication:

> Forget that commodities are good for eating, clothing, and shelter, forget their usefulness and try instead the idea that commodities are good for thinking; treat them as a nonverbal medium for the human creative faculty. (p. 62)

Of course, the idea that goods are non-verbal forms of communication through which we express our ideas about what is good and bad has an obvious relevance in some cases. The decision not to purchase South African oranges is well recognised as an expression of opposition to apartheid. Likewise in California in the 1970s, drinking Gallo wine and eating grapes and a particular type of lettuce indicated something very precise about your politics. But Douglas and Isherwood (1980) and Douglas (1977) go further than this by arguing that these are not isolated actions; there is a wholesale symbolic use of commodities:

> Consumption decisions are a vital source of the culture of the time . . . consumption is that very sphere in which culture is generated. Let me give you an example. The housewife comes home with her shopping basket. There are some things in it that she knows she is going to keep for her household, some for the father, and some she puts aside for the children. Other things she has bought for the special pleasure of her guests whom she is going to invite into her house. And then she is going to make decisions about what parts of the house she is going to invite people into, and what parts of them are available to one degree of outsiders, what parts are available to a more intimate group . . . and she makes decisions about how often she throws open her house . . . as well as how much of it, and what she offers – if it is music, or if it is food and drink, or if it is just drink and conversation. These sorts of choice are the mainspring of culture. They are not trivial choices at all, they are absolutely fundamental for the whole life of a people. In the end you should see the consumer's choices as moral judgements about everything: about what a man is, about what a woman is, how a man ought to treat his aged parents, how much of a start in life he ought to give his children, how he expects to grow old . . . All these are consumption choices and I have picked them to show you they are not at all trivial. . . . (pp. 292–3)

The hard-nosed economist might be forced to accept that goods are used communicatively as part of the response to the 'modern' predicament, and yet still doubt that much of the analysis of consumer behaviour turns on this observation. There are two remarkable books by Earl, (1983, 1986) which ought to persuade even the die-hard that there is something to be gained from these observations. For the moment, I shall mention some of the inferences drawn from Douglas and Isherwood (1980).

One which has already been noted in section 6.3 is how the communicative aspects of consumer decisions underline the relevance of interdependence, giving particular force to bandwagon effects and the like. A specific example in the applied literature where this insight has been used is in the explanation of the appearance of lagged dependent variables or lagged adjustments in aggregate consumption functions (see Deaton and Muellbauer, 1980, where the connection with Douglas and Isherwood is explicitly made):

This patterning of behaviour by households on other households takes time, particularly since there are recognition lags in perceiving what is the behaviour with which the individual identifies. These lags in interactions result, when aggregated, in current purchase levels being dependent on past ones. (p. 330)

Douglas and Isherwood also offer an explanation of why the savings ratio might vary across countries. In turn, this yields an understanding of why the fears about satiation and oversaving in the post-war period have proved unfounded. These fears were typically based on a desire-led model of consumption. If you begin with fixed desires and allow for economic growth, you are bound to get satiation at some point. But, once you also start with symbolic meaning in consumption and admit that change and innovation may be central to the construction of symbolic meaning for individuals, then the limits to consumption seem to vanish. Much like the holy grail, you can go on searching (i.e. consuming) for ever.

They also develop an analysis of how commodities are transformed from luxuries to necessities. There will always be luxuries because rank must be marked, they argue. However, not all luxuries filter down and become necessities as economic growth makes them more generally available. The future necessities which are drawn from today's luxuries are those which are what they refer to as goods 'with periodicity relieving properties'. Consumption activities have different periodicities, i.e. frequencies with which they occur. So, for instance, the activities around eating are high frequency. Shopping, cooking and washing must be undertaken with a high frequency whereas 'listening to music, has no such necessary high frequency. If you are engaged in high frequency activities then you have little opportunity to break off and do something different. High frequency activities are a source of inflexibility and bringing these inflexible periodicities under control is what rising income is all about in Douglas and Isherwood (1980). Put slightly differently, they are suggesting that today's luxury commodities which offer greater flexibility in the use of time, commodities which liberate people from a tight routine, are those which are seized on with rising income and become tomorrow's necessities.

Finally, Douglas and Isherwood throw a new light on advertising and the kind of information which is transmitted through this medium. One of the crucial pieces of information which is conveyed is who, i.e what type of person, consumes the product. In other words, they give information on the symbolic currency of the commodity and not just its physical properties. This helps explain why this is sometimes referred to as a period of lifestyle advertising (see Leiss, Kline and Jhally, 1986) because commodities are located in particular lifestyles. It also helps explain why successful advertising uses 'likeable' people to convey the message (see Lea, Tarpy and Webley 1987) and why the framing of the message is carefully constructed to bolster the self-esteem of the targeted group, and, indeed, why the activity of marketing more generally pays particular attention to the self-respect of the prospective purchasers (see Earl, 1983, 1986, where for example he draws our attention to the decision to leave eggs out of cake mixes because the need to add fresh eggs was thought to encourage the self-respect of prospective purchasers/cooks). Finally, it suggests another reason why some commodities might be heavily advertised, because symbolic meaning can change even when the physical properties of the commodity are unchanged and this change in symbolic meaning must be transmitted to consumers. Indeed, this may well help explain why some commodities (i.e. soft drinks) are heavily advertised when orthodox theories have difficulty explaining the phenomenon (see Schmalensee, 1987).

Plainly, altering the symbolic value of a commodity can be just as good a marketing strategy as changing its physical properties. And put like this, advertising which is aimed at altering symbolic values may make good business sense, but it also lends weight to the thought that advertising is manipulative because it creates wants. However, the perspective of expressive rationality also presents another side to this issue. People may exhibit complicity in such popular cultural change, because it offers opportunities for individual self-definition through innovation and change – again, this offers a different angle on the Scitovsky (1976) observation that we value change. Take, for instance, our alternating attitude to wooden toilet seats. This need not reflect some pathology or an advertisers' plot. In the 'modern' world this sort of circulation of values enables individuals to gain self-respect through the thought that they have in some degree created themselves.

I conclude this section with a final example from the economics literature which involves a sense of self-respect, where this sense specifically comes from social corroboration. This is Akerlof (1980). He argues that people do not just want to be rich, they want to be rich and famous. 'Being famous' here stands for a sense of self-respect; and people gain this feeling by following a social custom, where the sense of worth so derived depends positively on the degree of compliance within the community. Among other things, the model is used to explain why wage cutting may not happen despite the existence of unemployment.

8.5 Decision Making under Uncertainty

There is a growing formal literature on decision making in risky situations. It is a response to the accumulating empirical evidence which is at odds with the predictions of expected utility theory (see for instance the Allais paradox in section 6.4).

One strand of this literature, regret theory, was briefly discussed in section 6.4. Individuals in that theory work with an amended utility function which takes into account the likely regrets the individual will suffer when taking one course of action rather than another available one. As presented by Loomes and Sugden (1982), this is an observation on human behaviour which has some intuitive plausibility. But that is it: there is nothing more to commend the theory at the outset. However, I would want to argue that there is something more to it, which should command our attention. As I indicated in section 6.4, it can be regarded as a process of weighting two conflicting selves: the Promethean and the Epimethean selves. From this vantage point, the weighting is an act of judgement between the conflicting claims of two ways of making decisions in risky settings. Both seem plausible ways for deciding such matters to the individual, but they can conflict and the individual is called upon to exercise judgement. In short, regret theory could be regarded as an example of expressive rationality, because an 'uncertainty in the soul' has been added to the risk present in the decision environment.

Levi's work (1984, 1986) is another strand from this literature. The connection with expressive rationality here is even more straightforward because Levi refers to his theory as one of decision making in the presence of unresolved conflicts. The unresolved conflicts arise because of the presence of uncertainty (as opposed to risk). There are a number of probability distributions which could consistently be assigned to the outcomes associated with an action set, and there is no reason to prefer one to another. Alternatively, there are a number of consistent utility functions which could be used to rank outcomes, but there is no reason to choose between them. In these circumstances, he argues, expected utility theory gives no guidance for action and so you are forced back to some other criteria. He favours security and a maximin decision rule, or more generally a lexicographic maximin rule. This is exactly what I would call a procedural rule; and Levi demonstrates how its application might explain the Allais paradox and other pieces of anomalous experimental evidence.

There is one final reference that is obvious, but which ought to be made all the same. Unfortunately, considerations of space dictate that it must remain a reference only: this is Shackle. His specific theory of decision making has been closely scrutinised and has been criticised because it seems *ad hoc* in its specification of how people respond to uncertainty. Undoubtedly, the same criticism can be levelled against Loomes and Sugden, and Levi. But this criticism misses the point completely. The point is that if the conflicts which characterise genuine situations of uncertainty are taken seriously, there are only *ad hoc* ways of responding. *Ad hoc*ery, as the critics would have it, is a way of life; and long may it be so because it speaks to something quite fundamental about the human condition. It is, of course, Shackle's great merit that his analysis of decision making was always directly keyed into this wider vision of what it is to be a person.

I ought to add that in using the term *ad hoc* I am following the typical critic's usage in associating it with anything which cannot be reduced to instrumental rationality. An endorsement of *ad hoc*ery does not therefore amount to an 'anything goes' position. It is just that what is or is not *ad hoc* cannot be decided in advance through consulting instrumental rationality alone. Whether a particular decision rule ought to command our respect will depend instead on wider considerations, like whether it accords with a feature of expressive rationality, and like the support it receives from the psychological and sociological literatures and from the evidence emerging from experimental economics. And it is in the nature of these things that rules will change with history, so that the empirical support is historically contingent.

8.6 The Entrepreneur and Intrapreneurship

The entrepreneur has stood for many different things in the history of economic thought. Schumpeter (1934) famously treated him/her as the gambler who bought a new invention to the marketplace: he/she had a talent for exploiting an opportunity which had in all likelihood been created by someone else's innovation. For Hayek (1937), entrepreneurship is a more general capacity for acquiring and using information, while Leibenstein (1968) focuses on the ability to avoid inefficiencies within organisations. What is common to all these accounts of the entrepreneur is a particular skill for making decisions when the ordinary calculus of the instrumentally rational agent cannot gain a hold on the problem. Principally, in cases of entrepreneurship, it is a lack of information which undoes the instrumental calculation and entrepreneurship fills the gap. As such it sits uneasily with neoclassical economics because neoclassical economics seems to need such a 'person' if there is to be an explanation of how there are forces which promote an equilibrium and disturb it through the introduction of new technologies and the like, and yet it cannot explain this behaviour in its own terms.

Casson (1982, 1987) has recently described this particular capacity for decision making in terms of entrepreneurial judgement: 'The entrepreneur is defined as someone who specialises in taking judgemental decisions about the allocation of scarce resources. The essence of a judgemental decision is that there is no decision rule that can be applied that is both obviously correct and involves the use of freely available information.' (1987, p. 151)

In form at least, Casson's concept of 'judgement' is substantially the same as the one which was introduced in section 8.3. The incoherence which the entrepreneur faces is not exactly the same as that which arises from conflicting moral principles, but it is closely related to the problem of innovation and experimentation under the existential approach. In both instances, a coherence is created through the application of 'judgement': the central human capacity for making sense when there is no yardstick or rule which can be applied, for bridging the unbridgeable and acting.

This similarity is even plainer if we reflect on historical explanations which focus on the emergence of entrepreneurship. There it is typically argued (see Weber, 1976) that such capacity for judgemental decision making surfaces in cultures which stress individual autonomy. And this was precisely how I started developing the theme of expressive rationality. It was the concern for an individual identity and self-esteem that comes from reflecting and taking your preferences to be your own which set the modern problem and served to introduce the concept of 'judgement'. It is by appreciating these more general roots of entrepreneurship that we can understand Casson's (1987) further suggestion that 'the theory of the entrepreneur . . . is not the last step which renders the conventional theory of value complete, but the first step towards an economic theory which forms part of a wider integrated body of social science' (p. 153). In terms of the argument in this book, it does this by licensing expressive rationality.

In fact, recent discussions of entrepreneurship have been explicitly based on recognising that the attribute is one which is generally shared. This contrasts with the earlier treatments of entrepreneurship.

Traditionally, entrepreneurship has been regarded as a rather special skill which only a gifted few enjoy. There are the likes of Henry Ford with the blinding insight of mass production techniques and George Mestral whose mind leapt from the activity of removing burrs from trousers to the invention of velcro. But the message was: these people are not found on street corners; they are a rare species. Indeed, Schumpeter was extremely worried that the rise of the modern bureaucratic, corporate form would prove so inimical to entrepreneurs that they would be snuffed out. His reasons were straightforward. The hallmark of bureaucratic organisations was supposed to be the commitment to instrumental decision making. Such organisations are supposed to 'work' precisely because they do not allow conflicts to surface over ends; they reduce everything to 'technical'/ instrumental questions which are solved with the appropriate routines or procedures for means/ends decision making. There is no room for the wayward spirit who sits outside these routines, who breaks the rules, who addresses the conflicts between ends.

From the bureaucratic perspective, the management of motivation becomes a matter of manipulating the workforce. Management is about getting the decision context right, so that conflicts over ends do not surface.

You 'motivate' the workforce with an appropriate set of procedural blinkers. Not surprisingly, this leads management to build ever more byzantine corporate structures. As the world becomes more complicated and the possibilities for conflict more numerous, so the organisation grows in complexity with procedures and structures which are designed to cover any contingency which might befall the organisation. It is a Kafkaesque world which is created by the modern bureaucracy and the entrepreneurial spirit is quickly broken by it.

This traditional view of bureaucracies is so palpably false that MacIntyre (1981) refers to it as a 'moral fiction'. Conflicts between ends cannot be dissolved with a managerial sleight of hand; not all decision making can be reduced to the means/ends variety so praised by the traditional theorist of bureaucratic corporations. Whatever else, God was not an administrator, and it is nothing more than a moral fiction to pretend in this vein that managers are his apostles. In contrast, the recent 'cult of excellence'/ intrapreneuring literature sides with MacIntyre and turns this traditional wisdom on bureaucracies and entrepreneurship on its head.

This literature has attempted to distil the experience of the most successful US corporations into a theory of the determinants of entrepreneurship within corporations – sometimes referred to as intrapreneurship. In effect, the theory which emerges from this is based on the assumption that people are expressively rational. This is not the precise language of the famous Peters and Waterman (1982) bestseller, but it comes very close; and again the form of the argument is almost identical with that advanced at the beginning of this chapter. It goes something like this.

It begins by suggesting that the individual is built on a contradictory dualism: 'he needs to be a part of something and stick out'. To be more precise, in the corporate context, 'We desperately need meaning in our lives and will sacrifice a great deal to institutions that will provide meaning for us. We simultaneously need independence, to feel as though we are in charge of our destinies, and to have an ability to stick out.' (p. 56)

There will be more than a familiar ring to this! The argument then turns on a move which is a bit like the Rorty use of Freud's democratisation of the creative capacity. 'Excellence' can be generated in a corporation through a 'higher level of contribution from the "average" man' (sic) (p. 51). People are basically creative. We all have this capacity for 'judgement' because this is what gaining self-respect through individuation is about. Hence, if you want a successful corporation you must work with this grain of human nature. The project of a successful corporation is to tap into this basic impulse by encouraging creativity to surface in public actions at work rather than just in private fantasies/actions outside the workplace. It does this by recognising, consciously or unconsciously, that people will only expose themselves publicly in this way if they 'feel good about themselves' in the first place. The generation and preservation of self-respect is no easy thing, however, because we search for it in the contradictory space of both wishing to belong to and to stick out from the group. It is the old Groucho Marx syndrome of not wanting to belong to a club which would have you as a member; and the excellent corporation has found a way of laughing with Groucho all the way to the bank. In short, the excellent corporation is one which attends to the self-respect of its employees through a careful management of the dualism upon which this self-respect is constructed.

To make this more concrete in a way which draws out the distinction from traditional instrumentally rational approaches, consider one of the many examples cited by Peters and Waterman (1982), the case where there is the possibility of opportunistic behaviour by a part of the organisation. Suppose that the instrumentally rationally trained management perceives a potential conflict with its sales department because the sales department need to expend effort in their activity and so they are likely not to perform their activity well if left to their own discretion since they will wish to minimise their efforts. The instrumental management's response is to 'motivate' the sales department, by taking the discretion out of the situation through the imposition of high sales targets. Why then, ask Peters and Waterman, do the most successful corporations actually set very low sales targets? Their answer is that people perform better when they feel good about themselves, and most research points to positive reinforcement as a source of self-respect while negative reinforcement undermines self-respect. The virtue of low sales targets is the ample opportunity they afford for positive reinforcements, while high sales targets are a recipe for a dose of negative reinforcement and the generation of low self-respect.

Another example which focuses more closely on the dualism itself concerns the organisational form of successful corporations. They are, apparently, typically characterised, not by the Kafkaesque structures which might be expected from an evolving instrumental rationality, but rather by what is referred to as a 'loose–tight' fit: 'Excellent companies are both centralised and decentralised. For the most part they have pushed autonomy down to the shop floor or the product development team. On the other hand they are fanatic centralists around a few core values.' (p. 15)

Again the virtue of this arrangement is that it straddles the dualism neatly without denying either aspect. Their discussion of how these central values are conveyed and kept alive is also interesting because it involves recognising a rich in-house corporate culture where myths and stories play a crucial role in developing and sustaining these core values, thus reinforcing the Casson comment on how entrepreneurship does not complete orthodox theory but serves to relocate it in the wider social sciences.

8.7 Cognitive Dissonance

The next illustration of where the ideas of expressive rationality have surfaced implicitly is Akerlof and Dickens (1982), who use cognitive dissonance theory. They build a formal model where workers' evaluation of the hazards of working in a hazardous industry are revised downwards after the experience of working in such industries. The belief that the person is sensible and rational collides with the belief that the industry is hazardous, and the dissonance is removed by filtering out the evidence on the hazards. The result of this process is the sub-optimal use of protective equipment in hazardous industries when it becomes available.

They give a range of further illustrations where economic explanations might benefit from an application of cognitive dissonance theory. One concerns the economics of crime, and it brings out clearly the difference from a conventional instrumental account. Tullock (1974) is the standard bearer for the latter: 'Most economists who give serious thought to the problem of crime immediately come to the conclusion that punishment will indeed deter crime. The reason is perfectly simple. . . . If you increase the cost of something, less will be consumed. Thus, if you increase the cost of committing a crime, there will be fewer crimes. pp. 104–5)'

Evidence from the cognitive dissonance research yields a different interpretation, making Tullock, at best, only partially correct. Typically, this research shows that individual beliefs only change to remove cognitive dissonance when people cannot find any strong external reason for the action they are taking which is contributing to the dissonance. So, when you find yourself 'unconsciously' upholding the law, you are more likely to develop internal reasons for obeying the law when punishments are mild compared with when there are large punishments because large punishments provide a strong external reason for such legal behaviour. Consequently, the proposal for increasing punishments, whilst deterring crime, may not be the most effective way of achieving this aim. Given the costs of law enforcement, a more effective way of fighting crime may well be through encouraging internal reasons, self-motivation for obeying the law. Yet, it is precisely the growth of this motivation which will be undercut by the creation of a significant external reason for obeying the law in the form of large punishments.

This example has some relevance for the earlier discussion of 'excellence' in the corporation and the contrasting approaches to conflicts within the organisation. The high sales target solution is the direct analogue to Tullock's strategy of high punishment, and we can now appreciate a further reason why this is unlikely to be the strategy associated with 'excellence'. Within the corporation this is never going to be very effective because you cannot hope to specify targets to cover every contingency where such conflicts might arise. A corporation which can encourage its workforce to take on the objectives of the corporation will always perform better than one which moulds such conformity with a welter of finely tuned incentives, because this general identification with the corporation's objectives will apply to all settings and not just those that are covered by the high sales targets and the like. Of course, it goes further than this because this difference generates a completely different set of attitudes to change and flexibility. New settings and new opportunities are very threatening to a highly structured corporation precisely because the conflicts which are suppressed by the carefully calculated system of incentives will surface in novel situations for which the structure was not designed, whereas new situations pose no such problems for corporations which have encouraged a perspective of an identity of interest between the corporation and its component parts. Consequently, it would not be surprising to find that the corporation which has encouraged this perspective of mutuality is quicker to respond to change than the more structured variety.

8.8 Trust and Co-operation

A final example is drawn from economic explanations which rely on agents who are, broadly speaking, ethically motivated. This is one possible way of cashing in the idea of expressive rationality, and it completes the list of illustrations.

There are many situations where people seem to act in ways that can only be explained by allowing some sort of moral principle or allegiance to something other than self-interested preferences to motivate action. Akerlof (1983) gives a series of examples of such behaviour under the title of 'loyalty filters'. The argument is a familiar one: it revolves around the need for trust in situations which are particularly susceptible to opportunistic behaviour because it is impossible to write fully contingent contracts. Without such trust, either exchange in such situations is forgone or some second best arrangement must be accepted. Akerlof (1983) argues that such trust is generated by 'loyalty filters', i.e. the unconscious or conscious inculcation of non-self-interested values in children by their parents (and others). These values then act as signals to people who share these values that the person can be trusted, and the exchange proceeds unhampered by the doubts and worries about opportunism.

So, for instance, we have a model of how Quakers who typically rank low in terms of instrumental rationality, as far as the satisfaction of self-interested preferences are concerned because they subscribe to co-operation and honesty in all circumstances, are nevertheless one of the wealthiest minority groups in the USA. The Quakers can be trusted by virtue of these non-self-interested attributes and this enables them to make exchanges which are not available to the purely self-interested because it dissolves problems of opportunism. Of course, it is crucial here that these values stand above self-interested preferences. If they should be perceived as mere adjuncts to self-interest, playing a subordinate role, then they could not function in this way because once they become extensions of self-interest they fail to dissolve the problem of opportunism. Instead, they become liable to the interpretation of being part of an opportunistic deceit. The same point has been made, in effect, in the earlier discussion of multiple selves in section 6.4. The virtue of expressive rationality is exactly that it creates another dimension for individuals which can act in this manner by standing above ordinary self-interested preferences.

It is possible to generalise the role of expressive rationality here to the class of outcomes which Elster (1983b) refers to as 'states which are essentially by-products'. He has in mind states which by their very definition cannot be willed. You cannot act to achieve them because it undermines the objective that the action was designed to achieve. The example of love as a project was given in section 6.5; 'trying to be spontaneous' or 'trying to impress' are further examples of such self-defeating objectives. None of these may seem especially economic activities! But wanting to co-operate in a prisoner's dilemma game because it helps to satisfy self-interested preferences better is a perfect example, much closer to the economic home, of just such a state which cannot be willed.

Co-operation often poses a problem for self-interested individuals because the game of co-operation is a prisoner's dilemma. In section 5.4, it was argued that mere repetition of the game was not sufficient to remove the sub-optimal Nash equilibrium of the one-shot version of the game. It takes an additional belief either that the game will go on for ever with some small probability or that there is some positive probability that your opponent plays a non-instrumentally dominant strategy of defection. Again the virtue of recognising expressive rationality from an explanatory point of view is that it gives some foundation for the belief that your opponent might not play the instrumentally dominant strategy. He/she could for instance be guided by an ethical principle which valued co-operation highly.

There are innumerable examples of co-operative behaviour in economics, which fly in the face of the prisoner's dilemma, from membership of trades unions to 'tipping'. Hence, it is extremely useful to have a rationality framework which admits an explanation of such phenomena.

8.9 The Instrumental, The Procedural and The Expressive

This section is concerned with the relationship which exists between the three types of rationality which have been distinguished in this part of the book. As such, although the focus is still on expressive rationality in the 'modern' world, it constitutes something resembling a conclusion for the whole of the second part of the book.

It will be clear from the development of the argument about what is meant by expressive rationality that it need not undercut explanations which work through instrumental rationality. Instrumental rationality is still in place. In fact, it almost has to be in place if expressive rationality is to gain a purchase: otherwise why would people worry about whether some ends were worthy of being pursued if action had nothing to do with satisfying those ends. So, the expressive dimension of rationality merely opens a range of further explanations, rather than undermining those already offered by instrumental accounts. Some of the range of those explanations can be gauged from the examples in the previous five sections.

However, it may be tempting to go further than this on behalf of instrumental rationality, and claim that the expressive can be reduced to the instrumental with a suitable choice of the objectives which action is designed to satisfy. All we need is an objective of self-respect, and instrumental rationality has snuffed out the claims of expressive rationality. Although this may be a tempting move, it would be a mistaken one.

There are several ways in which the error of making this elision might be put. It is worth making some of them explicit because economists, by and large, do not recognise the particular claims of expressive rationality. Indeed, it is a standard move in the defence of neoclassical economics to redefine the objective function to include what otherwise appears as aberrant behaviour (see Becker and Stigler, 1977, and the discussion in sections 6.4, 6.5 and 6.6).

The first is an appeal to pragmatic considerations. It works backwards and notes that much of the explanatory power of expressive rationality, as in the last section, is gained by the possibility of putting distance between actions which are expressive and those that are instrumental. If you now close that gap, then you rule out that type of explanation. Granted the arguments of the previous section(s), this would be unfortunate, to say the least.

Fortune cannot always be relied on, however; and even if the consequences are uncomfortable, this would not constitute a decisive reason against the collapse of one into the other. A stronger reason for not eliding expressive with instrumental rationality is to be found in the discussion in the second and third sections. Put briefly, the conclusion from there is that the project of generating self-respect involves us in what might be kindly described as a mess. Either we are torn by ethical dilemmas and/or we are always trying something new: what coherence there might be to the preferences we hold at a moment in time is consequently very fragile. It relies on either arbitrary procedures of the mind, like cognitive dissonance removal mechanisms, and/or equally arbitrary social practices which throw up groups for us to communicate and reach temporary agreement with.

These procedures do not create coherence in the sense of a reconciliation of the conflicts which would enable us to recast the decision making procedure as satisfying some expanded set of preference orderings for two reasons. Firstly, they are a source of decision making in the presence of fundamental conflicts within the soul. They do not remove the inconsistencies; they merely provide a rule for acting in the presence of them. Witness Loomes and Sugden's agents using judgement in the face of regret: their objectives cannot be captured by a well-behaved set of preference orderings which they can then be construed as setting about satisfying. Secondly, it is precisely because there is no genuine reconciliation that anomalies get thrown up and we are forced to amend and innovate in our use of procedures. This means that self-respect cannot be slotted into a framework which requires well-ordered preferences because what is involved in the construction of self-respect is precisely an attack on any passing order of this sort. Self-respect is built on a subversion of the very ends which need to be in place if we are to talk about instrumental rationality.

This can be stated slightly differently, in a way which echoes an earlier theme in the discussion. It does not make sense to talk about action as being designed to maximise self-respect because there is not the information available which would allow the calculation of optimal actions in pursuit of this objective. It is the old conundrum of not being able to specify what would be the optimal acquisition of information when there is uncertainty. The description of what is involved in the notion of self-respect is premised on precisely this insight: it is a search for foundations in a world which has been deprived of them. And just as a model of optimisation broke down in the face of inadequate information, so does any attempt to turn self-respect into an objective which can thereby reduce expressive rationality to the instrumental variety. You need a different vocabulary to describe action which is motivated by expressive considerations because the language of optimisation cannot cope with it.

What is missing in the means-to-given-ends vocabulary of instrumental rationality is the open-ended nature of action. It is a process sense of rationality or a 'doing' rather than an 'achieving' model of human agency which we need (see also Habermas, 1985–6, who makes it a point about being communicative rather than purposive). One final way of describing the open-ended nature of some actions, which brings out why it cannot be reduced to instrumental rationality, is to say that expressively rational acts are ends in themselves. Acts which are ends in themselves are ones which are valued for the 'doing' rather than the 'achieving'. But the moment that you conceive of acts as ends in themselves, the space on which instrumental rationality went to work has disappeared. We are operating along a different dimension, and we need another concept of rationality to go with it: the expressive.

Putting matters like this helps to clarify further the relation between expressive and procedural rationality. In particular, it makes the following of procedures a genuinely more human activity than might at first seem to be the case. In loose terms, if expressive rationality is about 'doing' and procedures are guides to 'doing', then procedural rationality cannot be all that bad!

It is worth developing this thought a little more because it would be easy to have a rather more jaundiced view of procedures as some alien intrusion into the world of the individual. Consider the argument which initially placed procedural rationality on the agenda. It was the inability to explain institutions and information sets in exclusively instrumental terms which necessitated the introduction of procedures as a separate category and a new kind of rationality to go with them. Procedural rationality became a mark of our historical contingency because ultimately the procedures with which we operate could only be explained by invoking a particular historical narrative.

Viewed from this perspective, procedures might be regarded as some kind of unfortunate, albeit unavoidable, intrusion of history in the present or the grafting of something social onto the individual. Chapter 7 made it plain that this was not the only way of reading the relationship between the individual and society's shared procedures, but it is not really until this chapter that we can see why the intrusion view is grossly misleading.

The shared procedures of a society are crucial in facilitating communication in what is a continuing debate, engaged in by expressively rational agents, over what are the sources of value in our world. They are the building blocks for the exercise of expressive rationality. They are quite simply a resource we could not do without, unless we wish to deny an essential part of our nature. Indeed, it is rather more of a reciprocal relationship than this because the presence of procedures is actually an important ingredient in what I have taken to be the 'modernist' project.

To bring this out, let us go back to one of the crucial turns in the argument of this book which came from the observation in the discussion of procedural rationality that any actual shared set of procedures is likely to be arbitrary, in the sense that any of a number of such procedures once in place could have fulfilled the same co-ordinating function. The actual consequences of using one set of procedures rather than another are not the same, so there is a choice here which we can exercise collectively and which we must face unless we are to concede some priority to whatever history has left us. It is unclear what the independent claim of history might amount to here, and in so far as these shared procedures contribute to the development of the preferences of the individuals who use them (see section 6.3), then this choice is a part of the 'modernist' project. The choice of shared institutions is a part of the choice of who to be, which I have associated with the achievement of autonomy and self-respect.

In other words, once some reasons for playing the game are made internal to the game, then the recognition that there is a choice of which rules to use in the game is at the same time an acknowledgement that individuals face a choice of who they are to be. And it is this choice which lies at the heart of being expressively rational in the 'modern' age. Of course, this is not the only reason for choice. The point is to tie procedures more intimately with expressive rationality. It is not just that they are a crucial resource in responding to the uncertainty of how to choose, they also help to establish that there is a domain of choice.* In effect, the argument about the arbitrary nature of procedures is a particular example of the more general epistemic argument which set the stage for expressive rationality. In this particular case, what is demonstrated by the conclusion of arbitrariness is that the individual's preferences cannot be 'objectively' grounded in appeals to instrumental rationality alone. This strategy for gaining 'objectivity' will not work.

There is one final observation to be squeezed out of the nexus between the procedural and the expressive. It will be recalled that I linked, albeit somewhat loosely, procedural rationality with functional explanations and this complemented the intentional explanations generated by instrumental rationality. One problem with functional explanations concerned a possible presumption of an inadmissible teleology. Procedures were helpful here in substituting a teleonymy. Expressive rationality offers further support. It opens up the possibility, at least, of a 'true interest' variety of functional explanation. It is only a possibility because it would only make sense to talk of true interest if one accepted the ethical approach to the creation of self-respect.

Nevertheless, it would be a teleological functional explanation, where the teleology was perfectly admissible because it referred to the purposes

---

* This same argument might be made more directly with respect to the procedures of the mind if the choice of who to be is cast as a choice between multiple selves which is 'temporarily' resolved through the use of procedures which coordinate the 'actions' of each self. Any set of procedures might fulfil this function, and the individual in recognising the arbitrary quality of any particular set of procedures is recognising that there is a choice of who to be.

of individuals. It would remain a functional rather than an intentional explanation because the 'true' interests of the individual are not known to the individual. By definition, we do not know our 'true' interests under modernism; but those 'true interests' could still guide our selection of procedures. To balance this thought on behalf of the existential approach to 'modernity', I conclude by noting that just as true interests could provide a dynamic for the evolution of procedures, the accent on innovation and experimentation is also responsible for introducing a dynamism, albeit one which cannot be presumed to have any direction. There is only innovation and experimentation with this approach: it serves no greater goal (see the comment at the end of section 6.2).

8.10 Conclusion

This chapter completes the discussion of rationality and explanation in this part of the book. It has two purposes: to introduce the third kind of rationality used in social science explanation – expressive rationality – and to illustrate its use in economics.

Expressive rationality is the last and probably least familiar type of rationality. It reminds us that we sometimes act because the act is an end in itself. We are a 'doing' species as well as an 'achieving' one because our rationality leads us to recognise the uncertainty which must be entertained with respect to belief. Although less familiar, a range of examples of where it has been used, albeit implicitly, in economic explanations has been given. These ought to be enough to suggest that it is not an insignificant contribution to the explanatory canon of economics. Its deeper importance to economics perhaps comes through its intimate relationship to procedural rationality, sketched in the last section. This is apparent in the next part of the book when I turn to prescription in economics.

Let me conclude this chapter with a further illustration of the symbiotic relation between expressive and procedural rationality. It has the additional virtue of tidying up some unfinished business.

Towards the end of the introduction, when I sketched what was in store for instrumental rationality and neoclassical economics in this part of the book, I somewhat facetiously threw down a challenge to neoclassical economics – could it provide an explanation of laughter? The tone of the challenge was definitely tinged by a doubt that neoclassical economics could respond. To make the challenge something more than a cheap rhetorical trick, it is perhaps incumbent on me to give some idea about how an explanation might be advanced once expressive and procedural rationality are in place.

Douglas (1975) is again the source for guidance on how this might be done. This time it is her explicitly anthropological research which we can draw upon. She blends an account of jokes from Bergson, Freud and her anthropological analysis of culture. The common theme from both Bergson and Freud is that a joke is seen as an attack upon control. For instance, in Freud, it is when the normal monitoring system goes on holiday that the unconscious 'is allowed to bubble up without restraint, hence the sense of enjoyment and freedom'. This attack on control is then located in a culture where a complicated architecture of procedures and practices establishes a variety of public conventions, groups and institutions. The 'control' is the set of those conventions and institutions and a joke works by exploiting the cracks or inconsistencies which exist in that social system. Whereas the social conventions present the patterns of life as inescapable, 'the message of the joke is that they are escapable' (p. 103). The joke disorganises. But it does not do this in an unstructured way; it relies upon the cracks in the existing conventions, the paradoxes and the inconsistencies. 'If there is no joke in the social structure then no other joking can appear' (p. 98) is how Douglas puts it. This is what distinguishes an obscenity from a joke. Both present an alternative vision. 'Both consist of the intrusion of one meaning on another, but whereas the joke discloses a hidden meaning under the appearance of the first, the obscenity is a gratuitous intrusion' (p. 106).

In short, the joke is a symptom of expressive rationality; it comments on the arbitrariness of social conventions and expresses the creative possibilities of the situation. It works by reminding us of the elements of the project we have associated with expressive rationality. Indeed , we might say that joking is 'judgment' at play. Not unsurprisingly, the joker in Douglas's analysis closely resembles the entrepreneur in economics:

> Perhaps the joker should be classified as a kind of minor mystic . . . he is one of those people who pass beyond the bounds of reason and society and give glimpses of a truth which escapes through the mesh of structured concepts . . . the joker as god promises a wealth of new, unforeseeable kinds of interpretations. He exploits the symbol of creativity which is contained in a joke, for a joke implies that anything is possible. (p. 108)

Of course, there will be those who do not find an explanation of laughter relevant to economics. But life and economics cannot be too distinct . . . and who would want to claim that laughter had nothing to do with life? Only those, one suspects, who might think that entrepreneurship has nothing to do with economics!

Part III

RATIONALITY AND PRESCRIPTION

9 INSTRUMENTAL RATIONALITY AND WELFARE ECONOMICS

9.1 Introduction

Unlike the explanations in orthodox economics, it has long been recognised that there are major difficulties with the prescriptions offered by orthodox welfare economics. (I use the term orthodox here interchangeably with neoclassical to refer to theories which work exclusively with instrumentally rational agents.) So, there is not much to be gained here by simply parading these difficulties one more time: nobody will need reminding that orthodox welfare economics is in a bit of a mess (see Sen, 1979).

However, I argue in this chapter that these difficulties are not something separate to, or in addition to, those encountered by orthodox economic explanations in chapters 4, 5 and 6. They share a common source. Although the problems with orthodox welfare economics are not the same as those of neoclassical explanations, they are caused by the same impoverished vision of rational agency. It is the exclusive reliance on instrumental rationality which is to blame in both instances. Hence, this chapter lends general support to the argument of the book. We must work with an expanded conception of rational agency, not only to improve the scope of economic explanations, but also to add a prescriptive dimension to the discipline.

It will be clear why there might be a shared root cause to these difficulties if the relation between 'is' and 'ought' statements is read in such a manner that the former becomes one of the givens for the latter. Granted this reading, any doubt with respect to whether instrumental rationality 'is' exclusively the case is bound to undermine 'ought' statements which take this to be the way the world 'is'. Quite simply, the prescription, through being based on a partial picture of the way we are, will always be susceptible to the charge that: that might be what we ought to do if we were like that, but since we are not like that, it is really neither here nor there (see section 3.4).

However, as the explanatory gaps in the instrumental account are not well recognised, this has not been the typical form in which the problems of orthodox welfare economics have been appreciated. Instead, they have surfaced in a form which is more akin to what would be expected under the alternative reading of the relation between 'is' and 'ought'. Here what 'is' the case can be regarded as irrelevant to questions of what 'ought' to be. Questions of what 'ought' to be are purely normative and there is no reason why we should not include how we are to be rationally motivated within this discussion. In other words, under this reading, a welfare economics which starts with an assumption of agents as exclusively instrumentally rational need not be undermined by the observation that we are not: that is still the way we 'ought' to be, and the further prescriptions based on this still stand.

With this reading, the problem for a welfare economics based exclusively on instrumental rationality is that it does not yield determinate prescriptions. This is the form in which the problem has been encountered in the literature, and for my purposes it does not matter whether it arose in this manner because orthodox welfare economists thought (inadmissibly) that we were exclusively instrumental or merely believed we ought to be exclusively instrumentally rational. The point is that the orthodox welfare literature demonstrates neatly why, even under the alternative reading of the 'is'/'ought' relationship, the problems with welfare economics can be traced back to the invocation/presumption that we are or ought to be exclusively instrumentally rational.*

The next section sketches the difficulties encountered by orthodox welfare economics. It begins with Pareto optimality and the problem of applying this criterion without a social welfare ordering to say something about distribution. Voting of some sort, where agents have well-behaved preferences over social outcomes, is a natural response to this problem because it broadly keeps faith with instrumental rationality. But this method for constructing a social welfare function has run aground on the Arrow (1951) impossibility theorem.

The third and fourth sections develop two contrasting critiques of the Arrow-like construction of social welfare orderings. One is primarily

---

* Of course, in putting matters in this way, I am assuming that the argument from part II has been accepted in some measure. Just in case this is not the position, it is worth noting that this chapter can also be read as providing a modicum of support for that argument. In outline it goes like this. Both readings of the 'is'/'ought' relation are now possible since the inadequacy of the instrumental explanations is what is in doubt. The trouble with orthodox welfare economics is simply that it does not produce determinate prescriptions. Traditionally, what has prevented neoclassical explanations from being tarnished by this commonplace observation about its welfare economics is the positive/normative distinction. After all, put baldly, this distinction assigns the status of objectivity to explanation while reserving subjectivity and moral dispute for the normative realm. So, dispute in the latter is hardly surprising, or worrying as far as explanation is concerned because it lies on the other side of the methodological divide. However, it is precisely this distinction which cannot be maintained in the face of modern philosophy of social science (see chapter 2). Consequently, there is no longer a neat methodological prop which can be deployed to insulate neoclassical economics from the suspicion that some of the difficulties in welfare economics might also attach to their explanations.

associated with Sen and draws on the moral philosophy of Rawls (1972), while the other comes from what is sometimes referred to as the New Right, and this draws on the moral philosophy of Nozick (1974). These critiques have a surprising amount in common. Both find it useful to discuss the appropriate role for the State by reference to contracts which might be struck between individuals in some hypothetical original position. This is sometimes described as a 'contractarian' approach, and it is a method for making welfare statements which can also be found in Marxian economics (see Roemer, 1982b).

Furthermore, they share a common view of what is wrong with conventional welfare economics. It has got stuck in a rut because it works with such a thin conception of what it is to be a person. In particular, what is missing from the orthodox world is a recognition that people have 'rights' which are important and which stand independently of their preferences: people have a right to liberty that is ignored in the orthodoxy and which is ridden over roughshod in any calculation of social welfare based on preference satisfaction alone.

In the third section, it is argued that this move to incorporate 'rights' as well as preferences in the picture of people necessitates a change in the conception of rationality because 'rights' cannot be treated instrumentally as something which can be satisfied along with preferences. Instead, it requires a version of rationality which corresponds more closely to what has been described as expressive rationality in chapter 8. Hence, the critical welfare economics literature is not just pointing to the same source of failure as has been distinguished with respect to explanations; it is also suggesting similar remedies.

It is surprising that quite so much should be shared by these two critiques because they actually have sharply divergent perspectives on the question of what constitutes the public good and the resulting appropriate role for the State. In a nutshell, Sen provides an invitation to continue pursuing the holy grail of a social welfare ordering, while the New Right hopes to have put an end to the whole enterprise. The origin of this difference is to be found in their contrasting depiction and vision of, respectively, the hypothetical original position and how precisely the 'right to liberty' cashes in: Sen uses Berlin's (1958) positive sense of freedom while the New Right sticks with the Berlin negative conception of freedom (see section 8.1). In a way, these two differences are really just an alternative device for drawing out the difference between two familiar and different conceptions of the individual and his/her relationship to society. And the contractarian formula has merely fractured this difference into these two particular components.

Granted that the depiction of the individual is what is at stake in welfare economics, it is argued in the fourth section that the earlier discussion of rationality in explanation has a special relevance for this dispute. To be specific, it is concluded that once the full consequences of recognising that agents are not just instrumentally rational is taken on board from part II, there is a genuine paradox for the Nozickian conception of 'freedom'. There are many ways in which this paradox might be expressed: which is to be preferred will depend on precisely how the discussion with respect to explanation is conceived as relevant to a welfare dispute about what ought to be the case. One way, which echoes the conclusions in part II about the need for procedures that cannot be reduced to the outcomes of instrumentally rational actions and which consequently have a certain arbitrary quality, is to say the following. The Nozickian understanding of freedom involves making the individual a prisoner of a history which, in important respects, is arbitrary. Since freedom is often portrayed as a state where an individual is free from the exercise of the arbitrary will of others, this is strange to say the least.

9.2 The Impasse in Orthodox Welfare Economics

A word of caution makes sense at the outset. This section is not designed to offer anything more than a very rough and ready survey of orthodox welfare economics. Its main purpose is to sketch the impasse that has arisen in the orthodox welfare economics based on the vision of individuals as comprising a bunch of well-behaved preferences, which they are exclusively motivated to satisfy in an instrumentally rational fashion.

Once you begin with this picture of the individual, Pareto optimality looks like a natural criterion to use in judging what is good or bad about particular economic outcomes for society. After all, Pareto optimality is defined as a situation where there is no reallocation of resources which could make one person better off without at the same time making another person worse off, and the logic connecting this with individuals who are described as a bundle of preferences seems impeccable. An individual has preferences and is made better off through their satisfaction; a society is a collection of individuals; and so we ought all to be able to agree that a Pareto-optimal outcome is better for society than a non-Pareto-optimal outcome since it amounts to no more than an uncontentious efficiency requirement.

Indeed, Pareto optimality not only looks a natural welfare criterion to use in judging different social outcomes, it seems to be positively virtuous in not demanding any obviously controversial additional assumptions about what a society is and how you derive something 'social' like a social welfare judgement from a group of individuals.

With Pareto optimality in place, the demonstration in neoclassical general equilibrium theory that a competitive equilibrium is Pareto optimal becomes what is sometimes called the first fundamental theorem in welfare economics. To illustrate the theorem, and incidentally the role of instrumental rationality in the proof, we focus on a pure exchange economy.

It is assumed that each individual's preference orderings satisfy the standard conditions set out in section 3.2 and that there is a given initial distribution of goods/resources, no externalities and no public goods. Further, there is a competitive equilibrium which is defined by a price vector with only positive elements and a set of trades, one for each individual, such that the trade of each individual is instrumentally rational given the price vector and initial distribution; and the total amount of each good supplied equals the total demand.

The proof works by supposing the Pareto-optimal proposition is false. If this were the case then there is some alternative allocation which at least one agent, agent i, prefers to the competitive one whilst leaving all other agents indifferent. As i is instrumentally rational, it follows that the alternative allocation cannot lie within i's budget set as defined by the competitive price vector, given the assumption of no externalities and public goods. For all the other agents who are indifferent between the new allocation and the competitive one, it follows that the new allocation must either just satisfy their competitive budget constraints or violate them as well. The point is that, if the alternative allocation left a slack in the budget constraint, then these agents would not be acting in an instrumentally rational manner in the competitive equilibrium since they would be able to purchase the alternative bundle which leaves them indifferent and still have income which can be spent on purchasing other items to improve the bundle.

Let the alternative allocation of goods be given by the vector x_i for individual i, and the initial endowment be given by the vector y_i for individual i. The competitive price vector is p. The argument above concerning the consequences of Pareto optimality being false can be summarised as

$$p(x_i - y_i) > 0 \text{ for } i$$

and

$$p(x_k - y_k) \geq 0 \text{ for all } k \neq i$$

Summing over all agents l, it follows that there must be one good j such that

$$\sum_l x_{lj} > \sum_l y_{lj}$$

In other words, there must be one good under the hypothesised Pareto-superior alternative allocation for which demand exceeds supply, and so the hypothetical Pareto-superior allocation is not feasible.

This Pareto optimality result sets an agenda for welfare economics, and a literature to go with it. It revolves around the question of market failure: under what circumstances does a market fail to live up to its competitive ideal, and thus not deliver Pareto optimality? There are the classic cases of public goods and the presence of externalities which can cause a mischief with the invisible hand. And there is the corresponding literature on Pigovian tax and subsidy public policy interventions that are designed to internalise the externalities and which contrast with the Coasean approach where there is reliance on a kind of background public policy intervention to establish a particular common law framework for the remedy of torts.

This is a rich literature and it has touched upon some fundamental public policy issues, so it should not be discounted. For instance, there is the famous Lange–Lerner proposal for a species of market socialism, which claims among other things to be better able to deliver Pareto optimality when there are increasing returns to scale in production because firms under such a system can be ordered to attend to the necessary marginal conditions and ignore the associated loss which would occur under marginal cost pricing in these circumstances. Nevertheless, it has also proved to be a literature which has singularly failed to offer constructive guidance on the actual conduct of public policy.

Of course, one difficulty with public policy recommendations in this literature arises because of the theory of the second best (see Lipsey and Lancaster, 1956). I set this aside here since there need be nothing to tie this particular problem in with the underlying conception of the individual as a set of well-behaved preferences. Nor need it undermine a full blown Pareto-based approach to welfare statements: it only undermines the simple sort of policy prescription which says that, since a competitive equilibrium is Pareto optimal, any movement towards competitive conditions will constitute a Pareto improvement.

The so-called second fundamental theorem in welfare economics is really what does the damage to the Pareto criterion. This theorem demonstrates that any Pareto-optimal outcome can be achieved in a competitive equilibrium by a suitable redistribution of initial resources. On the negative side, this makes clear that the Pareto criterion itself is something of a blunt instrument for policy makers. There are any number of outcomes, each dependent on particular initial distributions of resources, which could satisfy the Pareto condition. Consequently, a public policy maker relying on Pareto optimality alone will not be able to distinguish one outcome as better than a number of other outcomes. This narrowing can only take place when the public policy maker is also able to make evaluations with respect to distribution. In short, it seems that policy makers must come to some conclusion over distribution before Pareto optimality comes into play.

On the positive side, it should be said, the second theorem does make clear that the matter of distribution can in some degree be separated from efficiency. But the nature of this separation has to be carefully noted lest it appear, in contradistinction to the above, that there is room for policy makers to pursue Pareto efficiency while remaining agnostic on matters of distribution. (See, for instance, the position adopted by Posner, 1977, in the law and economics literature which seems to work on the assumption that matters of distribution can be set on one side.) What the second theorem demonstrates is that the conditions which have to be satisfied for Pareto efficiency are independent of particular preferences on the matter of distribution; and, for any particular preferred distribution, the same competitive processes will guarantee the attainment of those conditions. In noting this separation and the sense in which the efficiency criterion is independent of distribution, nothing has been said to undermine the point that a pure concern for efficiency cannot produce a policy for policy makers to act upon. Efficiency alone puts the economy on the Pareto frontier: either implicitly or explicitly, the policy maker must choose a point on the frontier with reference to some other principle, most obviously one concerning distribution.

The inability of policy makers to be guided by the Pareto efficiency criterion alone is even clearer in a dynamic context since few dynamic changes leave no person worse off. Suppose, for instance, that some new technology is to be introduced. Most people might gain but it is difficult not to imagine at least one person, perhaps someone close to retirement whose skills become redundant and who does not have the time to retrain before that retirement, who will lose out under the proposed change.

Compensation tests appeared to offer a way out of such dilemmas whilst keeping faith with a pure Pareto criterion. They proposed that the change should be undertaken if those who gain can compensate those who lose and still remain better off (see Kaldor, 1939). But this leaves open an awkward question of how much compensation should actually be undertaken and an answer will demand a more active public policy position on matters of distribution. Furthermore, it is well known that compensation tests do not provide unambiguous advice on whether a change should be embraced. For example, consider the pair I and II of two-person utility possibility frontiers in figure 9.1. I gives the set of initial possibilities and point A is the particular position which obtains under current distributional arrangements. II gives the set of options made available after some change, the merit of which is to be evaluated using the compensation principle; and point B will obtain on II after the change if there is no alteration in the

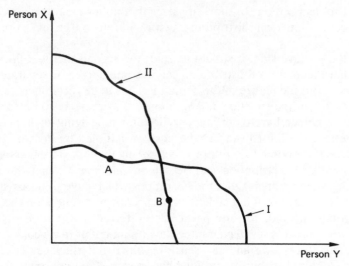

Figure 9.1   Compensation tests

prevailing distributional arrangements. Hence, the change from A to B fits the bill because it involves making one person better off while the other is worse off. Likewise, figure 9.2 depicts a similar kind of change and illustrates another problem with the compensation test criterion.

In figure 9.1, the compensation test suggests that the change should be undertaken, since X can be compensated for the switch while still leaving Y better off. However, exactly the same logic would endorse the reverse change of moving from B to A, as the economy's public policy makers consider the switch back from II to I. The compensation test licenses too much here, whereas in figure 9.2 it is unable to offer any evaluation of the switch from I to II because the possibility of compensation is not present. In short, the compensation test cannot be relied upon to supplement the Pareto principle and provide guidance for the policy maker in the dynamic setting where changes disadvantage at least one person.

So, to summarise, the pareto principle cannot guide public policy by itself. It selects a set of outcomes as efficient but it will not distinguish one of these as superior to another. This distinction must rely on some other principle. In particular, this principle would seem to have to reflect a judgement concerning interpersonal comparisons of utility since we shall be deciding whether a little more utility for A, bought at the expense of reduced utility for B, is desirable or not. This leaves a question concerning where the public policy maker is to get this principle from.

Traditionally this point is put in terms of the need for a social welfare

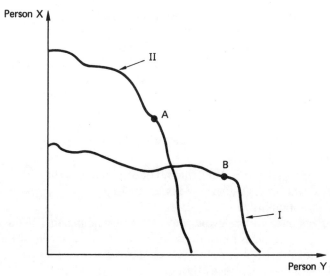

Figure 9.2   Compensation tests

function which can order the various possible Pareto outcomes, and the question becomes one concerning the origins of this function. Where does the social welfare function come from? And, in particular, is such a function consistent with the portrayal of individuals as a bunch of well-behaved preferences which they act to satisfy?

One candidate answer to this question allows for individuals to hold ethical preferences which define an ordering over these possible social states, and then proposes a constitutional mechanism for aggregating these individual preferences to arrive at a social assessment. At first sight this is likely to appear an attractive solution, not least because it seems to keep faith with the basic idea that individuals can be pictured as a set of preferences. Furthermore, it preserves the association with instrumental rationality and the understanding of action which flows from it, as agents can be depicted as 'voting' in an attempt to satisfy those preferences best. The only twist seems to be the rather novel inclusion of an ethical dimension to the 'bunch of preferences', but even this need not be so in any strict sense since 'ethical preferences' could simply reflect a selfish evaluation of each outcome according to the satisfaction of the individual's 'ordinary' preferences. They need only be 'ethical' in the sense that they are an ordering over social outcomes.

Of course, this approach might not avoid some of the tough interpersonal questions which would seem to be involved in deciding where to locate on the utility possibility frontier because there would still be an issue of which constitutional procedure to follow, and it is unlikely that such procedures would be neutral to the outcome. However, the matter does not really even get this far, because the proposal runs foul of the Arrow impossibility theorem. Arrow (1951) asks whether it is possible for any constitutional system to generate a social welfare ordering that satisfies the properties (i)–(v) below when individuals hold ethical preferences over these social states which satisfy the conditions of completeness, reflexivity and transitivity, as stated in section 3.2:

(i)   Unrestricted domain
(ii) Non-dictatorship (meaning that no one individual's choice between all pairs of outcomes should always be decisive)
(iii) Pareto optimality
(iv) Independence of irrelevant alternatives (meaning that if the preferences of individuals for options $\{x, y\}$ remain unchanged while preferences for other options change, the social welfare ordering associated with the new preferences should still rank $\{x, y\}$ in the same way as the old one)
(v)   Transitivity

These appear to be minimal and sensible sorts of conditions to place on a social welfare ordering, much as the conditions which are assumed with respect to individual preferences in chapter 3 seemed reasonable. Yet, Arrow's impossibility result demonstrates that there is no constitutional procedure which will satisfy all five conditions. In a sense the result is not a new one because it echoes the famous Condorcet voting paradox. This paradox may help to give some insight as to the origins of the Arrow result. It can be stated by considering a system of majority voting on pairs of options from $\{x, y, z\}$ when three voters exhibit the following preference orderings:

A: $[x, y, z]$
B: $[y, z, x]$
C: $[z, x, y]$

Majority voting yields xPy, yPz and zPx. In other words, an intransitive ordering is generated. Does such intransitivity matter? Yes, is the short answer because any individual or society which exhibited such intransitivity could, in principle, trade itself into poverty. Take a society that starts with outcome x in these circumstances: it should be willing to trade with another society and pay some fee to obtain the bundle z since zPx; once this trade is complete, it should be willing to trade with another society and pay some fee to obtain bundle y since yPz; and once this trade is complete, it should be willing to trade with another society and pay some fee to obtain bundle x since xPy. Thus, the society would end up where it started after this round of trades with bundle x, only it would be poorer to the tune of the three fees which it would have been willing to pay to facilitate each of the three sequential trades along the route to where it started. This is not a recipe for prosperity as the same cycle of trades will look just as enticing a second and third time, and so on, into poverty.

There is a line of defence for a voting approach which takes issue with one or other of the five conditions. For example, the independence of irrelevant alternatives has proved controversial; and the non-dictatorship might not seem quite so crucial once it is realised that it is only an 'as if' there were a dictator, in the sense of a coincidence between an individual and the social preference ordering, rather than an actual dictatorship which is being precluded. Nevertheless, the result is plainly worrying for the strictly instrumental approach to the construction of a social welfare function because at first sight none of the conditions seems obviously objectionable and worthy of relaxation.

In addition, a background issue, noted above, lurks over which constitutional procedure is to be followed once a 'possibility' result has been built on a relaxation of one or other of the conditions. Democracy comes in various forms and sizes and, unless we can be sure that all systems would generate the same social welfare ordering, we cannot just appeal to democracy in answering the question of where the social welfare ordering comes from. The problem has merely been displaced to a higher order question of how we come to choose a constitutional system, and this threatens to launch us on an infinite regress rather than provide a substantive answer to the question because we shall be asking further questions about the structure of the meetings to decide on constitutional procedures, and so on.

Finally, there is another problem to record that is related to the Arrow impossibility result, and which concerns the incentive to vote strategically. The Gibbard (1973) theorem demonstrates that under most voting systems there is an incentive for an individual to manipulate the system by voting strategically. The logic behind this theorem can again be appreciated with a reference to the Condorcet preferences set out above. Suppose these are the preferences of three individuals and there is a system of simple majority voting where the chair, A, has a casting vote in the event of a tie. Honest voting would produce a tie and A's casting vote would yield the choice of x. However, this is the worst outcome as far as B is concerned, and his/her position would be improved by voting strategically for z rather than y, as this produces a majority in favour of z, which B prefers to x.

This incentive to vote strategically is worrying as far as the construction of a social welfare function is concerned. The problem is really that, once individuals cease to vote honestly, it can no longer claim to be straightforward aggregation of the individual preferences on social outcomes; and if it cannot claim in some sense to represent 'average opinion', with what authority can it be used to impose one outcome on the whole of society? The difficulty is compounded further by the thought that matters would not stop here. There would be an incentive with B voting strategically in this fashion for A to follow suit and form a coalition with B to vote for y, as A prefers y to z. Nor would they stop here: this coalition could be threatened by one between A and C, and so on. In other words, there is no stable coalition which can be put together once the opportunities for strategic voting are appreciated, with the implication that such constitutional procedures need not generate a stable social welfare ordering.

In conclusion to this section, the approach to welfare economics which works with a picture of individuals as just a bunch of preferences and the allied sense of instrumental rationality finds itself in a bind. Pareto optimality is an obvious welfare criterion which follows from treating individuals as synonymous with a set of preferences, but by itself it is not decisive enough to single out one from a number of outcomes. We need a social welfare function if anything is to be made of the Pareto optimality criterion. But a democratic procedure cannot be relied upon with minimal changes to the underlying picture of individuals to generate this function. The agent cannot just be endowed with appropriate ethical preferences which are satisfied by voting instrumentally in the political arena to get a social welfare ordering and thus ease the individual-equals-preference set plus instrumental rationality account out of a prescriptive bind.

9.3   Sen and Capabilities

Two critiques of the Arrow type 'voting' approach to the construction of a social welfare ordering can be found in the literature, and they are important for this book because they contest the one-dimensional model of individuals found in the orthodox welfare economics. I focus first on an argument by Sen (1982a) which is directed at what he calls the informational content of the Arrow approach and then turn in section 9.4 to the criticism of the 'voting' approach which has been mounted by the New Right.

In effect, the Arrow approach only demands information on individual utilities (the ordinal representation of preferences). There is no need to consider any non-utility features of the outcome and there are no explicit interpersonal comparisons of utility. The framework simply searches for constitutional procedures designed to aggregate 'votes' which are based on individual utility (i.e. preference) information alone. At first glance, this may appear to be a positive advantage because any serious discussion of something like the foundations for making interpersonal comparisons of welfare looks likely to launch welfare economics into a morass of moral philosophy . . . from which it might never surface. But the temptation to avoid moral philosophy must be tempered by some realistic expectations of what might be achieved by the Arrow approach. Two examples help to bring out the prospective limitations: they concern cases where it is likely that most people would want a social welfare function to make certain sorts of distinctions, and yet the exclusive reliance on individual utility information will not permit these common-place judgements to be made. In one, Sen considers a redivision of the proverbial cake, by taking some from person 1 to be given to person 2 and person 3. This redivision occurs in two different cases, A and B.

> In case A, person 1 is very rich while 2 and 3 are poor, whereas in case B, person 1 is very poor while 2 and 3 are rich. . . . If each person prefers more cake to himself . . . then persons 2 and 3 prefer the change while person 1 disprefers it, in both cases A and B. Now the question: are the two cases of redistribution exactly similar? In the Arrow format they have to be . . . exactly the same judgement must be made in both the cases since the individual preference orderings are identical in the two cases. (Sen, 1982a, pp. 19–20)

Yet, most people would want to distinguish case A from case B. Hence, a framework which cannot draw such a distinction is beginning to seem a little strange. Indeed, Sen's observation is to the effect that, if the sparse informational format of the Arrow approach cannot distinguish between such obviously different cases as A and B, what possible chance can it have of being useful in more complicated examples? Of course, to make such a distinction will involve introducing other elements into the analysis, like interpersonal comparisons of utility. But, since it seems we would want to be able to distinguish cases like A from those of B, then so be it – and what is more, once they have been made, there is no problem proving possibility theorems (see Sen, 1970). In short, the problem is really that the informational basis of the Arrow calculation is too sparse, and what looked at first sight to be an advantage proves on reflection to be a handicap. As Sen (1982a) concludes: 'It does not belittle the outstanding importance of this elegant and far-reaching logical result . . . to note that an informational format that cannot distinguish between cases A and B is quite unsuitable anyway for welfare economics. More information is needed to deal with interest conflicts. The unsuitable, it transpires, is also the impossible.' (p. 20)

The other example focuses on the absence of non-utility information. It is really a variation on a charge that is regularly directed at utilitarianism, which sticks here as well because utilitarianism also only works with utility information. The point is that, by being concerned only with utility information, it is possible to construct situations which again will look decidedly odd to many people. For instance, if person 1 tortures person 2, then this would be an improvement under a utilitarian calculation, provided that the utility gain of the torturer outweighed the loss suffered by the victim. Or more generally, the outcome would be a Pareto improvement if the torturer was willing to pay more than the victim needed to be paid in compensation for the suffering. What is odd in this example is the admission of categories of action like torture which many people would be inclined to judge as a relevant factor in deciding between social outcomes. The evaluation of torture in the Arrow framework is reduced to its utility consequences, and hence it is possible to imagine situations involving torture being ranked above those where it is absent. What seems to be missing is a recognition of how human rights, like freedom from torture, enter into social welfare judgements independently of their utility content; and this can be traced directly to the exclusive use of utility information in the Arrow framework.

It is worth developing this distinction between utility and rights because it has been argued (see Ng, 1981) that rights of this sort are only valued because of their utility consequences. They are really no more than simple rules of thumb designed to serve the utility calculation, and consequently they should not be valued independently of those utility calculations – so the argument goes. Two considerations tell against this reduction of rights to utility satisfaction (see Sen, 1982b, for further discussion).

Firstly, many people would want to distinguish between a situation where someone consumes bundle a when the choice was $\{a, b, c\}$ and a situation where the same bundle was consumed and the choice set was $\{a\}$. For instance, it seems natural to grant a difference between sitting at home watching television when you could, say, have chosen to visit friends and sitting at home when there is no such alternative. Yet, from the vantage point of the consequentialist, utilitarian calculation, the person consumes a in both cases and this is all that counts. To make the distinction between the two requires some positive valuing of freedom quite independently of how such freedom might contribute to the satisfaction of preferences.

Sen (1985) refers to this as a positive valuation of 'capabilities' and it marks a sense of freedom which resides in knowing that you could have done something else. To construe this sense of freedom as a rule of thumb in the service of preference satisfaction, as in Ng (1981), does not seem to make any kind of sense. What is at stake is precisely not what preferences were satisfied but what preferences were not satisfied and which could have been satisfied had another outcome within the available set been chosen. To put it slightly differently, this 'right' to freedom does not have the same dimensions as preference satisfaction. Preference satisfaction is an attribute of particular outcomes within a choice set, whereas the 'right' to freedom is gauged by the variety within the whole choice set. Of course, this does not preclude the possibility that the evaluation of different choice sets according to the options available may well use the level of preference satisfaction under each option as raw material for a comparative assessment of different choice sets (see Sen, 1985 for further ideas on measuring capabilities). But such use of preference satisfaction data is a long way from the subordination of such calculations to the goal of preference satisfaction alone. It is the fact of taking account of 'what could have been', which is an operation of transformation on the raw data of preference satisfaction, that is important here rather than the possibility that preference satisfaction might be used as a common currency in such calculations. As such it constitutes a different yardstick for the evaluation of outcomes to preference satisfaction alone. One does not serve the other, as implied by Ng (1981): they are different components of an evaluation.

One possible counter to this line of argument is to redefine the boundaries of what generates utility to include this capability for exercising freedom. So, an evaluation which takes account of freedom can be subsumed under the general heading of utility maximisation or preference satisfaction, where utility or preference has now been defined with suitable width to include a preference for freedom in this capability sense. It is not clear that this liberal definition of utility undermines the substantive point that we have two yardsticks reflecting a vision of an individual which is now something more than the bunch of preferences, as usually understood. For instance, it seems likely that this same point would simply be made in the form of acknowledging that there are two different senses of preferences which comprise an individual now. It would then become a matter of taste as to whether the substantive point was made within a language which only admitted preferences or not.

A second consideration helps to bring out why the substantive point cannot be 'lost' with a suitable redefinition of utility, and why it is perhaps more sensible to use a different term like freedom, or more generally rights, to signal that individuals are being endowed here with a qualitatively new dimension. In effect, it is a replay of the argument made in section 8.9 with respect to why expressive rationality cannot be subsumed under instrumental rationality with a suitable redefinition of the individual's objectives.

The recurrence of this line of argument should not come as a surprise because Sen's sense of 'capability' corresponds closely with the Berlin (1958) positive sense of freedom, which I have linked to expressive rationality in the 'modern' world. We are concerned with the choice available, in part, because we wish to feel responsible for ourselves. We want to be autonomous beings who can reflect on our aims and purposes and take them to be our own; and it is simply not possible to stand back and reflect in this manner if we have undertaken a when the choice set was $\{a\}$. The concept of autonomy has no purchase in such circumstances. We did a because that was all there was; there is no possibility of construing the action as resonating with anything less prosaic than this. We can only begin to think of ourselves as reflective individuals concerned with autonomy if we choose a from a larger choice set like $\{a, b, c\}$. The capability of choosing is what underpins a reflective capacity; without it the project of autonomy cannot get off the ground and this explains in part why we value capabilities.

Now, to continue the argument of chapter 8, one of the crucial characteristics of the quest for autonomy is that it presupposes some uncertainty about what preferences, aims and objectives one should entertain. This is another way of appreciating why the choice set is important because it defines the options which might be tried in a process of learning through experimentation, in a quest for autonomy and self-respect. More importantly, once this uncertainty is recognised it undermines any discussion of this objective in terms of simple preference satisfaction because it is those very preferences which are in doubt. Just as expressive rationality could not be reduced to instrumental rationality, so a concern with 'capabilities' cannot be reduced to a preference, to be satisfied along with those for 'food, clothing and shelter'. Autonomy is a different kind of preference and it reflects a deep doubt and uncertainty about those other kinds of preferences for 'food, clothing and shelter'. In a nutshell, 'capabilities' matter because we wish to be able to shape our lives and this is an open-ended activity which cannot be fitted into the means-to-given-ends framework of instrumental rationality.

To summarise this argument, the criterion of preference satisfaction works on outcomes: it is an 'ends'-based criterion. Ng (1981) interprets rights like freedom as rules of thumb, 'means', which serve the 'end' of preference satisfaction. But this misses a crucial reason why we value rights. We value rights, like freedom in Berlin's positive sense, because we have doubts about the 'ends' we are pursuing. Rights do not serve a set of preferences like a rule of thumb; they reflect our concern for autonomy which will be revealed in the evolution of those preferences over time. This sets a concern for rights as separate from any one set of preferences which may establish 'ends' at a moment in time. Indeed, since one set of preferences at a moment of time will be the result of a particular historical pattern of evolution, it would make more sense to subordinate preferences to rights, rather than the other way round. But this is a large matter, and there is no need to make the stronger claim here. All that is required is that 'rights' stand independently of preferences at a moment in time.

Returning to the main theme of this section, the Arrow approach fails for reasons which at a second glance seem perfectly understandable, namely that its informational structure is too impoverished. In particular, it takes no heed of non-utility information like 'rights' and interpersonal comparisons of utility; and yet both these considerations appear to be crucial and unavoidable components of quite simple sorts of social welfare judgements. There remains the issue of how social welfare judgements utilising interpersonal comparisons and non-utility information might be made. We might all agree on how to draw a line between case A and case B in the cake redivision example, and we might all agree that a non-torture rule is to be respected; but how are we to deal with more difficult cases?

I make no attempt here to answer this question. But I do want to sketch the Rawlsian contractarian approach that Sen is sympathetic towards – partially to support the survey side and partially as a building block in the main argument. Rawls (1972) holds a strong position of equality with respect to primary social goods. These are the things which 'every rational man is presumed to want. These goods (liberty and opportunity, income and wealth, and the bases of self respect) normally have a use whatever a person's rational plan of life . . .' (p. 62). Now, although there is a presumption in favour of equality, inequality is permissible in so far as these inequalities make everyone better off: 'Imagine, then, a hypothetical initial arrangement in which all the primary social goods are equally distributed . . . if certain inequalities of wealth and organisational powers would make everyone better off than in this hypothetical starting situation, then they accord with the general conception [of justice]' (p. 62)

However, this possibility of trading equality for a bit of inequality, as long as everyone is made better off, is not possible according to Rawls when basic liberties are at stake. Rawls's formulation establishes a hierarchy between primary social goods, whereby basic liberties are paramount and cannot be traded for improvement with respect to the lesser primary social good of greater wealth. These liberties are, in effect, 'rights' which must be respected under all circumstances. The only difference here with Sen is that he wholeheartedly adopts the positive sense of liberty and so associates these paramount social goods with a wider set of 'basic capabilities' rather than just a set of basic liberties.

This is a small difference. What is interesting about the Rawlsian approach is the way he justifies this presumption towards equality. He uses a particular contractarian argument to motivate his position that inequality can only be justified if it makes everyone better off. This is of some interest because it sets the stage for the discussion of the New Right in the next section and it establishes another link with the earlier discussion of rationality. In general, contractarian arguments in support of a particular social outcome work by demonstrating how individuals would choose that outcome when starting from some hypothetical 'original position': this is what they would contract to have, so to speak, if they were given the opportunity of starting again. Rawls's version has a rather special 'original position': it has people deciding on the worth of different social outcomes from behind a 'veil of ignorance'. Each outcome for society is specified in terms of the distribution of goods and the utility function of each individual in that society; and these are known to the people in the 'original position'. What they do not know is which individual they will be in that society. This is the 'veil of ignorance' and it is introduced to ensure that the ordering of social outcomes which is so derived can be reasonably described as impartial, and worthy of the name of 'justice'.

Formally, the task that people face in the 'original position' can be characterised as decision making under uncertainty: each social outcome is a gamble, where the precise pay-off for a person is contingent on the random process which determines what individual they become under that social outcome. Rawls argues that the appropriate rule for decision making under uncertainty is maximin. Hence, each social outcome is judged and ranked according to the utility level of the person who is worst off under that arrangement; and so any movement away from a position of equality will only be chosen, and thus not violate the principle of justice, as long as it makes everyone better off.

The maximin criterion will not fit everyone's picture of rational decision making under uncertainty because it represents a rather strong position with respect to risk aversion. Alternatives in the form of expected utility maximisation need not produce the same ranking of outcomes. For example, using the notation $u(x, i)$ to describe the utility of individual i under outcome x, the maximin criterion is given by

$$xPy \text{ if } \min_i[u(x,i)] > \min_i[u(y,i)] \qquad (9.1)$$

in the choice between x and y, while the expected utility criterion is given by

$$xPy \text{ if } \sum_i u(x,i) > \sum_i u(y,i) \qquad (9.2)$$

under the assumption of an equal probability $(1/n)$ of becoming each of the possible n individuals.

It will be plain from this that, while (9.1) holds, (9.2) need not if the worst position in y, say j, is more than compensated for in this simple utilitarian addition by some superior position(s) for the other non-j individuals in y when contrasted with their position(s) under x. So, the precise decision over what outcome is to be preferred is necessarily linked to a prior decision over what constitutes a rational decision making procedure under uncertainty. There are a number of interesting results which can be obtained using this approach, by applying different instrumental criteria for decision making under uncertainty (see Harsanyi, 1955, and Sugden,

1981). For the moment, it suffices to note that this approach to generating interpersonal comparisons via a Rawlsian 'veil of ignorance' necessarily ties the welfare economics discussion into the earlier discussion of rationality. Since the argument of the previous part of this book is that there is much to be gained by working in economics with an expanded set of definitions of rationality, this linkage of the discussions promises to enrich welfare economics.

9.4 Nozick and the New Right

Paradoxically, the contemporary heirs of the Austrian tradition, who are sometimes labelled as the New Right, have come to much the same conclusion as Sen on the Arrow approach to the construction of social welfare functions. Their argument is typically developed in a slightly different way; nevertheless the critique of Arrow revolves around the same need to recognise 'rights' which is found in Sen. Where the New Right parts company from Sen is in the further inference that the whole project of constructing a social welfare function is misconceived. Taken seriously, this further inference undermines the promise which was held out at the end of the last section of developing welfare economics through the introduction of other kinds of rationality into Rawlsian 'veil of ignorance' decisions. Consequently, the argument of the New Right needs to be addressed before turning in the next chapter to how welfare economics might be influenced by the introduction of procedural and expressive rationality.

Most simply, the New Right draws attention to some well-recognised problems with constitutional procedures of the Arrow type. In particular, they can lead to the tyranny of minority groups by the majority in a society. Once this is recognised, it is not at all obvious what the claim of a democratic procedure is with regard to the generation of a social welfare ordering – why should one imagine that this is an appropriate way to go about constructing such an ordering when it can produce such obviously 'unjust' results? Minimally, it looks as if individuals must be granted some inalienable 'rights' if the tyranny over minority groups is to be avoided. In other words, the argument finds itself back at the same spot of bemoaning the poverty of a framework which depicts individuals only in terms of preferences and actions designed to satisfy them.

However, there is a more general principle that lurks behind this discussion of Arrowian social welfare functions, which the New Right also wishes to bring out. This concerns the very existence of a social welfare function: the New Right questions whether we really need one. Naturally, if we start with a government and set it the objective of acting in the public good we shall need a social welfare function. But, and this is the question the New Right wants to tease out, why charge governments with such authority in the first place?

In answering this question, the New Right also takes a contractarian position. Government action and authority will be legitimate in so far as it can be rationalised as the product of individuals contracting with each other to be served by such an authority. The difference in their approach resides in their original position: the one that sets the terms for the discussion of the type of contracts which might arise. It is not characterised by Rawls's 'veil of ignorance'. Instead, it is either a Hobbesian or Lockean state of nature (see Buchanan, 1986, and Nozick, 1974, respectively). This has quite dramatic consequences for the whole idea of a social welfare function. For instance, Nozick argues that only the classic nightwatchman state of liberal theory will evolve from the Lockean state of nature where agents are free to 'order their actions and dispose of their possessions and persons as they see fit . . .' subject only to the bounds of the law of nature which require that 'no one ought to harm another in his life, health, liberty or possessions' (p. 10). The state literally just acts as a mutual protection agency and adjudicates border disputes between individuals over property rights.

Nozick reaches this position by an argument which demonstrates how individuals might contract with each other to create such a minimal state. He then argues that there can be no justification for a state which has any expanded set of activities. In particular, there cannot be any justification for a state which sets about implementing some social welfare function in the name of the public good. In support of this further claim, he states a three-principle theory of justice:

1 justice in the original acquisition of a holding;
2 justice in the transfer of holdings;
3 a principle for rectifying an injustice which has been identified under (1) and (2).

It can be seen to reflect the basic commitment to freedom, in Berlin's negative sense of the absence of coercive or arbitrary restraint, that comes from the Lockean state of nature.

The centrepiece is (2). A just transfer/exchange according to this principle is any transfer/exchange which an individual voluntarily decides to undertake under the law established by the nightwatchman state. So, in the case where I have two knives and you have two forks, it would be in accordance with this principle of justice either if I keep the two knives which I have or if I exchange one knife with you for a fork, provided in both instances that I decided on the course of action voluntarily. In principle, it is just for me to do whatever I voluntarily decide to do with the knives; the only constraint is that I cannot plant the knife between your shoulder blades, as this will transgress the property rights you have to your body and which are protected by the minimal state. This is not an arbitrary or coercive restraint upon my actions because I have contracted with others to form a minimal state which polices property rights over a person's body in this manner.

This principle of justice in transfer will cover many of the cases concerned with the original acquisition of holdings under (1). An original acquisition will be just in so far as it is acquired as a transfer which was just under (2). In addition, everyone has a right to their own labour; and this combined with justice in transfer will cover most acquisitions. The exception will be those acquisitions which are not a transfer nor a product of labour, but which come from nature. Here Nozick argues that the acquisition of one of the gifts of nature, like water or minerals, by an individual is 'just' so long as the individual has done 'good capitalistic' things with the acquisition, with the result that everyone in the society is made better off through the acquisition. Nozick has little to say on the third principle, a point I shall return to in a moment.

Nozick terms this an entitlement theory of justice. Alternatively, it might be regarded as 'procedural', since outcomes are judged here according to the procedure which has generated them and not by virtue of any intrinsic features of the outcomes themselves. The procedures are just in so far as they respect the rights which individuals bring with them from the state of nature, namely the freedoms to make voluntary exchanges and transfers. Some care is required here: there is no presumption in putting matters in this way that a procedural sense of justice maps onto the procedural sense of rationality which was discussed in chapter 7 in any simple way, if at all. Nevertheless, what Nozick shares with procedural rationality is a general way of judging/deciding which is based on the way something was done rather than on the outcomes which it produced. The appreciation of this broad similarity helps to bring out Nozick's argument against a larger and more active state. The point here is that Nozick argues that larger and more active states typically rely on a theory of justice which is concerned with outcomes and these theories necessarily conflict with his own entitlement theory.

The conflict can be drawn out by imagining a state operating with some social welfare function. The social welfare function is an evaluation based on outcomes, and it will enable the state to decide and intervene in pursuit of, say, that distribution of income which generated the best available outcome. Now suppose that individuals 'set about their business', freely transacting as they please, in accordance with the entitlement theory. The distribution of income is bound to be upset by these actions: it would be

pure serendipity if the hurly-burly of these free trades happened to produce a new set of outcomes which corresponded to the best outcome
available, as judged by the social welfare function. Consequently, if the
state is to be moved by the social welfare function, it will have to intervene
again to engineer a new distribution of income to achieve the best possible
outcome in the new circumstances created by the trading which has ensued
since the last intervention. But, in so doing, it will undercut the entitlement
theory because the trades which were freely undertaken will be undone
and altered by these interventions.

In other words, it is not possible to hold simultaneously a theory of
justice which is based on outcomes and one which is based on entitlements.
You judge either according to 'ends' or according to 'procedures'. One
must give; and Nozick argues that it should be the one based on outcomes.
Since social welfare functions typically focus on outcomes and provide a
judgement in terms of end states or consequences, then this amounts to an
argument against the very idea of a social welfare function.

Once this is conceded, there seems little purpose in discussing how
alternative rationality postulates might enrich the derivation of a social
welfare function. So, is there anything wrong with the Nozick argument?
Should the book end here, with the thought that Nozick's procedural
considerations constitute an epitaph for welfare economics rather than a
new insight to take behind the 'veil of ignorance' in order to aid in the
production of a social welfare function?

Before answering this question, it would, perhaps, be helpful to go back
and tie up one loose end which has emerged in the argument. In the second
section, it was suggested that governments could not avoid using a social
welfare function; Pareto optimality did not provide a sufficient guide for
action/inaction. Consequently, it may seem rather puzzling to have arrived
at a position now where it has become possible, indeed some might argue it
has become imperative, to contemplate forsaking social welfare functions
altogether. The puzzle dissolves, however, once it is realised that Pareto
optimality itself need not be a desirable characteristic under the entitlement approach. As Sen elegantly demonstrated in his impossibility of
being a Paretian liberal result, sketched in section 8.3, the two principles
can conflict. For Nozick, the liberal principle embodying the commitment
to freedom, in the negative sense, is the primary one; and so even the
apparently innocuous objective of Pareto optimality cannot be presumed
to guide government action.

Put slightly differently, Pareto optimality is an end state/outcome feature
and it has no role in Nozick's purely procedural account of justice. So, the
problem of which Pareto-optimal outcome is to be chosen disappears: it
belongs to an end state theory of justice which no longer rules the roost.
Instead, what will justify where the economy is now is simply a history for

that economy, where the trades and exchanges faithfully reflect the first two principles of Nozick's theory of justice.

Let us return now to the main question. There is a hint of why Nozick may not be writing the epitaph for an outcome-oriented welfare economics in this sorting out of loose ends. Should the history of an economy prove upon inspection not to be consistent with the first two principles of justice, then the application of the third principle would be warranted; and, as Nozick himself acknowledges, such a principle would have to take the form of an intervention which was directed at altering outcomes. The third principle, in other words, licenses a social welfare function approach, at least on a once and for all basis if history has departed from the first two principles; and in so far as a society's trades continued to transgress the first two principles, there would be a continuing need for a social welfare function to guide rectifications. This line of argument at least provides an opening for social welfare functions. Nevertheless, their continuing relevance would seem to depend on society's failure to implement the first two principles: and it may be difficult to entertain this as likely. After all, once a society has accepted these two principles, it ought to be able to monitor actions at source and set the transgressions right immediately, the moment they are undertaken. Put bluntly, we cannot rewrite history, but at least we ought to be able to avoid making the same mistakes again once we have recognised the nature of the problem.

This is a tempting thought, but it is not without problems. To appreciate the difficulties which Nozick finds himself in, it is necessary first to question the full picture of the individual in Nozick's theory. Plainly, the person is endowed with rights, the right to Berlin's negative sense of freedom. But what else can be assumed about individuals? Can they be characterised by a well-behaved set of preferences? Do they have expressive concerns? Are they instrumentally and expressively rational?

It seems it would be difficult to associate the person in Nozick's theory with expressive concerns. A quest for autonomy is likely to do too much damage to the theory, since it will push the argument down the road taken by Sen, with its conclusion in favour of state activism. In particular, it is easy to see one difficulty here by recalling an argument from chapter 8. Expressive rationality cannot be divorced from procedural rationality: this is the inference which opens the way to a form of state activism justified with respect to individuals' expressive concerns. The full argument is in section 8.9, but the outline connecting it with state action goes something like this. Procedures often function as a language for making expressively rational statements or acts, and as such they are not neutral in their capacity to convey messages with expressive content. Or, more specifically, in so far as experimentation reflects an expressive concern, then procedures are not neutral in the encouragement they give to experimentation. Or a final way of putting it is that procedures can create reasons for action which are internal to those procedures, so in wanting to decide on your reasons for action you must address among other things those shared procedures which generate reasons for action. Consequently, there is a matter of choosing procedures which surfaces in support of expressive considerations. But the choice of procedures is not something which an individual can make alone. Typically, procedures work like conventions through a common acceptance, and this places the matter of their explicit choice in the arena of collective action. Hence, expressively rational individuals seem inevitably to be committed to an activist state because they will wish to make explicit public choices with respect to the procedures which serve their expressive concerns.

Of course, it might be possible to stretch a definition by making the concern with a negative sense of freedom into the only expressive consideration, thereby making the individual expressive in this sense. But this would not avoid the substantive issue, namely, that the person in Nozick's theory could not be coherently endowed with the kind of expressive concerns we have associated with the quest for autonomy and self-respect in chapter 8.

The possibility of endowing Nozick's individual with a well-behaved set of preferences and an instrumental sense of rationality looks much more propitious. This is the combination of rights and individual motivation which is typically found in liberal theory. Furthermore, it seems that this type of motivation lies at the heart of Nozick's derivation of the night-watchman state. Individuals would contract with each other for a mutual defence agency because this is the most efficient means for preserving individual property rights. Minimally, then, Nozick's individuals seem to have a preference for something like wealth which they act instrumentally in pursuit of, when they contract for the nightwatchman state.

However, there is a difficulty with this combination. In effect, it comes from the conclusion which was drawn to the discussion on instrumental rationality in chapters 4 and 5 and that served to introduce procedural rationality in chapter 7. It will be recalled that instrumental rationality by itself could not account for or explain fully the events of the social world. The explanations generated by instrumental rationality ultimately relied on agents following procedures which could not be simply reduced to the residue of previous actions by instrumentally rational agents: these procedures contributed a non-reducible element to explanation in economics. This argument can now be turned on Nozick.

As observed in chapter 7, procedural rationality is really a testament to our historical location as individuals, where history stands for something other than what might be rationally reconstructed in terms of the actions of instrumentally rational agents. From an instrumental point of view, history here is something arbitrary which a society brings to the present. Consequently, it is not a matter of fact, of contingency, whether a particular history for a society transgressed a principle of consisting of trades freely undertaken by agents pursuing the satisfaction of their preferences: as a matter of logic, it can never be so reduced.

It will be helpful, perhaps, at this stage to clarify exactly how the argument drawn from chapters 4, 5, 6 and 7 is being used here. The argument in that part of the book on explanation is now being used to draw out the logical implications of a theory of justice based on Nozick's principles. So, there is no attempt here to turn a discussion of 'is' into a discussion of 'ought': the analysis of 'is' questions is acting as a servant in exploring the logical implications of a particular theory of what 'ought' to be.

The logical implication is that history cannot be reduced to a series of freely undertaken exchanges between instrumentally rational agents: there is always another element in a history of transactions. This either makes Nozick's theory of justice incomplete as it stands, since we have no way of judging the justice of these procedural elements in history; or these procedural elements are covered by the third principle because they constitute transgressions of the first two principles, in which case there is a continuing need for the use of a rectification principle, and with it a social welfare function.

This logical implication can be expressed in a slightly different way to bring out the incoherence which now attaches to this commitment to the negative sense of freedom. The negative sense of freedom is important because individuals should be free to decide on their own courses of action. In particular, actions should be voluntarily undertaken and not coerced by the arbitrary will of others. Yet, from the point of view of individual preference satisfaction, no action resulting from individual choice is free from the arbitrariness which the non-reducible procedural element imparts to every decision setting. From the individual point of view we inherit a set of procedures which in some degree is arbitrary; to make freedom only count with respect to a given set of procedures is also then to make us a slave to a history which is unavoidably arbitrary. To stop short of questioning this arbitrariness in the name of a negative sense of freedom seems very strange. But, if we wish to bring the arbitrariness of a particular history into the ambit of choice, then we must embrace questions of choice with respect to procedures; and for the reasons sketched above this sets an agenda for a more activist state. Hence, a thoroughgoing commitment to the right to Berlin's negative sense of freedom when combined with instrumental rationality necessitates an activist state just as does the commitment to expressive rationality and a positive sense of freedom found in Sen.

This leaves us then with a question about what vision of the individual can be combined with a negative sense of freedom whilst still preserving the conclusion of a minimal state? If not a person with well-behaved preferences or expressive concerns, what kind of a person will inhabit Nozick's world?

9.5 Conclusion

It has been argued in this chapter that orthodox welfare economics runs into problems generating public policy prescriptions because it works with a picture of individuals as solely a bunch of well-behaved preferences, which they are motivated in their actions to satisfy in an instrumental fashion.

This diagnosis of the 'problem' with orthodox welfare economics is shared by both Sen and the New Right. Both would argue that as far as the picture of the individual is concerned what is missing is a conception of rights. In particular, individuals have a right to liberty that must be respected and which cannot be reduced to a species of preference satisfaction.

Where the two depart is in their conception of freedom. The New Right works with the Berlin negative sense, where freedom is judged through the absence of restraint, while Sen uses Berlin's positive sense of freedom in the form of reflective autonomy. This leads to different views with respect to the project of prescriptive economics and the role of the state. While the New Right would like to shackle the state, the Sen approach leaves open the prospect of constructing a rich prescriptive economics to guide an activist state.

Since what is at issue in the critique of orthodox welfare economics is the vision of the individual, it is not surprising that some of the strands of the argument from the previous part of the book have been redeployed in this chapter. In particular, it has been argued, on the basis of the earlier discussion about the need for procedural rationality, that the negative conception of freedom cannot be coherently appended to a conception of the individual as exclusively acting instrumentally to satisfy a bunch of well-behaved preferences. It makes a nonsense of the claim to freedom because it involves making the individual a prisoner of a history which is arbitrary.

This is particularly unfortunate for the New Right. If this connection cannot be coherently made between negative freedom and preference satisfaction, and a connection with expressive rationality is Sen territory, then it becomes unclear what kind of a person is being respected in the name of negative freedom when the state is assigned the minimal role of a mutual protection association. Instead, an activist state operating with a social welfare function appears to be an unavoidable consequence of recognising a right to liberty, however that right is construed. The need to construct a social welfare function will not go away.

This puts the emphasis of the argument on the damage done to New Right. More generally, this chapter is a complement to the central theme of the book: economics needs to work with an expanded conception of the individual, and canons of rationality to match. Instrumental rationality, with individuals as a bunch of well-behaved preferences which they act to satisfy, will not suffice. There are virtues in the simple and the economical, but in this instance it is a false economy. The richer vision is needed now, not only for explanation, but also for prescriptions in economics.

10 CONCLUSION

10.1 Introduction

This chapter concludes the book. It begins with a brief summary of the argument. The book has two objectives. One is to reveal the centrality of rationality assumptions to economic analysis: to bring out how they generate different types of explanations and prescriptions in economics. The other is to advance the claim of the often neglected procedural and expressive rationality assumptions: they need to be taken more seriously than is presently the case.

The last suggestion may sound innocuous enough, perhaps even vapid, and hardly the material from which barricades are made. But, serious means serious; and the suggestion should be read against the backdrop of a profession that is almost single-minded in its association of rationality exclusively with instrumental rationality. The specification of agents with well-behaved objective functions, which they set about maximising, is a knee-jerk reaction of the profession to almost every problem. And when procedural rationality is recognised it is treated as an ersatz version of the real thing: instrumental rationality has only been cut by the restricted computational powers of agents. Yet, procedural rationality stands for much more than this, as does expressive rationality; and together they are crucial for economics.

Procedural and expressive rationality are a testament to our social and historical location, and our self-conscious reflective capacities. They are, quite simply, an indispensable resource for the project of explanation and prescription in economics.

The next section provides a brief summary of the arguments from the previous chapters which support this conclusion. The last two sections give two final illustrations of how these other conceptions of rationality can contribute to explanation and prescription in economics.

10.2 A Restatement

Figure 10.1 has been reproduced from chapter 1; it encapsulates many elements from the discussion. Three rationality postulates have been distinguished: each is associated with a distinctive type of explanatory scheme; and they are also allied with two sorts of prescriptive statements. While instrumental and procedural rationality are linked with two well-

Rationality	Explanation type	Form of prescription
Instrumental	Intentional (supra- and sub- intentional causality)	Consequentialist (i.e. Pareto optimality, utilitarianism)
Procedural	Functional (cumulative causation, hysteresis)	Rights based (i.e. capabilities, exploitation)
Expressive	True interest, experimental	

Figure 10.1 Taxonomic summary

recognised forms of explanation in the social sciences, expressive rationality does not add a new form as such. It merely contributes a particular and distinctive twist to explanations which have the form of an intentional or functional one.

One of the objectives of the book has been to expose, in this manner, the skeleton of rationality which holds the body of economics together. However, the main objective has been to evaluate the various rationality postulates. In particular, I have been concerned with assessing instrumental rationality, and with it the claims of neoclassical economics, because I take the exclusive use of this rationality postulate to be a hallmark of neoclassical economics.

Instrumental rationality is a powerful rationality assumption. Not only is it the hallmark of neoclassical economics, but it runs through almost every kind of economic analysis. Yet, I have argued, it is also fatally flawed when used as the exclusive rationality assumption.

Doubtless this conclusion will surprise some economists. Indeed, at the outset, many economists would probably regard it as more than a trifle exaggerated. There are many potential lines of defence for neoclassical economics, and I cannot hope to have answered explicitly every possible counter. Nevertheless, I hope to have anticipated some of the more obvious moves, like hiding behind the positive/normative distinction and pleading the case for a division of labour in the social sciences; or like the naive empiricist move which attempts to subordinate the question of rationality assumption to the 'empirical evidence' alone. The upshot, I believe, is that the main charge stands and it ought to hurt neoclassical economics if it has pretensions to be a useful body of theory.

The charge is that an exclusively instrumentally based explanation and prescription in economics is incomplete. There is not a pure instrumentally driven explanation; nor is there a pure instrumentally grounded prescription. The instrumental notion of agency is simply too thin to support by itself either explanation or prescription in economics.

There is really one central argument that lies behind this charge, to my mind, and which I hope to have assembled in the book. It is the incompleteness with respect to explanation, which comes from not being able to explain the provenance of the institutions and information sets which agents both work within and go to work with. It is this argument which prevents neoclassical economics from claiming completeness with respect to explanation; it also signals the gaps in the account of human action which are responsible for the impasse in welfare economics, and it is this same argument, when replayed in a slightly different way, which undermines a Nozickian attempt to marry the negative sense of freedom with instrumental rationality to rescue welfare economics from that impasse.

Let me unpackage this a little bit more. When I say a useful theory, what I mean is a theory which will enable us to intervene in the world. I want a theory so that, through understanding the way the world is, I can better understand how to intervene to achieve what I want, where 'what I want' can be construed narrowly, ethically or in whichever way you want. In other words, a useful theory is never just explanatory: it must be capable of generating guidance for action as well; and public intervention/collective action is one of the crucial areas in which we need such guidance. Now, exactly how it helps generate prescriptions will depend on the reading of the relation between 'is' and 'ought'. But whichever way that relationship is conceptualised, the capacity of instrumental rationality to produce prescriptions is hopelessly compromised by the incompleteness that has been detected in its explanations. The prescriptions are tendentiously either partial or indeterminate (see chapter 9).

It must be acknowledged that the argument rests heavily on this definition of usefulness because it makes the capacity for producing prescriptions the important objective, and the charge of explanatory incompleteness hurts because it undermines this capacity. I take this sense of usefulness to be reasonably uncontroversial because it links knowledge, in the form of theories about the way the world is, with the service of human interest, in the broad sense of liberation from being the objects of unknown casual processes. However, I suppose there are those who are genuinely concerned with explanation for explanation's sake. I am bound to say that I have little sympathy for an attitude that economic theories are 'for the birds', or for the view that the discourse of economics is a game, where the reasons for playing it are wholly internal to that game. Nevertheless, I must acknowledge that they exist.

For these people, the charge seems to amount only to one of incompleteness in explanation; and consequently it is much weaker. Nevertheless, it still stands, since 'completeness' would remain a plausible, purely internal objective for theories. And I suspect that many economists will be surprised by how incomplete their theories are in this respect: much of what is distinctive in these explanations turns on the assumed non-instrumental features. However, there is more to the charge here, which is worth noting. It can be argued on the basis of the special relation between theories and action in the social world compared with the natural world that our theories help in some measure to create the world. Explanation for explanation's sake theorists may lament this aspect of the world, but our theories do get used to shape the world. Theories do become metaphors for living in some degree, is how the point was put earlier, and this sort of theorist cannot escape answering the normative question about whether their theories offer good metaphors for living. The question will arise even if they are only concerned in so far as their theories may, via the metaphor for living aspect, affect the quality of future theorists with whom to play. Taken in this minimal way, it seems to me that it would be pretty boring to play the game of economic theory with an exclusively instrumentally rational person: it would be much like playing the game of economics with a machine (recall Pareto's remark in chapter 6); and this should count against the exclusively instrumental theory.

Of course, it is not difficult to construe the consequences of the metaphor for living aspect of theories more widely and so come to even harsher verdicts on the exclusively instrumental version of rationality. But the point has not been laboured in this book because the genuine explanation for explanation's sake economist is a rare breed. And although the same argument applies to those economists who are more straightforwardly concerned with the policy relevance of their economic explanations, it has not been pressed as there is the more telling argument for them which links the incomplete explanation to the indeterminate prescriptions.

It has been argued that to fill the explanatory gaps we need two further senses of rational action: the procedural and the expressive. It will be obvious how this might help. At its simplest, whenever instrumental considerations alone are not sufficient, we can invoke the following of a procedure to produce determinacy. What is less clear is why such action should be deemed rational in a way that is different from instrumental rationality. For instance, why is procedural rationality not just an imperfect version of instrumental rationality, so that it is the nature of the imperfection which brings the determinacy and not some new form of rationality? Likewise, why not treat expressive rationality as a variant of instrumental rationality with the specification of an objective of self-respect?

The short answer to these questions is that neither move to incorporate both observations in an amended version of instrumentally rational action will work. The procedural and the expressive stand for features of human agency which actually undermine or straddle the neat means-to-given-ends framework within which instrumental rationality gains a purchase. You cannot fit all those features into the means/ends framework, and it is as simple as that!

There are a number of interlinking elements in the argument which support this conclusion. Take procedural rationality first. The point here is that when procedures are shared they speak to our social and historical location as individuals. The reference to social location is shorthand for the strand in Wittgenstein's discussion of language games which has been used at various points in the argument (see sections 2.5, 6.3, 7.1 and 8.9). Shared procedures/rules aid communication and co-ordination, but they also create new and additional reasons for following the procedures/rules. This is potentially disturbing for the instrumental version of rationality because procedures no longer neatly fit the Simon model of shorthand means which aid the achievement of given ends. Procedures threaten this means/ends framework by creating ends themselves. Thus action is no longer simply about satisfying given ends: it is also implicated in the creation of the ends which instrumental rationality takes as given. The full force of this point is felt when it is tied to the one about historical location. This link prevents the restoration of instrumental rationality in a dynamic sense because the current procedures cannot be simply related back to some previous ends which agents pursued.

The reference to history is shorthand for the compendium of non-instrumental features in decision making that have been responsible for the historical emergence of the shared procedures/rules/conventions/institutions which we now use. These contemporary shared procedures cannot be rationally reconstructed by appeals to instrumental rationality alone (see chapters 4 and 5). So it is not just a matter of actual histories exhibiting imperfections in instrumental decision making and this is why we observe non-instrumental features in the record of decision making. Instrumental rationality itself is not enough, even in a world of perfect calculators. Something which stands independently is required. Imperfection has to be built in from the beginning and not tacked on afterwards, if you like. This is a further reason why procedural rationality has to be recognised in its own right, and it meshes with the earlier one built around the recognition that procedures actually help to create some of the objectives we pursue instrumentally.

Another way of appreciating this difference is to turn the point about history into one about the existence of a sort of freedom which would otherwise go unnoticed. We face a choice with respect to our shared procedures. History presents us with a set of procedures/rules, but they cannot be justified in terms of preference satisfaction alone. Any of a range of institutions will aid preference satisfaction by acting as co-ordinating and communicating devices. In short, we have degrees of freedom in our choice of shared procedures. This is obviously important, as we have seen, in justifying an activist state, since these are choices which can only be made in an explicit fashion collectively. (Procedures work as co-ordinating and communicating devices through being shared and so the active choice of these procedures requires the apparatus of collective decision making.) But it carries something more than this. We need a way of talking about this choice which involves something other than preference satisfaction; and this has implications for our conception of rationality. This is the bridge to expressive rationality.

If the choice of shared procedures/rules/institutions helps in part to create the motives for people to use those procedures, then this choice is also, in part, a choice of who to be. This connects with what I have argued is the particularly 'modern' embodiment of expressive rationality: the concern for self-respect or autonomy, a feeling that can be linked to Berlin's (1958) sense of self-mastery which comes from having good reason for being the person that you are.

This concern for self-respect is not something that can be assimilated to instrumental rationality by a suitable redefinition of the ends pursued by the individual. The pursuit of self-respect is open-ended in a way that defies the means-to-given-ends framework. It is about the choice of ends in conditions of genuine uncertainty, i.e. conditions marked by apparently unresolvable conflicts between different ways of being. Action undertaken in these circumstances cannot be understood as satisfying a given end; it is about a provisional decision with respect to the ends themselves. Indeed, it would be more accurate to describe such actions as an end in themselves because they are a mark of our expressive rationality (see section 8.9).

In other words, procedural rationality adds a necessary social and historical dimension to human agency, and expressive rationality gives us the equipment to avoid this recognition turning us into cultural and historical dopes.

An alternative way of expressing this central argument is to say that a framework premised only on instrumental rationality is unable to theorise adequately two central features of the world which need to be understood: power and uncertainty. The kaleidoscope of failure can be turned, and the points about institutions and information reassemble as points about power and uncertainty. It is through the non-instrumental components of the analysis of institutions and information sets that we develop a richer understanding of the concept of power and uncertainty (see sections 5.6 and 7.6).

To complete the 360° movement of the kaleidoscope and see how these rather different ways of making the point amount to the same thing, I suggest a summary in the form that procedures both constrain and enable individuals who are procedurally and expressively rational, where part of what is enabled is the very experimentation with new procedures for doing things. The constraining side of procedures is a testament to the concept of power while the enabling element speaks to the existence of uncertainty.

Put in these ways, the charge against neoclassical economics, in one sense, is hardly new. Phrased in terms of power and uncertainty, it uses the language of Marxian and post Keynesian critiques. Equally, the prescriptive part of the indictment will come as no surprise to the practitioners of welfare economics. What I hope to have done, however, is avoid a jejune exercise of repetition by weaving a thread through a number of the contemporary criticisms of neoclassical economics which traces them back to a single source: the impoverished vision of human agency which underpins neoclassical theory. Let me put it this way. I believe that, whether we are discussing Keynesian economics, the macrofoundations of microbehaviour, new theories of choice under uncertainty, the economic success of Quaker groups, exploitation, the capabilities approach to welfare economics and a whole host of other topics which lie outside the neoclassical domain, we are actually shifting from a model of human agency which is based on instrumental rationality to one which shows features of procedural and expressive rationality.

Furthermore, I think it is important to note this shared shift in rationality assumptions for at least four reasons. Firstly, many economists are, I suspect, simply unaware that there is any significant alternative or complementary rationality postulate on offer, let alone present within their economic analyses. This seems important for selling an idea. An argument about the need to take other rationality assumptions more seriously is not a leap into the dark. It is a matter of bringing out something which is already a buried part of our current theoretical efforts (see chapters 7 and 8). As such, it ought to be perceived as less threatening than might otherwise be the case.

Secondly, since I regard knowledge as a servant of human interests, broadly construed, it seems to me that it is crucial for economics to demonstrate progress with respect to welfare economics. As indicated above, this will come both through progress in the explicit discussions of prescriptive propositions and indirectly through improvements in the explanations we have of our economy to service those policy discussions. On both counts, then, it is a pressing requirement, if welfare economics is to make progress, that we recognise the thicker notion of human agency implied by procedural and expressive rationality.

Thirdly, I believe that it adds force to each individual criticism of neoclassical economics to notice that it shares the same foundations as many other criticisms. The whole is greater than the sum of its parts in this instance because we are not dealing with a set of isolated jibes. Neoclassical economics is not just a bit flaky around the edges, vulnerable to a set of opportunistic attacks mounted from whichever corner suits the occasion. These are not *ad hoc* criticisms. Instead, each is a part of a coherent challenge involving, in one way or another, the substitution of a richer vision of the individual for the one-dimensional neoclassical species.

Of course, some care is required here not to oversell the coherence of the challenge. The coherence which exists is at an abstract level which recognises the irreducible role of procedures in social life and the meshing concern for self-esteem and autonomy on the part of the individual. There is no claim here that this can be reduced to a shared calculus of decision making – witness the range of options in the new literature on decision making under uncertainty. Rather, it is an agreement over the reasons why it is sensible to build specific features like bandwagon effects or regret etc. into the analysis of action which yields the coherence. The details of what has actually to be built in cannot be specified in advance: these details belong to the study of the procedures in use at the time; and as we have seen these are matters of historical contingency.

Nor is the claim to coherence to be identified with simplicity or stability. These are actually the virtues of the exclusively instrumental portrayal. Instead, the coherence I am referring to comes from a shared view of the patterns of incoherence which lie behind individual action. This may sound contradictory. But it need not be understood in that way. The point is precisely that life is necessarily more complicated than the instrumental vision will allow. This does not mean it loses all shape: it simply means that the shape cannot be reduced to that of an exclusively instrumentally rational person. The coherence, then, comes from the agreement with respect to the terms which can be used to describe this more complicated shape.

Finally, there is the relationship between economics and the other social sciences. Once the criticism is phrased in terms of rationality assumptions, there is a natural bridge between disciplines which would make the contribution of economics to the other social sciences almost the exact opposite of what it is currently presumed to be. At the moment, economics is typically regarded as demonstrating the power of instrumental rationality. It has no need for any sociological concepts which depart from this individualistic model of agency. Indeed, to demonstrate the point, it is moving out into traditional areas of sociological and political analysis with its model of instrumentally rational agency. In this fashion, I suspect it has given succour to a simple kind of individualistic analysis within the social sciences as a whole.

Now, it would be foolish to deny the explanatory power of instrumental rationality in economics (see chapter 3), just as it would be wrong to imagine that the emphasis on rationality in this book means that empirical evidence is to be ignored (see chapter 2). But the argument of the book has not been about substituting some other sense of rationality for the instrumental. It has been about recognising the limitations of this vocabulary and the need to introduce explicitly other senses of rationality, the procedural and the expressive. In fact, I think economics is very adept at demonstrating this conclusion. Consequently, it is sending the wrong message to the other social sciences when it supports a simple kind of individualism. Nowhere is this mistake clearer than in the marriage of instrumental rationality and the negative sense of freedom that marks the arguments for a minimal state by the New Right. This represents a version of individualism which economics often seems to support. Yet, economics should be doing the reverse: by exposing the limitations of the instrumental model, it should be revealing the weaknesses of this particular argument.

10.3   Explanation and Prescription I

There is a sort of simple view of social change – it even runs through some Marxist analysis – which asserts that poverty and blocked avenues of social mobility are the breeding ground of social change. Even if it is simple, it is also an appealing thought. When a set of social arrangements so obviously disadvantages a large group as to render them impoverished, with little prospect of advancement, it seems likely they will rebel against those arrangements. The idea is well captured in Marx's famous dictum about having nothing to lose but your chains. Naturally, there are some matters of detail, like how to overcome free-rider problems in collective action of this sort, but the proposition seems at first sight to be quite plausible.

However, it also appears to be one of the frequently observed paradoxes of the social world that the reverse often seems to be the case. It is exactly when arrangements become more equal and when opportunities for advancement branch out that disaffection grows. Boudon (1986) summarises:

> . . classical sociology is full of paradoxical statements of this sort. For Tocqueville greater equality tends to produce envious comparisons; as they become more equal individuals find their equality harder to bear. C. Wright Mills has also taken up this theme. For Durkheim individual happiness does not increase in direct ratio to the quantity of goods available . . . [it] has the form of a reversed U shaped curve. Again for Tocqueville dissatisfaction may grow when each person's opportunities begin to open and improve . . . Lazarsfeld observes the converse . . . when an individual's future is blocked, recriminations against the social system may well be weak. Stouffer's works show that individuals may well grow more discontented with the social system to which they belong as it offers them . . . better opportunities for success and promotion. (p. 171)

Boudon (1986) offers an interpretation of these paradoxical observations which revolves around what he calls 'the logic of relative frustration'. The basic idea is that people have reference groups and they judge the value of what they do or consume in relation to their reference groups. This judgement can lead to feelings of relative frustration when a person finds that he/she is not enjoying the same range of activities as his/her reference group.

Now, consider a very simple model of competition between individuals in a society where an individual can either enter a 'lottery/competition' for a stake c where there is a 'prize/benefit' of b with a probability of success that diminishes as the number of competitors rises or he/she can choose not to participate in the competition. As Boudon (1986) remarks, 'this very general structure characterises a whole number of situations in which there is competition: should I invest in order to try and be promoted to the rank of office head, given that the majority of my colleagues are doubtless driven by the same objective?' Alternatively, one might add as a further illustration, it also fits well the example of a firm considering whether to undertake an R&D programme designed to produce a new commodity. The firm knows that many firms already in related markets are similarly motivated and not all can succeed, with the probability of success declining as the number of firms embarking on such programmes increases. Not all can succeed at R&D for a variety of reasons: for instance, in the cases of consumer durables like video recorders or computer operating systems, those who get there first establish the industry standards, capture brand loyalties and so on, enjoying economies of scale, which puts the late arrivals at an impossible competitive disadvantage. In short, there is only the possibility of some finite number of new commodities filling this product niche and so the probability of success falls with the number of competitors.

Let x be the number of competitors, n the number of winners and N the number in the population. It follows that in equilibrium the expected return from competing must be equal to the return from non-competition:

$$\frac{n}{x} b - c = 0 \Rightarrow x = n \frac{b}{c} \qquad (10.1)$$

This condition can either be interpreted as defining the number x of people who will compete, or as defining the probability x/n that each individual will compete when they play a mixed strategy option in this game amongst themselves. Whichever interpretation is preferred, two groups will emerge (or can be expected to emerge) from this setting: the x competitors and the $N-x$ non-competitors. Within the group of competitors, there will be two sub-groups: those who succeed (n) and those who fail in the gamble $(x-n)$. It is the latter sub-group who, Boudon argues, will experience the feelings of relative frustration.

If we rearrange (10.1) to reveal the determinants of the relative size of this group within the population we have

$$\frac{x\text{-}n}{N} = \frac{n}{N} \left(\frac{b}{c} - 1 \right) \qquad (10.2)$$

From this it follows that the proportion of the population suffering relative frustration rises with increases in n/N, the proportion of winners in the population, and with increases in b/c, the size of the potential gain from entering the competition, provided that $(n/N)(b/c) < 1$. That is, relative frustration rises as long as the original number of competitors does not comprise the whole population. Once this level of competition has been reached, any rise in n/N must lower relative frustration, while a rise in b/c will leave the level unchanged.

This demonstrates nicely the Stouffer observation that disaffection, in the form of relative frustration, grows in a system where promotion (n/N) is more likely. Likewise, we can associate the size of nb with the growth of the organisation/society: nb is the overall gain which is available to competitors and the greater the growth in a society, *ceteris paribus*, the greater the pool of 'gains' which can be competed for. Alternatively, put this in terms of the corporation: its success in markets will determine the size of the surplus nb which can be made available for funding promotions in the organisation. In either interpretation, relative frustration increases as nb, the index of success/growth, rises.

Before pursuing this example, it is perhaps worth pausing to connect explicitly the Boudon model of relative frustration with the earlier discussion of procedural and expressive rationality, and to note how this might feed into prescriptive statements. Firstly, on the procedural side, we can associate the parameters of this example, b/c and n, with the procedures of a society or an organisation. This is plain in Stouffer's analysis of the police department: there will be procedures which govern promotion, a career structure that identifies the probability of promotion and the increment to income arising. Equally plainly, the organisation faces a choice with respect to these procedures and hence the parameters n/N and b/c, and it will be concerned amongst other things with the degree of disaffection they provoke. Likewise, in the example of R&D projects, the gains from success (b/c) can be altered by the taxation regime in an economy, and without taking the prescriptive discussion any further it would seem uncontroversial to assume that a government might be interested in the effect which its taxation scheme has both on innovative efforts and relative frustration. Innovative effort (x) is likely to interest governments because, in a more general setting discussed below, it will plausibly influence the number of successes (n); and relative frustration here will be important because it is an index of the financial fragility of firms in a particular industry since it captures the proportion of firms who find themselves in a weak financial position because they have expended the resources on innovation without reaping the rewards. As such it is a guide to likely changes in industrial structure.

The phenomenon of relative frustration itself can best be understood with reference to the expressive sense of rationality. This is not to imply that expressive rationality can be reduced to relative frustration, but there are some obvious connections. In general terms, the concern with making sense of the world can lead people to find causal connections between events where none exists. It is one of the frequent observations in the experimental psychological literature that people do not accept that events which are driven by stochastic processes are stochastic by nature. Instead, they introduce causal explanations for what are in effect the patterns of chance (see Steinbruner, 1974). For instance, sports fans will often talk about winning/losing streaks to describe the phenomenon where winning/losing today seems to make it more likely that you will win/lose again tomorrow because your confidence soars/wanes. In fact, there are very few winning/losing streaks in sports which do not occur with a frequency and duration that you would expect from simple stochastic models where teams have a stable probability of winning each game that they play (see Kahneman, Slovic and Tversky, 1982).

In short, we are constant strivers after an order in the universe and this leads us to look for an order or reason even when none exists, as in the case of this competition where winners and losers are decided by luck. This means that we are likely to find a reason for failure in these circumstances, and the most likely reason is to be found within the self and to lead to a consequent diminution in self-respect.

To be more specific, it might be argued slightly differently. Individuals who enter the competition and lose face a challenge to their self-esteem and this leads to feelings of disaffection. The losers have competed, and in terms of most schemes of justice they will seem to have lost for no good moral reason. This sense of disaffection can be further analysed by noting that this failure has placed them in a position of cognitive dissonance: their own self-image confronts the experience of failure. Two possibilities for reconciliation are present: either the individuals lower their own estimate of their worth, i.e. self-esteem drops; or they find an external explanation for their failure in the form of faulty competition rules, and the disaffection attaches to these arrangements. The latter is, then, more probable when there is a large proportion of failures because the sharing of failure by a significant group is likely to point away from the idiosyncrasies of individual character to the shared participation in a game with 'unfair' rules.

So, to summarise the connections: the procedures of a society are implicated in the terms of the competition and relative frustration can be understood by reference to expressive rationality. Finally, if individuals, say, use Rawls's veil of ignorance technique for making prescriptive statements and the individuals are expressively rational, then they will be interested, among other things, in how much relative frustration there is under different procedural arrangements.

· Before using this simple model to generate some further understanding of the Tocqueville paradoxes, two points of generalisation should be noted.

Firstly, a word is in order about the consistency between the hypothesis that relative frustration matters, and the theory of individual decision making that has been built into the model. This is not the place to attempt a specific formulation of decision making by expressively rational agents: this has already been eschewed in the discussion of chapter 8. However, it is known from the discussion of that chapter that there are variety of specific hypotheses, and it is possible to gesture in their direction by placing a slightly different interpretation on the otherwise apparently conventional decision making rule present in the model. (This has the further benefit of keeping the analysis as uncontroversial as possible.) In particular, some evaluation of the benefit b can be taken to represent the concern which individuals have for experimentation/innovation, to take the existential approach to self-respect, and the stake c can be construed as a risk premium, where the risk is the prospect of the failure, which is valued because of the consequences failure has for self-esteem. In other words, c captures the individual's desire to safeguard self-esteem through the avoidance of failures and b captures, in part, the pursuit of self-esteem through experimentation.

Secondly, it is possible to endogenise the number n of winners in a variety of ways. Perhaps the most appealing is to make it an increasing function of x, the number of competitors. In the case of the organisation considering the promotion procedures, this makes sense because the number of individuals competing for promotion might reasonably have an effect on the success of the organisation and hence the amount of surplus which is available for expenditure on promotions. Likewise, with R&D it seems sensible to make the number of 'winners' an increasing function of the number of firms 'trying'. In these circumstances, the only procedural choice variable is b/c. The proportion of experimenters/competitors is given implicitly by

$$\frac{x}{N} = \frac{f(x)}{N} \frac{b}{c} \qquad (10.3)$$

where $n=f(x)$. Assuming a solution for x from (10.2) within the interval given by the population size, and $f'>0$, $f''<0$, then it is easy to demonstrate that relative frustration grows in the population as b/c increases.

To conclude this section, one obvious prescriptive inference can be drawn from this more general model. In so far as the policy maker is concerned with promoting the number of successes, the growth of the organisation or whatever, then it will make sense to increase the incentive from experimenting/competing by stretching the ratio b/c. This, so to speak, is no different from the conventional argument that lies behind policies which improve the incentives to risk taking. However, in so far as the policy maker is also interested in minimising the relative frustration, i.e. the disaffection which can either result in lowered self-esteem or opposition to the very procedures of the organisation/society, then the policy maker will wish to reduce incentives. This provides a different motive for reducing incentives to the traditional concern which is stated in terms of the principle of equity.

10.4 Explanation and Prescription II

The model of the previous section treated the population as comprising N identical individuals. It can be complicated by allowing for several different groups of individuals in a society. This enables the effects of inequality between groups to be studied.

Suppose there are two groups, denoted by subscripts 1 and 2. They are distinguished by having different costs c for entering the competition and different proportions of 'winners', n/N. Group 2 is designated as the subordinate group because the proportion of winners drawn from this group is smaller and because the cost of entering the competition is higher. The difference in costs of entry can be regarded as a reflection of the static dimension of stratification. For example, a static measure of stratification is the existing inequality with respect to wealth holdings between the groups and it is commonly assumed that poorer groups attach a higher risk premium to failure. In turn, the difference in the proportion of winners could be picking up the dynamic aspect of stratification in a society, by capturing the different chances of success between groups.

The equations

$$\frac{x_1}{N_1} = \frac{n_1}{N_1} \frac{b}{c_1} \tag{10.4}$$

$$\frac{x_2}{N_2} = \frac{n_2}{N_2} \frac{b}{c_2} \tag{10.5}$$

define the equilibrium proportion of competitors/experimenters for each group; and

$$\frac{x_1 - n_1}{N_1} = \frac{n_1}{N_1} \left(\frac{b - 1}{c_1} \right) \tag{10.6}$$

$$\frac{x_2 - n_2}{N_2} = \frac{n_2}{N_2} \left(\frac{b - 1}{c_2} \right) \tag{10.7}$$

give the respective levels of relative frustration.

Two interesting features of such a stratified society are revealed here which relate back to the earlier paradoxes of Tocqueville et al. Firstly, it can be noted that the proportion of experimenters from the subordinate group will be smaller than the proportion from the dominant one and this will tend to legitimise the inequalities with respect to the distribution of rewards. Since there is a rough correspondence between reward and effort here, it could be read as 'reward has followed effort' when, in fact, the reverse is the case. Secondly, the relative frustration of the dominant group is greater than that of the subordinate group, so those who are actually disadvantaged by the procedures of a society are less likely to feel disaffected from those procedures.

These observations might help explain both why an unequal set of procedures does not always generate a reaction among those who are disadvantaged and why the attacks on those procedures are often led by members of the group which is actually advantaged by those procedures. In particular, it can be shown that a movement towards equality in the form of $dn_1 < 0$ and $dn_1 = -dn_2$, or a zero sum redistribution of wealth which has the same but opposite linear effect on the cs, will lead to an increase in the relative frustration of the subordinate group and a diminution of that amongst the dominant group. In short, there is support for Tocqueville's observation that increased equality often has the perverse effect of increasing the disaffection amongst the disadvantaged group whose position has actually been improved by the movement towards greater equality.

Again this model of how the effects of stratification within a society feed through to reinforce/undermine that stratification can be made more general by allowing for the 'rewards' n_i of a group to depend on the 'efforts' x_i of that group, as above. The analysis carries over as before.

Let us turn explicitly to the prescriptive implications. It will not be obvious from what has been said that there need be any clear impact on the overall level of relative frustration in a society as a result of redistribution since the relative frustration of the two groups moves in opposite directions. However, it is possible to say something more specific in the general case where n depends upon x. In particular, it is easy to demonstrate that in so far as a redistribution from poor to rich is justified on the traditional incentive grounds because it leads overall to a greater number of successes, then the overall level of relative frustration in the society will also rise.

Group 1

		E	NE
Group 2	E	$b - c_2, b - c_1$	$-c_2, 0$
	NE	$0, -c_1$	$0,0$

Figure 10.2   Co-ordinating experimentation game

This parallels the earlier insight for a society where individuals are not stratified into groups, and suggests a general proposition that in so far as relative frustration matters to policy makers it will constitute a new reason to set against the traditional argument that increasing inequality helps to create the incentives which encourage greater experimentation and, with it, growth.

As a final illustration, consider the case where the probability of success is not determined competitively: rather it is governed by a synergistic process. Suppose for instance that when members from different groups meet, they can either behave experimentally (i.e. use some new cultural convention) or non-experimentally (i.e. use the tried and tested convention for dealing with intergroup communication). The return from each strategy depends on the strategy pursued by the member of the other group. To capture the idea of synergy: each i enjoys a return of $b-c_i$ if both experiment, and 0 if neither experiment; while he/she just incurs the cost c_i of experimenting if he/she experiments while the member of the other group does not. In other words, there is a co-ordination game between members of the two groups with a matrix of pay-offs given by figure 10.2.

I now assume, as before in the analysis of repeated play of such games, that the probability of a group 1 member experimenting is p and this is revised upwards or downwards according to the relative success of the two strategies. Success depends on the probability q of group 2 members experimenting, and this probability is revised in the same fashion and so depends on p. The dynamics of the evolution of p and q are given by the phase diagram in figure 10.3.

There are two stable equilibria: $[1, 1]$, $[0, 0]$. Either everyone experiments or nobody does. In this case, as you might expect from the synergistic setting, there is no trade-off between the number of successes and the level of relative frustration. There is no relative frustration with either equilibrium, but the $[1, 1]$ equilibrium brings higher returns (everyone is a success compared with no successes at $[0, 0]$). Public policy will want to increase the chances of achieving $[1, 1]$ rather than $[0, 0]$. Which is achieved will depend on the initial $[p, q]$ pairs. Anywhere in the area

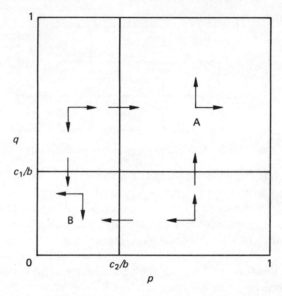

Figure 10.3   Repeated play of the experimentation game

designated A shoots the society to [1, 1], while anywhere in B yields [0, 0]. Hence, any public policy that increases the size of area A while reducing that of B will increase the chances of achieving the [1, 1] solution.

It can be easily demonstrated that, if risk aversion falls but at a diminishing rate as wealth increases and if wealth differences are the source of differences in c, then a redistribution of wealth from the rich group 1 to the poor group 2 will increase the size of A−B.

Hence, it would seem on the basis of these three examples that the recognition of expressive and procedural rationality in welfare economics is likely to favour policies of equality. Of course, these examples tender only hints of how welfare economics might be concretely affected by expressive and procedural considerations, and so the conclusion must necessarily be qualified. What need not be qualified, however, is the more general conclusion which has been drawn from the acknowledgment of procedural and expressive rationality in this book. This is that questions of state activism cannot be avoided. Quite simply, we have a concern for freedom which necessitates that matters of collective choice must always be addressed in a society.

REFERENCES

Akerlof, G. (1970) 'The Market for "Lemons": Quality Uncertainty and the Market Mechanism'. *Quarterly Journal of Economics*, 84, 488–500.
Akerlof, G. (1980) 'A Theory of Social Custom, of which Unemployment May be One Consequence'. *American Economic Review*, 80, 749–75.
Akerlof, G. (1983) 'Loyalty Filters'. *American Economic Review*, 73, 54–63.
Akerlof, G. and Dickens, W. (1982) 'The Economic Consequences of Cognitive Dissonance'. *American Economic Review*, 72, 307–20.
Alchian, A. (1951) 'Uncertainty, Evolution and Economic Theory'. *Journal of Political Economy*, June, 211–22.
Alchian, A. (1971) 'Information Costs, Pricing, and Resource Unemployment', in E. S. Phelps et al., *Microfoundations of Employment and Inflation Theory*. London: Macmillan.
Aronson, E. (1972) *The Social Animal*. San Francisco, CA: W. H. Freeman.
Arrow, K. J. (1951) *Social Choice and Individual Values*. New Haven, CT: Yale University Press.
Arrow, K. J. and Hahn, F. H. (1971) *General Competitive Analysis*. Amsterdam: North Holland.
Axelrod, R. (1981) 'The Emergence of Co-operation amongst Egoists'. *American Political Science Review*, 75, 306–18.
Axelrod, R. and Cohen, M. D. (1984) 'Coping with Complexity: The Adaptive Value of Changing Utility'. *American Economic Review*, 74, 30–42.
Backus, D. and Driffill, J. (1985) 'Inflation and Reputation'. *American Economic Review*, 75, 530–38.
Barro, R. J. and Gordon, D. B. (1983) 'Rules, Discretion, and Reputation in a Model of Monetary Policy'. *Journal of Monetary Economics*, 12, 101–21.
Barro, R. J. and Grossman, H. I. (1971) 'A General Disequilibrium Model of Income and Employment'. *American Economic Review*, 61, 82–93.
Becker, G. S. (1965) *Economics of Discrimination*. Chicago, IL: University of Chicago Press.
Becker, G. S. (1968) 'Crime and Punishment: an Economic Approach'. *Journal of Political Economy*, 80, 813–46.
Becker, G. S. and Stigler, G. J. (1977) 'De Gustibus non est Disputandum'. *American Economic Review*, 67, 76–90.
Beckerman, W. (1965) 'Demand, Exports and Growth', in W. Beckerman et al., *The British Economy in 1975*. London: NIESR.
Begg, D. (1982) *The Rational Expectations Revolution in Macroeconomics: Theories and Evidence*. Deddington: Philip Allan.
Berlin, I. (1958) 'Two Concepts of Liberty', reprinted in *Four Essays on Liberty* (1969). London: Oxford University Press.
Bernheim, D. (1984) 'Rationalizable Strategic Behaviour'. *Econometrica*, 52, 1007–28.
Bernstein, R. J. (1983) *Beyond Objectivity and Relativism*. Oxford: Basil Blackwell.
Binmore, K. (1987) 'Modeling Rational Players: Part I'. *Economics and Philosophy*, 3, 179–214.

226   REFERENCES

Binmore, K. (1988) 'Modeling Rational Players: Part II'. *Economics and Philosophy*, 4, 9–55.
Binmore, K. and Dasgupta, P. (1986) *Economic Organisations as Games*. Oxford: Basil Blackwell.
Blanchard, O. and Summers, L. H. (1986) 'Hysteresis and European Unemployment', in *NBER Macroeconomics Annual*. Cambridge, MA: MIT Press.
Blanchard, O. and Watson M. (1982) 'Bubbles, Rational Expectations and Financial Markets', in P. Wachtel (ed.), *Crises in the Economic and Financial Structure*. Lexington, MA: Lexington Books.
Blaug, M. (1980) *The Methodology of Economics: Or How Economists Explain*. Cambridge: Cambridge University Press.
Blume, L., Bray, M. and Easley, D. (1982) 'Introduction to the Stability of Rational Expectations Equilibrium'. *Journal of Economic Theory*, 26, 313–17.
Boudon, R. (1986) 'The Logic of Relative Frustration', in J. Elster (ed.), *Rational Choice*. Oxford: Basil Blackwell.
Bray, M. (1983) 'Convergence to Rational Expectations Equilibrium', in R. Frydman and E. S. Phelps (eds), *Individual Forecasting and Aggregate Outcomes*. Cambridge: Cambridge University Press.
Bray, M. (1985) 'Rational Expectations, Information and Asset Markets: An Introduction'. *Oxford Economic Papers*, 37, 161–95.
Buchanan, J. M. (1975) *The Limits of Liberty*. Chicago, IL: University of Chicago Press.
Buchanan, J. M. (1986) *Liberty, Market and the State*. Brighton: Wheatsheaf.
Casson, M. (1982) *The Entrepreneur: An Economic Theory*. Oxford: Martin Robertson.
Casson, M. (1987) 'Entrepreneur', in J. Eatwell, M. Milgate and P. Newman (eds), *The New Palgrave: A Dictionary of Economic Theory*. London: Macmillan.
Chatwin, B. (1987) *Songlines*. London: Cape.
Caldwell, B. J. (1982) *Beyond Positivism*. London: Allen and Unwin.
Clarke, E. H. (1971) 'Multipart Pricing of Public Goods'. *Public Choice*, 29, 65–70.
Clarke, R. N. (1983) 'Collusion and Incentives for Sharing Information'. *Bell Journal of Economics*, 14, 383–94.
Coase, R. H. (1937) 'The Nature of the Firm'. *Economica*, 4, 386–405.
Cohen, G. A. (1978) *Karl Marx's Theory of History: A Defence*. Oxford: Oxford University Press.
Cohen, G. A. (1982) 'Reply to Elster on "Marxism, Functionalism and Game Theory"'. *Theory and Society*, 11, 483–496.
Collard, D. A. (1978) *Altruism and the Economy*. Oxford: Martin Robertson.
Cornwall, J. (1978) *Modern Capitalism: Its Growth and Transformation*. Oxford: Martin Robertson.
Deaton, A. and Muellbauer, J. (1980) *Economics and Consumer Behaviour*. Cambridge: Cambridge University Press.
Dixit, A. (1980) 'The Role of Investment in Entry Deterrence'. *Economic Journal*, 90, 95–106.
Douglas, M. (1975) *Implicit Meanings*. London: Routledge and Kegan Paul.
Douglas, M. (1977) 'Beans Means Thinks'. *The Listener*, 8 September, 292–3.
Douglas, M. (1982) *In the Active Voice*. London: Routledge and Kegan Paul.
Douglas, M. (1986) *How Institutions Think*. London: Routledge and Kegan Paul.
Douglas, M. and Baron Isherwood (1980) *The World of Goods: Toward an Anthropology of Consumption*. Harmondsworth: Penguin.
Dreyfus, H. (1987) 'Husserl, Heidegger and Modern Existentialism', in B. Magee (ed.), *The Great Philosophers*. London: BBC Books.

Duhem, P. (1914) *The Aim and Structure of Physical Theory*. Princeton, NJ: Princeton University Press.

Earl, P. (1983) *The Economic Imagination*. Brighton: Wheatsheaf.

Earl, P. (1986) *Lifestyle Economics*. Brighton: Wheatsheaf.

Elster, J. (1978) *Logic and Society*. Chichester: Wiley.

Elster, J. (1979) *Ulysses and the Sirens*. Cambridge: Cambridge University Press.

Elster, J. (1982) 'Marxism, Functionalism and Game Theory'. *Theory and Society*, 11, 453–82.

Elster, J. (1983a) *Explaining Technical Change*. Cambridge: Cambridge University Press.

Elster, J. (1983b) *Sour Grapes: Studies in the Subversion of Rationality*. Cambridge: Cambridge University Press.

Elster, J. (1985) *Making Sense of Marx*. Cambridge: Cambridge University Press.

Evans, G. (1983) 'The Stability of Rational Expectations in Macroeconomic Models', in R. Frydman and E. S. Phelps (eds), *Individual Forecasting and Aggregate Outcomes*. Cambridge: Cambridge University Press.

Freeman, R. and Medoff, J. (1979) 'Two Faces of Unions'. *Public Interest*, Fall, 69–93.

Friedman, A. L. (1977) *Industry and Labour: Class Struggle at Work*. London: Macmillan.

Friedman, M. (1953) *Essays in Positive Economics*. Chicago, IL: University of Chicago Press.

Frydman, R. (1982) 'Towards an Understanding of Market Processes: Individual Expectations, Learning and Convergence to Rational Expectations Equilibrium'. *American Economic Review*, 72, 652–68.

Frydman, R. and Phelps, E. S. (1983) *Individual Forecasting and Aggregate Outcomes*. Cambridge: Cambridge University Press.

Fudenberg, D. and Maskin, E. (1986) 'The Folk Theorem in Repeated Games with Discounting or with Incomplete Information'. *Econometrica*, 54, 533–54.

Gibbard, A. (1973) 'Manipulation of Voting Schemes: a General Result'. *Econometrica*, 41, 587–602.

Giddens, A. (1979) *Central Problems in Social Theory*. London: Macmillan.

Giddens, A. (1982) 'Commentary on the Debate'. *Theory and Society*, 11, 527–39.

Goodhart, C. and Crockett, A. (1970) 'The Importance of Money'. *Bank of England Quarterly Bulletin*, 10, 159–98.

Gordon, R. J. (1982) 'Why US Wage and Employment Behaviour Differs from that of Britain and Japan'. *Economic Journal*, 92, 13–44.

Green, H. (1971) *Consumer Theory*. Harmondsworth: Penguin.

Groves, T. (1973) 'Incentives in Teams'. *Econometrica*, 41, 617–33.

Habermas, J. (1985–6) *The Theory of Communicative Action*. Cambridge: Polity Press.

Hahn, F. (1980) *Money and Inflation*. Oxford: Basil Blackwell.

Hahn, F. (1987) 'Information, Dynamics and Equilibrium'. *Scottish Journal of Political Economy*, 34, 321–34.

Hahn, F. and Solow, R. (1986) 'Is Wage Flexibility a Good Thing?' in W. Beckerman (ed.), *Wage Rigidity and Unemployment*. London: Duckworth.

Haltiwanger, J. and Waldman, M. (1985) 'Rational Expectations and the Limits of Rationality: An Analysis of Heterogeneity'. *American Economic Review*, 75, 326–40.

Hammond, P. J. (1976) 'Changing Tastes and Coherent Dynamic Choice'. *Review of Economic Studies*, 43, 159–73.

Hargreaves Heap, S. P. (1986) 'Risk and Culture: A Missing Link in the Post

Keynesian Tradition'. *Journal of Post Keynesian Economics*, 9, 267–79.

Hargreaves, Heap, S. P. (1980) 'Choosing the Wrong "Natural" Rate: Accelerating Inflation or Decelerating Employment and Growth?'. *Economic Journal*, 90, 611–20.

Hargreaves Heap, S. P. and Hollis, M. (1987) 'Great Expectations'. *Tijdschrift voor Politieke Ekonomie*, 10, 8–29.

Hargreaves Heap, S. P. and Varoufakis, Y. (1987) Multiple Reputations in Games with Uncertain Horizons. Economics Research Centre Discussion Paper No. 22, University of East Anglia.

Harsanyi, J. C. (1955) 'Cardinal Welfare, Individualistic Ethics and Interpersonal Comparisons of Utility'. *Journal of Political Economy*, 63, 309–21.

Harsanyi, J. C. (1975) 'The Tracing Procedure: A Bayesian Approach to Defining a Solution for n Person Non-co-operative Games'. *International Journal of Game Theory*, 5, 61–94.

Hayek, F. A. (1937) 'Economics and knowledge'. *Economica*, 4, 33–54.

Hayek, F. A. (1969) *Studies in Philosophy, Politics and Economics*. New York: Simon and Schuster.

Hayek, F. A. (1973) *Law, Legislation and Liberty* (three volumes, the first was published in 1973, the others in 1976 and 1979). London: Routledge and Kegan Paul.

Heilbroner, R. (1988) 'Economics without Power'. *New York Review of Books*, 3 March.

Hintikka, J. (1967) 'Cogito, Ergo Sum', in W. Dewey (ed.), *Descartes*. London: Macmillan.

Hirsch, F. (1976) *Social Limits to Growth*. London: Routledge and Kegan Paul.

Hobson, A. (1988) *The Dreaming Brain*. New York: Basic Books.

Hodgson, G. (1988) *Economics and Institutions*. Cambridge: Polity Press.

Hollis, M. (1983) 'Rational Preferences'. *Philosophical Forum*, 14, 246–62.

Hollis, M. (1987) *Cunning of Reason*. Cambridge: Cambridge University Press.

Isaacson, D. L. and Madsen, R. W. (1976) *Markov Chains: Theory and Applications*. Chichester: Wiley.

Kahneman, D., Slovic, P. and Tversky, A. (eds) (1982) *Judgement under Uncertainty: Heuristics and Biases*. Cambridge: Cambridge University Press.

Kahneman and Tversky, A. (1979) 'Prospect Theory: An Analysis of Decision under Risk'. *Econometrica*, 47, 263–91.

Kaldor, N. (1939) 'Welfare Propositions of Economics and Inter-personal Comparisons of Utility'. *Economic Journal*, 49, 549–52.

Kaldor N. (1970) 'The New Monetarism'. *Lloyds Bank Review*, 139, 1–18.

Katouzian, H. (1980) *Ideology and Method in Economics*. London: Macmillan.

Kelly, G. A. (1955) *The Psychology of Personal Constructs*. New York: Norton.

Keynes, J. M. (1936) *The General Theory of Employment Interest and Money*. London: Macmillan.

Kreps, D. and Wilson, R. (1982) 'Reputation and Imperfect Information'. *Journal of Economic Theory*, 27, 253–79.

Kreps, D., Milgrom, P. Roberts, J. and Wilson, R. (1982) Rational Co-operation in the Finitely Repeated Prisoners' Dilemma'. *Journal of Economic Theory*, 27, 242–52.

Kuhn, T. S. (1970) *The Structure of Scientific Revolutions*. Chicago, IL: Chicago University Press.

Kuran, T. (1987) 'Preference Falsification, Policy Continuity and Collective Conservatism'. *Economic Journal*, 97, 642–61.

Lakatos, I. (1978) 'Methodology of Scientific Research Programmes', in J. Worral and G. Currie (eds), *Philosophical Papers* volume 1. Cambridge: Cambridge University Press.

Lancaster, K. J. (1966) 'A New Approach to Consumer Theory'. *Journal of Political Economy*, 74, 132–57.

Latsis, S. J. (ed.) (1976) *Method and Appraisal in Economics*. Cambridge: Cambridge University Press.

Lea, S., Tarpy, R. and Webley, P. (1987) *The Individual in the Economy: A Survey of Economic Psychology*. Cambridge: Cambridge University Press.

Leamer, E. E. (1983) 'Let's Take the Con out of Econometrics'. *American Economic Review*, 73, 31–43.

Leibenstein, H. (1968) 'Entrepreneurship and Development'. *American Economic Review*, 58, 72–83.

Leijonhufvud, A. (1968) *On Keynesian Economics and the Economics of Keynes*. London: Oxford University Press

Leiss, W. Kline, S. and Jhally, S. (1986) *Social Communication in Advertising*. London: Methuen.

Levi, I. (1984) *Decisions and Revisions*. Cambridge: Cambridge University Press.

Levi, I. (1986) 'Paradoxes of Allais and Ellsberg'. *Economics and Philosophy*, 2, 23–53.

Levine, A., Sober, E. and Olin Wright, E. (1987) 'Marxism and Methodological Individualism'. *New Left Review*, 162, 67–84.

Lipsey, R. (1963) *An Introduction to Positive Economics*. London: Weidenfeld and Nicolson.

Lipsey, R. J. and Lancaster, K. (1956) 'The General Theory of the Second Best'. *Review of Economic Studies*, 24, 11–32.

Loomes, G. and Sugden, R. (1982) 'Regret Theory: An Alternative Theory of Rational Choice under Uncertainty.' *Economic Journal*, 92, 805–24.

Luce, R. and Raiffa, H. (1957) *Games and Decisions*. New York: Wiley.

Lukes, S. (1974) *Power: A Radical View*. London: Macmillan.

MacIntyre, A. (1973) 'The Idea of a Social Science', in A. Ryan (ed.), *The Philosophy of Social Explanation*. Oxford: Oxford University Press.

MacIntyre, A. (1981) *After Virtue*. London: Duckworth.

Malinvaud, E. (1977) *The Theory of Unemployment Reconsidered*. Oxford: Basil Blackwell.

Marglin, S. (1974) 'What Do Bosses Do?'. *Review of Radical Political Economy*, 6, 60–112.

Marx, K. (1950) 'Preface to A Contribution to the Critique of Political Economy', in *Selected Works* volume 1. London: Lawrence and Wishart.

Marx, K. (1967a) *Capital* volume 1. New York: International Publishers.

Marx, K. (1967b) *Capital* volume 2. New York: International Publishers.

Marx, K. (1975) 'Contribution to the Critique of Hegel's Philosophy of Law', in *Collected Works* volume 3. London: Lawrence and Wishart.

Marx, K. (1978) 'Class Struggles in France', in *Collected Works* volume 10. London: Lawrence and Wishart.

McAleer, M., Pagan, A. and Volker, P. (1985) 'What will Take the Con out of Econometrics?' *American Economic Review*, 75, 293–307.

McCallum, B. T. (1980) 'Rational Expectations and Macroeconomic Stabilization Policy'. *Journal of Money, Credit and Banking*, 12, 716–46.

McCloskey, D. (1983) 'The Rhetoric of Economics'. *Journal of Economic Literature*, 21, 481–517.

230   REFERENCES

Mises, L. von (1949) *Human Action: A Treatise on Economics*. London: Hodge.
Mises, L. von (1962) *The Ultimate Foundation of Economic Science*. Princeton, NJ: Van Nostrand.
Muth, J. F. (1961) 'Rational Expectations and the Theory of Price Movements'. *Econometrica*, 29, 315–35.
Nell, E. (ed.) (1980) *Growth, Profits and Property*. Cambridge: Cambridge University Press.
Nelson, R and Winter, S. (1982) *An Evolutionary Theory of Economic Change*. Cambridge, MA: Harvard University Press.
Nelson, R. and Winter, S. (1975) 'Factor Price Changes and Factor Substitution in an Evolutionary Model'. *Bell Journal of Economics*, 6, 466–80.
Nelson, R. and Winter, S. (1978) 'Forces Generating Industrial Concentration under Schumpeterian Competition'. *Bell Journal of Economics*, 9, 524–48.
Ng, Y. K. (1981) 'Welfarism: A Defence against Sen's Attack'. *Economic Journal*, 91, 527–30.
Nozick, R. (1974) *Anarchy, State and Utopia*. Oxford: Basil Blackwell.
Okun, A. (1975) 'Inflation: Its Mechanics and Costs'. *Brookings Papers on Economic Activity*, 2, 351–90.
Okun, A. (1981) *Prices and Quantities*. Washington, DC: Brookings Institute.
Olson, M. (1982) *The Rise and Decline of Nations*. New Haven, CT: Yale University Press.
Osborne, D. K. (1976) 'Cartel Problems' *American Economic Review*, 66, 835–42.
Parfitt, D. (1984) *Reasons and Persons*. Oxford: Oxford University Press.
Parijs, P. van (1981) *Evolutionary Explanations in the Social Sciences*. London: Tavistock.
Paris, P. van (1982) 'Functionalist Marxism Rehabilitated'. *Theory and Society*, 11, 497–511.
Peters, T. and Waterman, R. (1982) *In Search of Excellence*. London: Routledge and Kegan Paul.
Pollak, R. (1970) 'Habit Formation and Dynamic Demand Functions'. *Journal of Political Economy*, 78, 60–78.
Popper, K. (1963) *Conjectures and Refutations: The Growth of Scientific Knowledge*. London: Routledge and Kegan Paul.
Posner, R. (1977) *Economic Analysis of Law*. Boston, MA: Little and Brown.
Quine, W. V. O. (1961) 'Two Dogmas of Empiricism', in *From a Logical Point of View*. Cambridge, MA: Harvard University Press.
Radner, R. (1980) 'Collusive Behaviour in Non-Cooperative Epsilon Equilibria of Oligopolies with Long but Finite Lives'. *Journal of Economic Theory*, 22, 136–54.
Rawls, J. (1972) *A Theory of Justice*. Oxford: Oxford University Press.
Roemer, J. (1979) 'Divide and Conquer: Microfoundations of a Marxian Theory of Wage Discrimination'. *Bell Journal of Economics*, 10, 695–705.
Roemer, J. (1982a) 'Property Relations vs. Surplus Value in Marxian Exploitation', *Philosophy and Public Affairs*, 11, 281–313.
Roemer, J. (1982b) *A General Theory of Exploitation and Class*. Cambridge, MA: Harvard University Press.
Rorty, R. (1986) 'Contingency of Language', 'The Contingency of Selfhood' and 'The Contingency of Community', in *London Review of Books*, 17 April, 8 May, and 24 July.
Rorty, R. (1987) 'Posties'. *London Review of Books*, 3 September.
Sah, R. K. and Stiglitz, J. E. (1986) 'Architecture of Economic Systems: Hierarchies and Polyarchies'. *American Economic Review*, 76, 716–27.

Samuelson, P. (1958) 'An Exact Consumption–Loan Model of Interest with and without the Social Contrivance of Money'. *Journal of Political Economy*, 66, 467–82.

Sargent, T. J. (1978) *Macroeconomic Theory*. London: Academic Press.

Savage, L. J. (1951) 'The Theory of Statistical Decision'. *Journal of American Statistical Association*, 46, 55–67.

Schelling, T. C. (1984) 'Self Command in Practice, in Policy, and in a Theory of Rational Choice'. *American Economic Review*, 74, 1–11.

Schelling, T. C. (1980) 'The Intimate Contest for Self Command'. *Public Interest*, 60, 94–118.

Schotter, A. (1981) *Economic Theory of Social Institutions*. Cambridge: Cambridge University Press.

Schumpeter, J. A. (1934) *The Theory of Economic Development*. Cambridge, MA: Harvard University Press.

Scitovsky, T. (1976) *The Joyless Economy*. New York: Oxford University Press.

Schmalensee, R. (1987) 'Advertising', in J. Eatwell, M. Milgate and P Newman (eds), *The New Palgrave: A Dictionary of Economic Thought*.

Selten, R. (1975) 'Re-examination of the Perfectness Concept for Equilibrium in Extensive Games'. *International Journal of Game Theory*, 4, 22–5.

Selten, R. (1978) 'Chain Store Paradox'. *Theory and Decision*, 9, 127–59.

Sen, A. (1970) *Collective Choice and Social Welfare*. San Francisco, CA: Holden-Day.

Sen, A. (1979) 'Personal Utilities and Public Judgements: Or What's Wrong with Welfare Economics?' *Economic Journal*, 89, 537–50.

Sen, A. (1982a) *Choice Welfare and Measurement*. Oxford: Basil Blackwell.

Sen, A. (1982b) 'Rights and Agency'. *Philosophy and Public Affairs*, 11, 3–39.

Sen, A. (1985) *Commodities and Capabilities*. Amsterdam: North Holland.

Simon, H. A. (1976) 'From Substantive to Procedural Rationality', in Latsis (1976) (ed.) *Method and Appraisal in Economics*. Cambridge: Cambridge University Press.

Simon, H. A. (1978) 'Rationality as Process and as Product of Thought'. *American Economic Review*, 68, 1–16.

Simon, H. A. (1982) *Models of Bounded Rationality*. Cambridge, MA: MIT Press.

Smith, A. (1976) *Wealth of Nations*. Chicago, IL: University of Chicago Press.

Starmer, C. and Sugden, R. (1987) Violations of the Independence Axiom: An Experimental Test of Some Competing Hypotheses. Economics Research Centre Discussion Paper No. 24, University of East Anglia.

Steedman, I. and Krause, U. (1986) 'Goethe's Faust, Arrow's Impossibility Theorem, and the Individual Decision Taker', in J. Elster (ed.), *Multiple Self*. Cambridge: Cambridge University Press.

Steinbruner, J. D. (1974) *The Cybernetic Theory of Decision: New Dimensions of Political Analysis*. Princeton, NJ: Princeton University Press.

Stigler, G. (1964) 'A Theory of Oligopoly'. *Journal of Political Economy*, 72, 44–61.

Sugden, R. (1981) *The Political Economy of Public Choice: An Introduction to Welfare Economics*. Oxford: Martin Robertson.

Sugden, R. (1986) *The Economics of Rights Co-operation and Welfare*. Oxford: Basil Blackwell.

Taylor, C. (1983) *Social Theory and Practice*. Delhi: Oxford University Press.

Thaler, R. and Shefrin, H. (1981) 'An Economic Theory of Self Control'. *Journal of Political Economy*, 89, 392–406.

Tullock, G. (1974) 'Does Punishment Deter Crime?'. *Public Interest*, 36, 103–11.

Weber, M. (1922) *Economy and Society*. New York: Bedminster Press.
Weber, M. (1976) *Protestant Ethic and the Spirit of Capitalism*. London: Allen and Unwin.
Wiggins, D. (1976) *Truth, Invention and the Meaning of Life*. British Academy.
Williamson, J. (1978) *Decoding Advertisements*. London: Marion Boyers.
Williamson, O. E. (1975) *Markets and Hierarchies: Analysis and Anti-Trust Implications*. New York: Free Press.
Winch, P. (1958) *The Idea of a Social Science and its Relation to Philosophy*. London: Routledge and Kegan Paul.
Wittgenstein, L. (1953) *Philosophical Investigations*. Oxford: Basil Blackwell.

Index

action/structure, 87, 89–90, 143
advertising, 130, 162–3
Akerlof, G., 20, 115, 163, 169, 170
Alchian, A., 122, 131, 133
Allais paradox, 108, 163–4
altruism, 93
Aronson, E., 114
Arrow, K., 42, 96, 149, 182, 190–4
auctioneer, 51
Austrians, 2, 29–31, 199
autonomy, 5, 10, 103, 110, 149–50,
    166, 168, 175, 195–6, 203–6, 213,
    215
Axelrod, R., 82, 109

Backus, D., 105, 106
Bakke decision, 159
bandwagon, 96–103, 141, 161, 215
Barro, R., 20, 105
Baye's rule, 58–9
BBC, 99
Becker, G., 70, 109–10, 115, 133, 172
Beckerman, W., 141
Beethoven, L., 31
Begg, D., 58
Berlin, I., 149, 150, 183, 195–6, 200,
    203, 205–6, 213
Bernheim, D., 126
Bernstein, R., 34, 159
Binmore, K., 121, 126, 128
Birt, J., 99
Bismark, 107
Blanchard, O., 64, 141
Blaug, M., 15, 22–3, 29
Blume, L., 60
Boudon, R., 216–18
bounded rationality, 118–19
Bray, M., 59, 60
Buchanan, J., 73, 77, 200

Caldwell, B., 15
capabilities, 192–8
Casson, M., 165, 168
centipede game, 127

chain-store game, 47–8, 65, 67, 84–5,
    105, 107
Chatwin, B., 77
chauvinism, 152–3
chicken game, 79
Clarke, E., 66, 123
Clarke, R., 68
class, 50, 87
    see also stratification
Coase, R., 53, 86, 186
cognitive dissonance, 114–15, 169,
    173, 219
Cohen, G., 134
Cohen, M., 109
Collard, D., 93, 95
collective choice/action, 87–8, 118–21,
    141, 146, 175, 204, 213, 216, 224
common knowledge, 47, 126
communication, 99–103, 113, 116, 158,
    160–3, 173–4, 212–13, 223
compensation tests, 187–9
Condorcet paradox, 190–1
consequentialism, 6, 152, 194, 209
    see also pareto optimality;
    utilitarianism
consumer theory, 41–2, 45, 99–102,
    160–3
contractarianism, 183, 197–8, 200–1
contradictory desires, 110–12
    see also individual, conflict and
    uncertainty within; preferences
conventions, 63, 71–2, 80, 90, 99, 116,
    121, 142, 144, 177, 204, 223
Cornwall, J., 141
cosmology, 148
    see also expressive rationality
counter factuals, 126–7
Crockett, A., 20
culture, 27, 100, 102, 116, 148, 157–8,
    161, 163, 166, 168, 177, 223
cumulative causation, 121, 140, 147

Dasgupta, P., 126
Davidson, D., 155

234   INDEX

Deaton, A., 42, 161
Debreu, G., 107
Dickens, W., 115, 169
Dixit, A., 50
doing vs achieving, 173–4, 176
Donne, J., 111
Douglas, M., 135, 157, 160–2, 175–6
Dreyfus, H., 157
Driffill, J., 105, 106
Duhem, P., 19, 21, 22
Durkheim, E., 216

Earl, P., 161, 163
Easley, D., 60
economics, and other social sciences,
   relationship between, 1, 121,
   143–6, 215–16
economist as technician *see* neutrality
   in economics; positive and
   normative economics
Edgeworth, F., 51, 93
efficiency wages, 98
Elster, J., 9, 43, 51, 109, 110–15, 120,
   128, 131, 134–5, 138, 145, 146,
   183
emergent property, 121, 142
empiricist methodology, 1, 2, 7,
   15–29, 32–5, 151, 209
Enlightenment, 16, 18
entrepreneur and intrapreneurship,
   165–70, 177
ergodicity, 139–43, 145
ethics, 152–3, 170
   see also preferences, ethical
Evans, G., 62
evolutionary games, 70–85, 223–4
existentialism, 5, 111, 150, 152, 153,
   160, 166, 220
experimental explanation, 5, 176, 209
   see also self creation
explanation and prescription, 8–10, 53,
   91–2, 181, 207–24
   see also positive and normative
   economics
explanatory scope, 1–5, 7–11, 40, 43,
   56, 71, 80–1, 88–92, 115–16, 172,
   210
exploitation, 50, 214
   see also stratification
expressive rationality, 4–8, 16, 34,
   101, 148–77, 183, 195, 199,
   203–24

falsificationism, 22–3
feminism, 7, 152–3
   see also stratification, gender
Festinger, L., 114
financial markets, 63–5, 122, 124
firms in general equilibrium, 53, 86,
   137
Folk theorem, 65
freedom, 10, 80, 90, 112, 118, 146,
   149, 177, 183–4, 194–6, 200–1,
   205–7, 212–13, 224
Freeman, R., 123
Freud, 40, 113, 154–5, 167, 177
Friedman, A., 87
Friedman, M., 15, 17–18, 22, 132, 133
Frydman, R., 59, 62
Fudenberg, D., 65

game theory, 46–51, 62, 64–5, 121,
   126–8
   see also evolutionary games
Gibbard, A., 191
Giddens, A., 89, 134
God, 85, 131, 151–3, 167
Godel, K., 127–8
Goodhart, C., 20
Gordon, D., 105
Gordon, R., 123
Green, H., 93
Grossman, H., 20
Groves, T., 66, 123

Habermas, J., 151, 173
Hahn, F., 20, 21, 42, 44, 63, 65, 69,
   70, 89, 96, 122
Haltiwanger, J., 60
Hammond, P., 107
Hamnett, K., 99
Hargreaves Heap, S., 48, 56, 68, 141
Harsanyi, J., 82, 128, 198
Haydn, J., 31
Hayek, F., 30–1, 56, 68, 165
Hegel, G., 110
Heidegger, M., 157
Heilbroner, R., 143
Heller, J., 111
hermeneutics, 16, 27
hierarchy *see* stratification
Hintikka, J., 111
Hirsch, F., 98
historical materialism, 134
history, 65, 69–71, 74, 79, 89, 117–19,